U0035596

Teaching English using the Internet and the Multiple Intelligences Approach

丁廣韻　著

封面設計：實踐大學教務處出版組

出 版 心 語

近年來，全球數位出版蓄勢待發，美國從事數位出版的業者超過百家，亞洲數位出版的新勢力也正在起飛，諸如日本、中國大陸都方興未艾，而台灣卻被視為數位出版的處女地，有極大的開發拓展空間。植基於此，本組自民國 93 年 9 月起，即醞釀規劃以數位出版模式，協助本校專任教師致力於學術出版，以激勵本校研究風氣，提昇教學品質及學術水準。

在規劃初期，調查得知秀威資訊科技股份有限公司是採行數位印刷模式並做數位少量隨需出版〔POD＝Print on Demand〕（含編印銷售發行）的科技公司，亦為中華民國政府出版品正式授權的 POD 數位處理中心，尤其該公司可提供「免費學術出版」形式，相當符合本組推展數位出版的立意。隨即與秀威公司密集接洽，出版部李協理坤城數度親至本組開會討論，雙方就數位出版服務要點、數位出版申請作業流程、出版發行合約書以及出版合作備忘錄等相關事宜逐一審慎研擬，歷時 9 個月，至民國 94 年 6 月始告順利簽核公布。

這段期間，承蒙本校謝前校長孟雄、謝副校長宗興、王教務長又鵬、藍教授秀璋以及秀威公司宋總經理政坤等多位長官給予本組全力的支持與指導，本校多位教師亦不時從旁鼓勵與祝福，在此一併致上最誠摯的謝意。本校新任校長張博士光正甫上任（民國 94 年 8 月），獲知本組推出全國大專院校首創的數位出版服務，深表肯定與期許。諸般溫馨滿溢，將是挹注本組持續推展數位出版的最大動力。

　　本出版團隊由葉立誠組長、王雯珊老師、賴怡勳老師三人為組合，以極其有限的人力，充分發揮高效能的團隊精神，合作無間，各司統籌策劃、協商研擬、視覺設計等職掌，在精益求精的前提下，至望弘揚本校實踐大學的校譽，具體落實出版機能。

實踐大學教務處出版組　謹識

2007 年 4 月

FOREWORD

One of the most common problems facing teachers of English as a Foreign Language in Taiwan, where English is compulsory for all university students, is how to improve student-learning in large-group teaching. Kuang-yun Ting, finding herself in such a situation, decided to research the advantages of using Internet resources and the Multiple Intelligences Approach (MLA) in the English classroom. Her study, which can be followed in this publication, has concentrated on an English listening course. It is an example of research in action and is valuable for other teachers of English in that it illustrates the richness of the Internet as a teaching resource and the importance of the MLA when planning a class so as to present one's material in a way, which will motivate and interest students and thereby enhance learning. Kuang-yun Ting describes not only her success but also her disappointment with certain results and offers either an explanation or indicates an area for further research.

Her research is thus important because of its contribution to pedagogical research and because it provides useful practical advice for other teachers, who are either hesitant about using the Internet or who are seeking to maximise its efficiency in the classroom.

Keith Cameron

Professor emeritus, University of Exeter, UK

Honorary Associate Editor, Computer Assisted Language Learning

Preliminary Remarks

This book explores a teacher's use of Internet resources and the implementation of multiple intelligences in an English listening course setting. The approach taken for the use of these Internet resources involved the application of multiple entry points (which are considered as a practical form of Gardner's multiple intelligence theory), to investigate how links between theory and practice might be strengthened.

Four areas are discussed: (1) how the teacher used website resources more effectively as teaching materials for learners of English in a language classroom, (2) the extent that web page design appeared more likely to engage learners, (3) how the teacher implemented the theory of multiple intelligences in a web-assisted language learning setting, and (4) the ways in which the website resources and multiple intelligences-inspired instructions shaped language learning. The research methodology in this study was that of individual teacher action research.

The results confirm that Internet resources, combined with multiple intelligences-inspired approaches, provided a flexible form of learning. The participating students generally benefited from the potential of website materials and displayed their understanding in a range of forms. Internet resources were therefore confirmed as valuable learning materials. In addition, the applications inspired by the multiple entry points, provide more opportunities for learners to become involved in in-depth learning when using these resources. The findings also suggested how teachers can incorporate Internet resources in English courses. Several class activities were introduced, showing how website materials may be incorporated, alongside the theory of multiple intelligences, in the context of Computer Assisted Language Learning. The findings also indicated that multiple intelligences-inspired instructions may not help learners to prepare for standardised tests though they may help us form more authentic assessments of their learning potential. In conclusion, consideration is given to pedagogical matters, such as opportunities for teachers to become involved in computer assisted language teaching training and to discuss the implementation of a multiple intelligences approach in the classroom.

Many people have helped me along the way to make this book a reality and a success. I like to acknowledge with enormous gratitude the help and support of Dr. Keith Postlethwaite, for showing me different ways of approaching research problems, for his advice, his encouragement and for making me a better researcher. Also, many thanks to Professor Keith Cameron, who has the difficult task of being the long-time reader for this book, and who stayed in close contact with me throughout this arduous process. In addition, my thanks to Dr. David Carter, for developing my understanding and use of methodology and Mr. Roger Haesevoets, for proofreading this book. Finally, many thanks to my research participants for their valuable comments on the courses and teaching material. Their feedback provided me with information that helped me refine my teaching practice and helped me gain more insight of how theory can be applied.

CONTENTƒ

Teaching English using the Internet and the Multiple Intelligences Approach

CHAPTER $\boxed{1}$

INTRODUCTION

1.1 Research Motivation

Computer Assisted Language Learning (CALL) has been implemented for some time in language teaching. However, research has shown that teachers still get frustrated when attempting to integrate the Internet into their English teaching in the classroom (Bax, 2000; Debski & Gruba, 1999; Gunn & Brussino, 1997). Debski and Gruba's (1999:229) research shows that instructors use the words '*stress, frustration, and problem*' to describe their experiences with computers. The accessibility and usability of a network-based environment are still inadequate: a criticism that has been made by Taiwanese as well as other second language teachers (Linder, 2004; Singhal, 1997; Yang, 2001; Yu & Yu, 2002). In fact, Gunn and Brussino (1997:21) make explicit what many language teachers think:

teachers with full workloads and satisfactory outcomes from existing methods of course delivery are not necessarily motivated to venture into the uncharted waters of technology-based developments which are sometimes hard to access, often unreliable and always costly.

With no experience in using a computer as a teaching tool, teachers must spend a great deal of time sifting through useless information on the Internet (Toyoda, 2001). Teachers often worry that their technical competence is insufficient to manage competently a CALL course. When teachers run into technical problems, the whole teaching process may be halted. According to my own observations in CALL classrooms, language teachers' perceptions of CALL can greatly diminish its benefits. The main problem in implementing CALL is that technology-related resources, e.g. language learning programmes and the Internet, are not used in a flexible way. There are two practical questions of which teachers often face the network connection and students' learning attitudes.

The Network Connection

The problems encountered in using modern technology, ranging from inter-connectivity to unstable systems, are unavoidable. The most difficult issue for the language teacher is knowing where the technical problem lies. In addition, when a whole class tries to access the same website simultaneously, the speed of the network server can reduce considerably, and switching to the next website may take a considerable amount of time. During a lesson, with limited time, accessing large files or graphics can be very time consuming due to the long response time. These factors are likely to be a very discouraging influence on teaching and the learning progress.

Students' Learning Attitudes

A number of researchers have explored how the World Wide Web displays visual elements and text to enhance teaching and learning listening or reading (Hanson-Smith, 1999). However, students may access other websites during the lecture or task. They may simply surf a succession of homepages, instead of building on basic language knowledge and employing skills via the World Wide Web. More specifically, it can be difficult to persuade students to take web-based lessons seriously as it is easy for them to surf other websites. It is impossible for one teacher to monitor all students' screens.

In view of these difficulties, this research project is undertaken to explore how CALL might be used in more varied ways, using website materials as resources for teachers to use in a full class teaching situation.

1.2 Purpose of the Study

The research tries to demonstrate how teachers may create rich learning opportunities via certain website features, while being able to manage their classrooms in a computer assisted language learning context. Moreover, the considerations of how teachers can present learning materials in a concrete way and help learners with a variety of approaches are the other focus in the study. Therefore, a teaching approach inspired by Howard Gardner's theory of multiple intelligences is conducted in this study.

The theory of multiple intelligences stresses different ways of learning and expressing learner understanding. In reality, the principle fits well with the current emphasis on computer assisted language learning. The application of the MI theory has been applied in English language teaching for a while (Christison, 1996; Pirie, 1995). The main idea is that learners will value their own strengths and involve promising learning. The idea of computer assisted language learning is that learners have more choice to select what they need and how they engage with materials. Moreover, the obvious pedagogical advantage of the Internet is the availability of material on the websites. The World Wide Web is like a virtual library which attracts language teachers' attention. Moreover, the Internet facilitates the use of a specific language in an authentic setting. Students can access current information in which the target language is spoken. This kind of authenticity is often mentioned in the field of second language learning (Sanderson, 1999).

In addition, the theory of multiple intelligences can be regarded as rich instructional framework, while computer technology and the Internet can be thought of as rich materials. Therefore, the study tries to bridge the gap between the two powerful facilities and explore in which way they can promote better understanding for learners and enhance their language learning.

1.3 An Outline of the Project

In this research, the principal aim is to explore how English learning may be supported through the use of website resources and MI-inspired instruction. Accordingly, the processes of professional learning are examined in order to improve the practice. In all, this project comprises eight chapters.

Chapter 2 reviews the literature in the area of second language acquisition, the theory of multiple intelligences (MI), and Computer Assisted Language Learning (CALL). The Internet provides a wide range of teaching resources. The CALL literature enables teacher to distinguish good resources from other criteria such as readability. However, teachers remain unsure about how to use these good resources. A great deal of research has applied multiple intelligences to English teaching indicates that second language acquisition is actually compatible with the theory of multiple intelligences. Examples are given, such as task-based learning, project-based learning and authentic learning materials. Moreover, the review explores of how the theory of multiple intelligences can be used to design a practical approach, known as multiple entry points. Selecting this approach is expected to help teachers plan a course syllabus around promoting understanding by providing examples for using multiple entry points to create a climate for in-depth learning. Meanwhile, the criteria of web design are mentioned based on the issues of readability, multimodal presentations, and source evaluation which are often emphasised in Computer Assisted Language Learning settings. Therefore, the review aims to bridge the gap between the principles of MI and CALL.

Chapter 3 outlines the research stance, which consists of an interpretative study, designed to facilitate an in-depth understanding of teaching practice. The design of the study includes the setting of the courses, the background of the participants, and the instruments used in the data gathering process. The action research methodology is used to explore the ways in which professional learning may be put into practice. This study was conducted by an individual action researcher/teacher. Accordingly, each cycle of every stage is detailed in the following chapters.

Chapter 4 focuses on the practice of using the first website in the listening comprehension course for the four groups involved. It also describes how the entry point approach, a practical form of multiple intelligences, was implemented within the teaching context. Initial problems, discovered in this application, are also reported.

Chapter 5 offers ways to amend the problems found in Chapter 4, via the application of the second website, which contained richer information. At the same time, the analysis of participants' feedback is presented in order to improve the next stage of the practice.

Similarly, Chapter 6 introduces the process of the third action research cycle. It also reports on learners' feedback of the third website used in the classroom. Specifically, the practice of classroom activities is addressed.

Chapter 7 reveals the findings gathered from the research questions, raised by the study. A discussion of these research questions follows.

The final chapter summarises the effects of website resources and multiple entry points, an intelligences-inspired instructions, on my own learning and professional development. Further, the study provides recommendations for further study and implementation in the field of multiple entry points and the use of computer technology in English teaching. The whole research is written in the first person. The idea is to attempt to make more transparent impact of the teacher and the research role.

CHAPTER $\boxed{2}$

LITERATURE REVIEW

2.1 Introduction

This chapter is concerned with second language acquisition, multiple intelligences, and computer assisted language learning. Stephen Krashen (1985), an educator in second language acquisition, argues that learners acquire language best when they are given comprehensible input. Howard Gardner (1983), another educational theorist, proposes the theory of Multiple Intelligences and argues that if teaching is flexible and pays attention to the range of intelligences, more students will gain a better understanding of what is being taught. In recent developments of Computer Assisted Language Learning (CALL), the Internet and its World Wide Web have been shown to enhance opportunities to help learners' understanding from a diverse environment.

Accordingly, this chapter sets out the issues to consider in combining second language acquisition theory and multiple intelligences research literature, so as to create a guide for the elaboration of web-assisted language-teaching courses. First, it discusses the impact of Krashen's input hypothesis on second language acquisition.

Second, it introduces the theory of Multiple Intelligences provided by Howard Gardner in the early 1980s. It then explains the application of the Multiple Intelligences theory to English teaching. After that, the review explores the entry points based on MI theory and explains how they map on to some issues of second language teaching including comprehensible input, task based learning, and project work.

Third, a brief history of the development of computer assisted language learning, is discussed based on three categories: structural CALL, communicative CALL and integrative CALL. The review subsequently discusses web design and website resources. Meanwhile, the guidelines of website selection for English listening classes are provided. Further, this review bridges the gap between the application of multiple intelligences and the practice of computer assisted language learning by using website resources and entry point instructions in English teaching.

2.2 Inputs into Second Language Acquisition

The study of second language acquisition is concerned with how learners acquire a second language, and which factors may influence that process. While different theories emphasise different aspects of second language acquisition, Gass (2003:229) claims that input is '*a highly important factor in acquisition*'. In other words, input plays a significant role and its quality can influence learners' interest in learning a second language. It may determine whether learners want to continue their learning and help them to construct their knowledge of a second language. Input theory is therefore particularly important. The discussion of input will be explored in terms of authentic input, visual material input, and the issue of multimodality.

2.2.1 Comprehensible Input

With regard to the input theory, Krashen mentions that language is acquired by '*understanding messages*' or by '*receiving comprehensible input*' (Krashen, 1985:2). His notable input hypothesis is referred to as $i+1$ (input + 1). In his input hypothesis, Krashen declares that if learners are at level i, the input should be at level i+1. Learners must be provided with appropriate input which contains structures beyond their current level of competence. In this way, learners should be able to construct new meanings with what they already know about the language, contextual information, and extra linguistic information. Krashen's input hypothesis emphasises that comprehensible input is a fundamental requirement in acquiring a second language. The studies show that the principle of comprehensible input can elicit a higher level of learners' interests and that learners are more likely to enhance their vocabulary and grammar knowledge (Rodrigo et al., 2004). Further, Krashen (1985: 4) states that learners acquire second languages if their '*affective filters are low enough to allow the input in*'. These affective filters include a lack of self-confidence, lack of motivation, and anxiety. In brief, learning occurs when learners are able to produce competent output after receiving a sufficient quantity of the appropriate input.

2.2.2 Input and Interaction

Krashen's input hypothesis has been criticised by interactionist scholars who believe language is acquired through the process of interaction or negotiation (Ellis, 1994; Mitchell & Myles, 1998). They argue that Krashen's input hypothesis is not well-explained and does not include input coming from other learners. Mitchell and Myles (1988:126) argue that the theory is not clear about '*how the learner's present state of knowledge (i) is to be characterised*'. The other question is '*whether the 'i+1' formulation is intended to apply to all aspects of language, from lexis to phonology and syntax*' (Mitchell & Myles, 1998:126).

Gass and Selinker (1994:150) accept that Krashen's definition of comprehensible input is necessary, but they argue that Krashen's input hypothesis '*is not specific as to how to define levels of knowledge*'. Further, they go on to say that Krashen does not explain what a '*sufficient quantity of the appropriate input*' (Gass & Selinker, 1994:150) is. Gass and Selinker provide an interaction hypothesis, which includes the following three parts (Gass & Selinker, 1994:219):

(1) comprehensible input is necessary for acquisition;

(2) conversational interactions (negotiation) makes the input comprehensible;

(3) comprehensible output aids learners in moving from semantic processing to syntactic processing.

As Gass & Selinker argue, learners' ability to understand the message is through a series of adjusted interactions; this is the process of language learning.

Likewise, Ellis and He (1999) reach a similar view in their research regarding how interaction contributes to second language acquisition. Their study found that interaction involving conversation between learners and the teacher provided far more opportunities for learning. Learners should be provided with the opportunity to talk with each other. It enables learners to interact in second language learning (Ellis, 1994). The modifications of interaction help learners obtain better comprehension and greater vocabulary acquisition.

Apart from native speakers, the input should not be seen to embrace only oral exchanges in the target language, but also to include all the possible sources of input, such as learning material in second language classrooms. Apart from the oral input, other studies suggest that task-based learning approaches (Long & Crookes, 1992) help learners acquire better comprehension. From interactive tasks, learners are able to produce longer sentences and negotiate meaning more often than in teacher-fronted instruction (Doughty & Pica, 1986).

A similar point is made by Lightbown and Spada (1999:122), saying that learners should be provided with the opportunity '*to engage in meaningful activities*', so that '*they are compelled to negotiate for meaning*'. That is, the quality of comprehensible input is achieved by a series of negotiations. From communicating problems to negotiating solutions, the process makes input comprehensible to learners. When learners are involved with meaningful activities, such as negotiating meaning in order to express their ideas and to clarify their opinions, learners arrive at '*a mutual understanding*' (Lightbown and Spada 1999:122). In summary, a second language is acquired after learners experience a series of procedures, e.g., repetition, clarification, and confirmation, to gain understanding. These processes help learners master their own learning and complete a task or project.

2.2.3 Input from Task Based Learning

In recent years, much research has discussed how task-based approaches can help students adapt their comprehension techniques and thereby facilitate second language learning (Ellis, 2003; Long & Crookes, 1992). An important element is that tasks enhance the value of input for the learners. Ellis (2003) discusses three types of input-enhancement tasks: structure-based production tasks, comprehension task, and consciousness-raising tasks. The principle of all these three focused tasks is to help learners produce, notice and understand targeted structures (Ellis, 2003).

Willis (1996:24) points out that all the tasks are '*goal-oriented*' which focus on understanding and conveying meanings. When learners are doing tasks, it means that they are '*using language in a meaningful way*' (Willis, 1996:24). As for the framework of task-based learning, Willis (1996) suggests three stages for a task activity: pre-task, task cycle, and language focus. It is shown in Table 2.1.

Table 2.1 Task Stages Adopted from Willis (1996:38)

Pre-task	Introduction to topic and task	
Task cycle	Task ↓	Students do the task. Teachers monitor and offer comments.
	Planning ↓	Students prepare their report. Teachers correct linguistic section.
	Report	Students present their reports. Teachers give comments and summaries.
Language focus	Analysis	Students examine and discuss specific features of the text or transcript of the recording.
	Practice	Teacher conducts practice of new words, phrases and patterns occurring in the data, either during or after the analysis.

In pre-task preparation, teachers usually introduce the topics to create interest in doing a task and give students clear instruction on what they are going to do. The task cycle consists of linguistic practice by using language resources, group discussion, and task performance in oral or written forms. Once the task is finished, teachers give feedback by highlighting language forms used during the report phase for analysis. Apart from teachers' feedback, students may be required to participate in peer evaluation at the report stage. The last phase of the task based learning framework is the focus on language. Language analysis activities are designed for learners to focus on specific language use, e.g., words, phonology, context meaning (Willis, 1996). In addition, language practice activities aim to help learners practise a specific language skill such as listening.

As Skehan (1996) notes, task-based instruction can engage learners in learning through doing. In this way, learners are actively involved in the acquisition process.

In contrast, some researchers mention a number of critiques of task-based approaches to instruction (Sheen, 1994; Skehan, 1996). For example, Sheen's (1994) study indicates that learners may not be aware of the errors they have made in the tasks.

2.2.4 Input from Authentic Material

Studies of second language teaching have come to refer to 'authenticity' as *'the language that has been actually used by native speakers for any real purposes'* (Rost, 2002:123). Accordingly, authentic material which includes *'real context'* and *'real language'* can motivate learners at all levels (Rost, 2002:124). The material is able to engage students' attention, provides vast amounts of comprehensible input and keeps affective filters low (Sanderson, 1999; Secules et al., 1992). Secules et al. (1992:480) show that learners can benefit from videos, which provide *'the dynamics of interaction'* from native speakers with different accents or gestures. Real life literacy resources, which include newspapers, radio broadcasts, the Internet, advertisements, and daily life magazines, are regarded as authentic materials. Sanderson (1999) points out that authentic material keeps students informed about what is happening in the world. For many students, *'the ability to read and understand English language newspapers for work purposes represents a very real and tangible goal to aim for'* (Sanderson, 1999:3).

However, teachers need to have a clear view of their objective in using authentic material. Some teachers find that authentic material is *'too difficult for the students to handle'* (Rost, 2002:125). Teachers need to make sure students understand those materials and justify what students are actually doing with authentic tasks. Further, the reflective question is whether students use language more effectively at the end of the activity. The activity may be wonderful and creative, but it may not lead to students learning language structures or increasing their linguistic knowledge. Teachers may simply be guiding students through activities with the assumption students are learning.

2.2.5 The Input of Visual Material for Language Learning

Some research has shown that second language learners' comprehension may be enhanced when the provision of visual information is increased (Mueller, 1980; Ur, 1984). For language learners at an elementary level, input can be made more comprehensible through a variety of strategies, such as the use of visuals, or linguistic simplification. Krashen (1985) suggests that teachers use visual aids, such as pictures and objects, when providing context. Pictures are generally used to elicit word recognition and text comprehension of materials, especially at lower levels. Learners understand the language forms via flashcards or storybooks with illustrations. Studies have shown that pictures are able to support teaching processes in reading and writing in the language (Calhoun, 1999; Wright, 1989).

Calhoun (1999) describes a Picture Word Inductive Model that immerses students in how language works. When students observe an item or an action in the picture, they connect the picture with a word. Then, they note the spelling of the word and make connections with word recognition. Calhoun explains the instruction of the Picture Word Inductive Model as a repeated instructional pattern. Students see the item, listen as the teacher reads the word and then pronounce the word, to reinforce word recognition. Calhoun (1999) also suggests that the Picture Word Inductive Model can be applied to older beginners to construct their language vocabulary.

Similarly, Wright (1989:2) raises three points concerning the contribution of learning by pictures:

1. They increase '*interest and motivation*'.
2. They develop '*a sense of the context of the language*'.
3. They represent '*a specific reference point or stimulus*'.

In brief, appropriate pictures can motivate beginning learners to gather information and to identify words and story plots.

Flashcards are often used by teachers of English to help elicit new vocabulary or phonemes for beginners. Flashcards used as a learning resource keep students interested and help them to understand selected vocabulary. In other words, teachers may use the image processing of flashcards to help students to translate the meaning of words. One example of this use is the set of authentic phonic cards published by the Letterland Company (http://www.letterland.com).

Their phonic card is designed in pictorial style using picture cues for letter shapes (Wendon, 1993). Each card has one letter, or a mixture of letters, with a focal point for presenting a spelling pattern on one side and a story outline on the reverse. Through the interesting story recounted on each card, beginning learners' cognitive skills are reinforced. In order to exemplify this point, take the 'h' story in Letterland as an example. The phonic of 'h' represents 'Hairy Hat Man'. Mr. H does not like noise. When Hairy Hat Man meets noisy Sammy Snake (s), he will tell Sammy Snake to be quiet by saying 'sh' (Figure 2.1).

Figure 2.1 Examples of Phonemes and Graphemes in Letterland Flashcards

McFarlane (1998) shows convincingly that children are captivated by the characters via the stories of Letterland. With pictorial cards, teachers can get children's attention and stimulate their curiosity. Learners can also repeat the sound spontaneously after the story has been told. My belief in the efficiency of pictorial flashcards comes from working with older beginners in a local community. The above set of pictorial flashcards helped such learners to identify phonetic patterns and letter shapes. Take 'h' as an example again. The stories of the related flashcards, th, ch, gh, sh, and wh were told together to reinforce learners' impression of 'h' in a consonantal cluster. With the story-telling approach, learners understood the phonetics of the cluster and remembered the phonetic changes. Not only young learners but also older beginners associated the letter with an attractive picture that they had already been familiarised with, in order to develop a new concept. Thus, with the aid of still pictures, linguistic skills were learnt through a combination of narrative and natural experience.

Similarly, pictures on websites tend to attract beginners and help them make sense of the words of the accompanying text (Ikeda, 1999). Research shows that the pictures related to a story help the understanding of that story. In contrast, pictures without any connection to a story do not facilitate comprehension (Ting & Cameron, 2004). These research results suggest that not every picture is equally helpful. For example, cartoons and pictures which introduce purely decorative elements are not as efficient as simple relevant illustrations in enhancing learning.

2.2.6 Input in Multimodality

Multimodality implies multiple forms of communication, such as images, words, and actions, all dependent on each other to create a holistic meaning. According to Kress and Leeuwen (1996), a multimodal text is an integration of several modes of communication such as images, printed text, and the spoken word in order to convey a message. In other words, multimodality refers to the situation where one individual mode depends on other modes to complete a communicative process. Without text, an image would not make much sense. Similarly, without spoken words, a text may not make an impression. Each mode is regarded as a semiotic contribution to facilitate meaning (Kress, 2003). From this point of view, images not only represent material reality, but also provide an interpersonal interaction creating a relationship between the viewer and what is being viewed (Kress & Leeuwen, 1996).

Moreover, Mayer explains (1999:615), *'when instructional messages are presented in pictorial form'*, learners are able to choose *'relevant features to pay attention to, thereby forming a series of mental visual images'*. Thus, they build up *'the images into a coherent structure* (Mayer, 1999:615). Further, *'when instructional messages are presented in verbal form'*, learners can select *'relevant words to pay attention to, thereby forming a collection of mental word sounds'*. Once again, learners are able to construct *'the words into a coherent structure'* (Mayer, 1999:615). Finally, learners mentally *'integrate the visual mental model and the verbal mental model with each other and with existing knowledge'* (Mayer, 1999:615). This is entirely consistent with the principle of using multimodal presentation to support language learning where images associated with spoken language help clarify the target meaning.

As for multimodality in the context of information technology, Snyder (2001:119) explains that *'the written, oral and audiovisual modalities of communication are integrated into the same electronic system – multimodal hypertext system made accessible via the Internet and the World Wide Web'*. Similarly, Unsworth (2001:12) points out:

> *The interaction of the peculiar affordances of computer-based and networked technologies and the multimodality of electronic format texts have the effect of multiplying potentially new literacy practices'.*

Websites often incorporate a diversity of images and audio files into their designs. Accordingly, learners' learning experiences are effected within a visual, aural and interactive environment. It is the impact of diverse communicative sources which promotes student learning. Using multimodal input helps learners to tailor their learning according to their own preferences. The issue of multimodality may also be considered as a question of design as it draws attention to *'a range of semiotic meaning-making resources, including the verbal, the visual, and the technological'* (Maun & Myhill, 2005:20). Such a notion of design is closely related to the criteria for the construction of good web pages. These criteria will be discussed in this chapter, section 2.4.3.

2.2.7 Comments

This section has introduced the input hypothesis in second language acquisition and tries to identify what it is that makes different types of input comprehensible to learners. The importance of input in learning a second language is due to learners not only needing to receive knowledge but also to understand what they learn. If they do not sufficiently comprehend input, they easily forget what they have been taught or lose interest in it. While input is regarded as an important element in acquiring a second language, the next question concerns the sources of the input.

Recommendations for task-based learning and the use of authentic material in the classroom, described earlier in this chapter, rest on the understanding that they tend to enhance input comprehensibility. The premise is that teachers should design a meaningful task and/or choose appropriate authentic materials which are suitable for their learners' use. The importance of this input is in helping learners to build on their strengths and to apply them to learning a second language when needed. However, teachers need to be aware of their learners' levels and requirements. Material may be authentic, but learners may give up learning if the material adopted is too difficult. In fact, multimodal formats could be used to facilitate learning from otherwise difficult authentic sources.

When good input designed with reference to the issues discussed above, is used a new question arises: why are some kinds of language learners successful, while others are not? According to the traditional definition of intelligence, learners with higher linguistic or logical-mathematical abilities, learn better. If this idea applies to second language learning, the barrier of low linguistic ability can reduce learners' self-confidence, raise anxiety, and affect learning. Such a construct, however, has limited utility for educationalists who are interested in inclusive models of pedagogy. In contrast to traditional intelligence concepts, Gardner (1983) proposes a multiple intelligences theory, which encourages everybody to learn in line with their own strengths. The issue of multiple intelligences is discussed in the next section.

2.3 The Theory of Multiple Intelligences

The theory of multiple intelligences was developed by Howard Gardner, who argues that traditional ideas about intelligence should be significantly reformed (Gardner, 1983). He is not satisfied with the traditional view of intelligence, which focuses on linguistic and mathematical intelligences and the notion that children's strengths and weaknesses can be measured by the intelligence quotient (IQ) test. Instead of intelligence being a single capacity described with an IQ score, Gardner redefines the term of intelligence as an engine to '*fashion products*' in real life situations (Gardner, 1993:7). He claims that human intelligences are various. As he states, (1993:15):

> *We are all so different largely because we all have different combinations of intelligences. If we recognize this, I think we will have at least a better chance of dealing appropriately with the many problems we face in the world.*

As Gardner defines it, intelligence should be considered a plurality of capacities (Armstrong, 2003). He uses a variety of sources to support the theory of multiple intelligences. His criteria for defining a specific kind of intelligence include: (Gardner, 1999:36-40):

1. The potential of isolation by brain damage

2. An evolutionary history and evolutionary plausibility

3. An identifiable core operation or set of operations

4. Susceptibility to encoding in a symbol system

5. A distinct developmental history, along with a definable set of expert "end-state" performances.

6. The existence of idiot savants, prodigies, and other exceptional people.

7. Support from experimental psychological tasks

8. Support from psychometric findings

By using these criteria, Gardner (1983) identifies at least seven different forms of intelligence located in different areas of the brain. Each intelligence represents a set of capacities which can either work independently or together. In reality, these intelligences work in many different combinations and ways. In other words, when learners are engaged in learning linguistic skills, other intelligences are very important even if those intelligences are not in evidence in the context. These seven intelligences are manifested differently, in different people. In Table 2.2, a brief definition of each intelligence is shown, as defined by Gardner (1999) and completed by Armstrong (2000).

Table 2.2 Summary of Gardner's Multiple Intelligences

Type of Intelligence	Core Components
Linguistic intelligence	*It involves sensitivity to spoken and written language, the ability to learn languages, and the capacity to use*

	language to accomplish certain goals. (Gardner, 1999:41) *The capacity to use words effectively, whether orally or in writing. This intelligence includes the ability to manipulate the syntax or structure of language. (Armstrong, 2000:3)*
Logical-mathematical intelligence	*It involves the capacity to analyze problems logically, carry out mathematical operations, and investigate issues scientifically. (Gardner, 1999:42)* *The capacity to use numbers effectively and to reason well. (Armstrong, 2000:2)*
Spatial intelligence	*The ability to form a mental model of a spatial world and to be able to manoeuvre and operate using that model. (Gardner, 1993:9)* *The ability to perceive the visual-spatial world accurately and to perform transformations on those perceptions. (Armstrong, 2000:2)*
Bodily/kinaesthetic intelligence	*The ability to solve problems or to fashion products using one's whole body, or parts of the body (Gardner, 1993:9)* *Expertise in using one's whole body to express ideas and feelings and facility in using one's hands to produce or transform things (Armstrong, 2000:3)*
Intrapersonal intelligence	*A correlative ability, turned inward. It is a capacity to form an accurate, veridical model of oneself and to be able to use that model to operate effectively in life. (Gardner, 1993:9)* *This intelligence includes having an accurate picture of oneself (one's strengths and limitations). (Armstrong, 2000:3)*
Interpersonal intelligence	*The ability to understand other people: what motivates them, how they work, how to work cooperatively with them (Gardner, 1993:9)* *The ability to perceive and make distinctions in the moods, intentions, motivations, and feelings of other people. (Armstrong, 2000:3)*

Musical intelligence	Musical intelligence entails skill in the performance, composition, and appreciation of musical patterns. (Gardner, 1999:42) The capacity to perceive, discriminate, transform, and express musical forms. (Armstrong, 2000:3)

Adapted from Gardner (1993:8-9), (1999:41-42) and Armstrong (2000:2-3)

After proposing the above seven forms of intelligence, Gardner (1999) points out that there may be one or more other forms of intelligence, such as naturalist intelligence. In referring to naturalist intelligence, Gardner (1999:48) wrote:

A naturalist demonstrates expertise in the recognition and classification of the numerous species – the flora and fauna – of his or her environment.

Campbell and Campbell mirrored Gardner's definition of naturalist intelligence as *'one who specializes in recognizing and classifying natural and human-made phenomena'* (Campbell & Campbell, 1999:5).

According to Gardner (1993:32), *'an intelligence can serve both as the content of instruction and the means or medium for communicating that content'*. Gardner gives an example about learning mathematical principles. For students whose strengths are not in logical-mathematical intelligence, the teacher can use *'an alternative route to the mathematical content'* (Gardner 1993:33). In other words, the teacher may start an activity with a spatial presentation or *'a bodily-kinaesthetic metaphor'* to initiate learning

(Gardner 1993:33). In this way, students may be encouraged to use their preferred intelligences to master the target subject. As Gardner (1993:7) emphasises, intelligence is *'the ability to solve problems, or to fashion products'*.

2.3.1 Critique of Multiple Intelligences Theory

The theory of Multiple Intelligences (MI) theory has literally inspired a mountain of response and has been criticised by scholars especially in the field of psychology (Aiken, 1988; Herrnstein & Murray, 1994; Sternberg, 1985). Aiken (1988:196) argues that the MI theory is *'based more on reasoning and intuition than on the results of empirical research studies'*. Herrnstein and Murray (1994:18) make a similar observation that MI theory lacks *'psychometric or other quantitative evidence'*. Sternberg (1996:479), a critic of MI theory, argues that *'hard evidence for the existence of these separate intelligences has yet to be produced'*. Moreover, Sternberg (1985:1114) claims two problems of MI theory to be:

(1) Factorial evidence has shown that the various abilities are not independent;

(2) It is not clear exactly what each intelligence consists of, especially because this theory, like other map-based theories, does not specify processes.

Sternberg points out that the multiple intelligences may be better *'referred to as multiple talents'* (Sternberg, 1985:1114). This view is supported by Morgan (1992 cited in Kezar, 2001:144) who argues that Gardner's definition of these multiple intelligences is actually *'what are commonly called gifts or talents'*. Meanwhile, they question the legitimacy of MI theory because there is no specific test to measure the seven intelligences. Moreover, some educators question how to put the theory into practice (Klein, 2003; White, 1998). In brief, the general critical view is that the concept and the empirical evidence of multiple intelligences are not sustained by psychologists.

2.3.2 Gardner's Response to Criticism

To clarify the ideas of his MI theory, Gardner has responded to these criticisms many times in his writings and in public debate (Checkley, 1997; Gardner, 1995). He (1999:80-89) claims that there are seven 'myths' of multiple intelligences described as follows.

Myth 1. *Now that eight or nine intelligences have been identified, researchers can –*
and perhaps should create a variety of tests and secure the associated scores.

Myth 2. *An intelligence is the same as a domain or a discipline.*

Myth 3. *An intelligence is the same as a learning style, a cognitive style, or a working style.*

Myth 4. *MI theory is not empirical. (A variant of this myth alleges that MI theory is empirical but has been disproved.)*

Myth 5. *MI theory is incompatible with g (general intelligence), with hereditarian accounts, and/or with environmental accounts of the nature and causes of intelligence.*

Myth 6. *By broadening the term intelligence to include a broad spectrum of psychological constructs, MI theory renders the term and its typical connotations useless.*

Myth 7. *There is a single 'approved' educational approach based on MI theory.*

Gardner has provided feedback on each of these myths (= assertions). For example, with regard to myth 1, Gardner points out that his concept of multiple intelligences has grown from his accumulating knowledge about the human brain, but *'not from the result of a priori definitions or factor analyses of test scores'* (1999:80). Nevertheless, regarding myth 4, contrary to the criticism of no empirical research, Gardner argues that MI theory has been researched with empirical evidence and has been *'revised on the basis of new empirical findings'* (1999:85). The most important myth in connecting with this study is myth 7. With regarded to this, Gardner accepts that *'MI theory is in no way an educational prescription'* (1999:89), rather he concludes that *'educators are in the best position to determine whether and to what extent MI theory should guide their practice'* (1999:89). Overall, Gardner (2004:214) claims that MI theory derives from *'an evolutionary perspective'* and *'the way of thinking is consistent with how most biologists think about the mind and the brain'*. Nevertheless, Gardner's MI theory is still the subject of open warfare in the psychological field in recent years. The main reason is that psychologists criticise the theory on the grounds that it is not based on clear psychometric evidence (Nettelbeck & Young, 2002).

2.3.3 Implications of Multiple Intelligences Theory - Multiple Entry Points

According to Gardner's theory of multiple intelligences (MI), learners vary in intelligence across a combination of seven or eight different areas. Gardner does not actually prescribe any specific methodology for developing these multiple intelligences. Instead, he (1991) suggests ways in which the theory of multiple intelligences may be applied to promoting broader educational goals. One important application of MI is to assist in understanding teaching and learning processes. Gardner acknowledges that a high student-teacher ratio in a classroom using a single textbook can present a challenge for any teacher attempting to individualise instruction and meet the diverse needs of students. Therefore, he recommends that teachers should structure their presentation of material in a variety of ways so as to help students achieve understanding and initiate learning. Gardner therefore suggests a multiple entry point approach, to help students achieve understanding and initiate learning (see below). He claims:

Any rich, nourishing topic - any concept worth teaching - can be approached in at least five different ways that will map onto the multiple intelligences. (Gardner, 1991:245)

Gardner regards the main topic as a room, with at least five doors (entry points). These entry points can '*help teachers introduce new materials in ways in which they can be easily grasped by a range of students' intelligences*' (Gardner, 1991:245). Gardner's idea of multiple entry points is to promote learners' understanding of a new concept via multiple perspectives. He suggests that a skilled teacher can '*open a number of different windows on the same concept*' to contribute towards student understanding (Gardner, 1991:246). Accordingly, students must be provided with opportunities to put their comprehension into practice. This indicates that teachers' instruction should focus on how to draw on students' interests and strengths to carry out their school task. For example, if teachers introduce a linguistic concept, visual demonstration can at least capture students' attention and initiate their learning.

From 1991 to 2006, Gardner described several types of multiple entry points including aesthetic, existential/foundational, experiential, fundamental, hands-on, interpersonal/ collaborative, musical, narrative/narrational, quantitative/numerical, and social. Gardner's (1991) original entry points were narrational, logical-quantitative, foundational, aesthetic and experiential approaches. Each point can map onto certain intelligences as shown in Table 2.3.

Table 2.3 Gardner's Multiple Entry Points

Entry Point	Description
A narrational entry point (aligned to linguistic intelligence)	Presenting material through stories or narrative about the concept in question.
A logical-quantitative entry point (linked to logical intelligence)	Presenting concept by invoking numerical considerations or deductive reasoning processes.
A foundational entry point (map onto logical intelligence)	Examining the philosophical and terminological facets of the concept.
An aesthetic entry point (associated with spatial intelligence)	Presenting material by emphasising sensory or surface features that will appeal to – or at least capture the attention of -- students who favour an artistic stance to the experiences of living.

An experiential entry point approach (related to logical intelligence)	Conveying the concept by engaging activities, such as building, manipulating and carry out experiments. It is a hands-on approach.

Adapted from Gardner (1991: 244-247) and Gardner (1999: 169-172)

As Gardner explains:

> *An entry point perspective places students directly at the center of a disciplinary topic, arousing their interests and securing cognitive commitment for further exploration. (Gardner, 1999:172).*

Many teachers have used the multiple intelligences as entry points into lesson content (Campbell, 1997). Advocates of the MI theory claim that the entry-point activities '*draw on MI's conception of pluralistic intelligence by emphasising multiple entry points into the class material*' (Kallenbach and Viens, 2002:58). Kallenbach and Viens (2002:58) explain that '*entry points refer to activities that engage students in a particular subject area or content*'. In order to attract students' attention and help them achieve better understanding of the main subject, teachers need to present a topic using multiple approaches which is a '*component of effective teaching*' (Gardner, 1999:178).

2.3.4 Application of Multiple Intelligences to English Language Teaching

Although the theory of MI is questioned by many psychologists, it is widely applied in education, including English language teaching (Baum et al., 2005; Davis et al.1998). Educators from many countries have used the MI theory as a framework for instruction (Woods, 2004). The main reason is that MI theory suggests that everyone can learn well if their potential strengths are exploited. This constitutes a further reminder for teachers that learners differ. This idea is in contrast with theoretical models such as IQ which tends to imply that potential is restricted to a relatively small group of pupils who happen to score well on this single test. This emphasis on the potential of all students to learn, albeit in different ways, is central to the values of many teachers. Indeed, the correlation between MI ideas and the values commonly held by teachers may explain the popularity of the MI theory among educationists despite the criticism from psychologists.

According to the MI theory, learners' strength in one area might facilitate performance in another (Krechevsky & Gardner, 1990:232). In other words, those who are weak in the linguistic and mathematical intelligences can still learn well through the potential of their other intelligences. Therefore, flexibility in the teaching approach is necessary. It seems that multiple entry points provide a theoretical framework to enable teachers to recognise the potential of all pupils and provide this flexibility. This approach to the application of MI theory is supportive of English language teachers who argue that the main use of the theory of multiple intelligences is to *'help us increase the variety of exercise types we offer our students'* (Davis et al., 1998:132).

A number of studies have explored how MI theory may be applied practically in English classrooms from different perspectives

(Berman, 1998; Haley, 2004; Smagorinsky, 1995; Tanner, 2001). For example, in a literature lesson, Simeone (1995) adopts kinesthetic approaches involving role play, picture guessing games and free writing. Take picture guessing games as an example. One student makes some sketches on the board which relate to the proverb, '*A bird in the hand is worth two in the bush*'. Then, other members of the team attempt to guess the proverb. From Simeone's (1995) observation, students who are often poor in written examinations are outstanding with picture conceptualisations. This suggests that ability to conceptualise picture could be used to promote learning during a course.

Another example is provided by Kallenbach and Viens (2002), who maintain that students taught by MI-inspired instruction, are more confident in taking greater control of their own learning. In addition, Christison (1996) addresses the diversity in her English classroom by keeping a weekly checklist of multiple intelligences. Another researcher speaks of increased motivation and greater engagement by students in learning (Ko, 2002). To sum up, the above studies provide evidence of the compatibility between MI theory and second language learning.

2.3.5 Multiple Entry Points versus the Input Theory

One concern of input theory is how learners can understand a language through a variety of mediums (see section 2.2.6). As Meskill notes (1999:142),

Language learning is facilitated by use of the target language in content-rich and purposeful ways while an active awareness of the forms and functions of language used is maintained.

This principle matches the concept of entry points, which provides comprehensible input to a core subject. As stated by Krechevsky and Seidel (2001:51), *'the more ways a teacher can explain or teach a topic or concept, the more likely that both the teacher and the students will understand it deeply'*. This kind of presentation not only promotes learning by learners, but also allows teachers to present the same material in a variety of ways. Brualdi (1996) summarises that teaching in this manner, activating a wide assortment of intelligences, can facilitate a deeper understanding of the subject material. The above points show that both input theory and multiple entry point approaches have certain similarities concerning the use of a range of teaching methods to enhance learners' understanding. Accordingly, it is possible to compare the relationships between multiple entry points and input theory, as the following table indicates.

Table 2.4 The Input Theory versus Multiple Entry Points

The Input Theory		Multiple Entry Points
How is the input made comprehensible?	Aims ↔	Which method helps learners acquire a new concept?
Providing comprehensible input through authentic material, rich visual information, and problem-solving tasks.	Principles ↔	Promote learners' understanding of a new concept via multiple perspectives.

Comprehensible input can elicit a higher level of learners' interests.	Approach ↔	Start a lesson with the simplest way of gaining initial access.
Project work, task-based activities	Application ↔	From project work, students learn in ways which best suit them.

Several studies of English as second language have focused on applying multiple entry points in the language classrooms (Simpson, 2000; Simeone, 1995). Simpson (2000) applied the MI-inspired approach to an English composition class through seven activities. After the teacher explained the constructs of the paragraph in English (linguistic intelligence), students were required to draw a diagram to represent the paragraph structure (spatial intelligence) and to share their diagrams with one another (interpersonal intelligence). After that, they presented the structure of a paragraph using physical action (bodily-kinaesthetic intelligence). Free writing about the comparison between English and learners' native language was required as homework (intrapersonal intelligence). In the next class activity, students created a crossword puzzle using the structure they had learned from the previous lesson (logical-mathematical intelligence). Meanwhile, they wrote a song with the constructs used in the paragraph (musical intelligence). The findings indicate that students liked to learn in this manner, asking questions about topic sentences, following content, and writing a concluding sentence to their paragraphs.

Authentic and real-life learning activities are learner-centred so learning through these activities becomes more interesting. When students realise the purpose of what they are doing, they become highly motivated. While at the same time, their language skills are naturally utilised. In other words, when students are engaged in a task, it means that they construct their knowledge and develop a product by interacting with material, technology and other people.

2.3.6 MI-inspired Approaches versus Task Based Learning Activities

Kallenbach and Viens (2002) point out that multiple intelligences-inspired tasks can be authentic for students in dealing with real life problems. They explain that the authenticity of a task reveals the '*real problems and products highlighted in MI theory's definition of intelligence*' (Kallenbach and Viens, 2002:58). Learning is meaningful when students are allowed to choose activities compatible with their intelligence strengths.

Christison (1996) emphasises that many teachers of English as a second language (ESL) believe in the importance of diversity in the classroom, so MI theory is often applied in the English language classroom. Berman (1998) designed a series of classroom tasks based on each specific intelligence type. In reality, his lesson plans are similar to activities in ESL textbooks and have often been applied in classrooms. Activities including information gap, pair work, matching, guessing, searching, arranging and small group work all require students to use different intelligences.

In addition to these small tasks, project based learning reflects MI theory in that it involves learners using different intelligences. As Krechevsky and Seidel (2001:53) mention:

Projects offer students the opportunity to solve problems or create products – the definition of intelligence according to Gardner. In project work, the intelligences function as means, rather than goals.

Fried-Booth (1986:7) points out that '*project work helps to bridge the gap between language study and language use*'. Learners have to use what they have learned in the classroom and also use the language in real life situations. Fried-Booth (1986:9-10) suggests several stages for developing project work, including:

stimulus, definition of the project objective, practice of language skills, design of written materials, group activities, collating information, organization of materials, and final presentation.

That is, students need skills to plan, organise, negotiate, and perform the task. In other words, they require not only linguistic intelligence but also logical or spatial intelligence to create a presentation. When they negotiate, they are utilising both interpersonal and intrapersonal intelligences. They organise the project and do the presentation with spatial and logical-mathematical intelligences. Such project work requires students to exert their strengths in a variety of intelligences. Overall, using MI-based instruction enables students to take more control of their learning and build on their strengths by tailoring tasks to their own interests. MI inspired instruction appears to be compatible with a task-based learning approach. The following table shows the similarity of ideas expressed between MI inspired instruction and task-based learning approaches.

Table 2.5 MI-inspired Instruction versus Task-Based Learning Approaches

MI inspired instruction		Task-based learning
Help students recognise their own strengths in order to understand a concept and complete a task	Aim ↔	A task is an activity where the target language is used by the learner for a communicative purpose (goal) in order to achieve an outcome. (Willis, 1996)
To provide learners with multiple ways of exploring main ideas of a topic to promote understanding.	Approach ↔	The verbal or non-verbal information supplied by the task, e.g., pictures; a map, written text. (Ellis, 2003:21)
Multiple entry point activities- Problem solving activities Project activities	Type ↔	Jigsaw tasks, Information-gap tasks, Problem-solving tasks Decision-making tasks Opinion exchange tasks (Richards, 2001:62)

2.3.7 Comments

The theory of multiple intelligences tends to encourage those students experiencing difficulties when learning a second language. In the traditional model, the measurement of language learners' potential is based on intelligence quotient (IQ) tests. Many studies show '*IQ scores were a good means*' of predicting how well a language learner would learn (Lightbown & Spada, 1999:52). In other words, high IQ scores are related to the successful learning of a second language. However, in a model of multiple intelligences, everyone can learn to the best of their ability, weakening this correlation between language achievement and IQ.

Many teachers define MI theory as a new method of instruction. They follow the MI categories and design a syllabus to include all multiple intelligent aspects. These kinds of lesson plans can actually be regarded as a resource book of practice activities. Like Berman's book (1998), each activity in each unit can be regarded as supplementary, rather than the main teaching material. The problem in this book is that those activities, which are categorised at elementary level by Berman, are actually more suited to intermediate users of English. The activity contains a wide vocabulary and many complicated sentences. Further, the multitude of place names and characters, mentioned in this book, are mostly related to the UK, such as Buckingham Palace, the British monarchy and the Loch Ness Monster. Perhaps only teachers with a British background should adopt this kind of activity in their language classroom. Also, students who do not know Britain may find such topics of little or no interest. Therefore, although the MI principles may be broadly valuable, the current practical expression of those principles in books and material deserves further development.

Another study devoted to MI, written by Lazear (1991), can be considered as a sourcebook for expanding different intelligences. It offers various ideas about how to improve learners' multiple intelligences. Each chapter describes how to activate a specific intelligence via content-based lessons in a classroom setting. The instructions in the book are clear and are helpful for teachers who like to establish task-based learning activities. Apart from the chapter on linguistic intelligence, this kind of book actually has few benefits for language learning. For example, Lazear outlines a '*Story Grid for Creative Writing*' to emphasise creative writing in the chapter on linguistic intelligence. He suggests teachers assign students to groups, with four roles: *'recorder'*, *'encourager'*, *'organizer'*, and *'reporter'* to *'write a story outline for a TV show which links the circled items on the grid in a single story'* (Lazear, 1991:16). This task can be a good reference for language teachers who like using task-based learning. However, the other activity for recognition, creation or reproduction of rhythm, to activate musical intelligence, may be helpful for facilitating language learning. The difficulty here is that many language teachers may not be familiar with rhythm and may not feel confident enough to undertake a rhythm activity even if they know that such an activity would be a useful language task.

In reality, this kind of sourcebook focuses on how to amplify musical or other intelligences, rather than using potential learner intelligences to enhance language learning. When language teachers want to adopt the framework of multiple intelligences in their teaching, they should select tasks related to language learning. For example, if a rhythm task is linked to appreciating poetry, it is an appropriate aim in language teaching. In contrast, if rhythm is applied to develop musical intelligence, it is not a convenient focus for a language lesson. Trying to teach students how to develop all the intelligences may not be appropriate in a language lesson. In brief, it is not perhaps the task but the purpose for which the task is being performed that is crucial.

To put it more simply, the idea of MI sourcebooks is a valuable one, but the context of my research did not allow me to exploit them fully. In the sourcebooks, the theory of multiple intelligences is used to design teaching that will increase a specific intelligence. However, the MI theory adopted in my research was through the form of one of its practical implications, i.e., the multiple entry point approaches to help students learn English.

Gardner (1999) clarifies that the MI concept is neither a learning style nor a new teaching methodology. The application of MI theory in my research is to remind teachers that students are diverse and that a subject can be taught in more than one way. It is not possible for a teacher to address all the individual MI profiles of each student. Instead, a syllabus design with multiple perspectives can help students understand their own intelligences and manage their own learning. This reminds teachers that they should be aware of the principle of MI and be flexible in its implementation.

Gardner (1983:391) mentions that '*the potential utility of computers in the process of matching individuals to modes of instruction is substantial*'. Veenema and Gardner (1996) explain that technology can enhance understanding to '*help more students form rich representations of an event and cultivate deeper understanding*', meaning that technology can provide a range of entry points for students to exhibit their own understanding. This notion is actually echoed in the principle of Computer Assisted Language Learning (CALL), which attempts to create a learning environment with multiple perspectives in which learners feel motivated. The issue of CALL is discussed in next section.

2.4 Computer Assisted Language Learning

In section 1.2, the application of CALL in Taiwan was discussed. In this section, a wider range of CALL literature will be reviewed. Integrating computer technology into the language classroom promises many benefits, due to advances in computer software and the Internet. Moreover, one of '*the most significant Internet event in the 1990s*' is the creation of the World Wide Web which provides rich information (Fox & Johnson, 2001). Accordingly, the addition of the World Wide Web sets the stage for second language learning. As Warschauer (2000) defines it, the development of computer assisted language learning (CALL) can be divided into three main stages: structural CALL, communicative CALL, and integrative CALL, each stage corresponding to a certain level of technology and certain pedagogical theories. Structural CALL is based on behaviourist learning and communicative CALL on the communicative approach, while integrative CALL is based on a content-based approach.

We begin this section with the history of CALL and a discussion revolving, specifically, around current practices of the World Wide Web in the language classroom. A review of how the input theory of second language acquisition relates to CALL practice is then addressed. Finally, how the theory of multiple intelligences relates to website resources in language teaching is discussed.

2.4.1 The History of Computer Assisted Language Learning

Warschauer (2000) defines the development of computer assisted language learning (CALL) as having three stages: structural, communicative and integrative, which is in line with his perspectives of language learning and teaching. It is shown in Table 2.6.

Table 2.6 Warschauer's Three Stages of CALL

Stage	1970s-1980s: Structural CALL	1980s-1990s: Communicative CALL	21st Century: Integrative CALL
Technology	Mainframe	PCs	Multimedia and Internet
English-Teaching Paradigm	Grammar-Translation & Audio-Lingual	Communicative Language Teaching	Content-Based
View of Language	Structural approach	Cognitive approach	Socio-cognitive approach

Structural CALL

As Warschauer (2000) explains, the first stage of CALL development was influenced by behaviourism. The behavioural learning process involves '*habit-formation, which was brought about by imitation, reinforcement and repetition of behaviour*' (Littlewood, 1994:17). At this stage, CALL material heavily relies on a behaviourist instruction which follows drill and practice methods (Beatty, 2003). The computer programme provides game-like exercises and a second-try opportunity for students. Students meet the challenge, solve the problem and attain a score as a result. This type of program is designed with a large amount of drill activities and learners have to give answers in a certain form. The program then provides immediate feedback for reinforcement. In other words, the pedagogical objectives in this type of CALL are focused on improving specific areas of learners' grammatical knowledge (Chapelle, 1996). With a computer-assisted grammar system, students learn grammatical structure through the traditional structure-based approach.

Communicative CALL

The second stage of CALL development is influenced by the communicative approach, representing a shift from teacher-fronted to learner-centred learning. The principle of the communicative approach is that *'language techniques are designed to engage learners in the pragmatic, authentic, functional use of language for meaningful purposes'* (Brown, 1994:245). At this stage, the design of computer-based instruction corresponds to cognitive theories which recognise that learning is a creative process of discovery, expression, and development (Warschauer, 2000). Accordingly, the computer software attempts to follow the principles of communicative approaches. These software programmes are based on problem-solving or information exchange types, where learners use the language to share information, discover sequences or locations and determine answers. The target is that learners understand the content and complexity of the language through the tasks used.

Bax (2003) argues against Warschauer's definition of the term 'communicative CALL' by saying that communication and interaction are too limited in CALL. As Bax mentions, this communication is too limited because it only happens between computers and students. Bax's view is similar to many teachers' points of view that learners actually interact with a machine. These teachers identify *'the computer is not yet a good conversation partner'* (Hanson-Smith, 1999:192).

However, some research has given interaction in the CALL context a wider expectation (Hémard, 2003; Murray, 1987; Smith,

2003). Murray (1987:14) claims that the use of the computer does not simply mean '*face-to-face*' interaction between learners and machines. Interaction is not provided by the technology itself and does not happen in terms of learners and computers only, but encompasses the entire learning situation. It would be better to say that a computer is a tool which does not provide of its own accord any communication or interaction for learners. It is the material on the Internet or the software which provide interactive activities for learners. Moreover, it is essential that teachers take great pains when designing a lesson and preparing an activity so as to ensure that the most effective use is made of these learning opportunities.

Integrative CALL

The third stage of CALL development adopts an integrative approach that can be introduced by two innovations, multimedia and the Internet. The advantage of multimedia is that it combines reading, writing, speaking and listening activities in one single package. Moreover, learners exercise a high degree of control over their progress by going through the learning material. Research has proved that computer technology provides many benefits for the acquisition of English language skills. For example, a multimedia programme provides '*naturalistic language input punctuated by drawings, animations, and sound effects*' (Hanson-Smith, 1999: 196). These functions allow learners to access input with their preferred learning modes in a variety of ways such as reading or listening (Hanson-Smith, 1999).

In tandem with the development of the Internet, CALL has developed a multi-perspectives role with the unique ability to deliver authentic material that meets the needs of the individual learner. As Kern and Warschauer (2000) point out, network-based language teaching has been transformed into a new form of CALL. Networks now provide students with many more opportunities to learn and to use the target language, such as online courses, discussion groups, or collaborative learning exchanges. These content-based or project-based activities can integrate the four language skills in ways that a coursebook never can. Learners are given an opportunity to use the target language to share information via electronic mail or discussion boards, which may be defined as active use of the language. Moreover, learners have become active participants in learning and are encouraged to be explorers and creators of language rather than passive recipients of it (Brown, 1991).

Much research has discussed how the Internet and its related facilities, e.g. web integration, email, mailing lists and discussion groups provide greater potential for language learners (Isbell & Reinhardt, 2000; Kitao & Kitao, 2001, Tsou et al, 2002). One of the Internet services attracting the attention of many language teachers is the World Wide Web, and it does so because it constitutes a virtual library. The World Wide Web is regarded as a source of ready-made material in primary visual and verbal modes. The multiple sources available include written words, pictures, sounds and movement, which teachers can readily turn into usable curriculum resources. However, because of the multiplicity of choice on the World Wide

Web, finding a quality source for classroom material is becoming more and more difficult. The multimodal input from the World Wide Web and the issues of web design will be reviewed in the following sections.

2.4.2 Input from the World Wide Web

The World Wide Web environment is considered to be a powerful input resource, because the input from written texts is supplemented by '*pictures, graphics, animations, video, and sounds*' (Hanson-Smith, 1999:189). Many current websites are designed using several modes, including visual, textual and audio modes, in order to facilitate a reader's understanding of the web content. In the multimodal applications on the Web, the verbal and the visual are combined in new ways to enhance meaning (Snyder, 2001). While the World Wide Web employs multi-sensory information to enhance interaction with users, the problem still remains that reading from a screen is different from reading a printed text. Readers cannot read from a screen for an extended period of time. They may have difficulties reading an article from the screen, especially if the website fonts are too small or if the text and background colours do not have sufficient contrast. A research study into interest thresholds reports that print material has to be assimilated within 13 seconds in order to capture attention and the most critical threshold was found to be visual interest (Burmark, 2002). Therefore, it can be deduced that the attention of students working with poor website displays will quickly lapse. Normally, users would change to another web page if the page they are looking at fails to catch their attention within 13 seconds or less; in class they may simply stop concentrating. That is to say, people tend to give up reading the contents of a web site, if it is not visually attractive enough to quickly engage their attention. These observations lead us to a discussion of various issues concerning a web design.

2.4.3 Web Design Issues

Choosing websites for this research should take into account the users. This section explores the issues which should be given attention. Norman (2002) offers four basic suggestions for a user-centred design which are:

1. *Make it easy to determine what actions are possible at any moment.*
2. *Make things visible, including the conceptual model of the system, the alternative actions, and the results of actions.*
3. *Make it easy to evaluate the current state of the system.*
4. *Follow natural mappings between intentions and the required actions; between actions and the resulting effect; and between the information that is visible and the interpretation of the system state. (Norman, 2002: 188)*

Norman's recommendations remind us that the designer has to be aware of facilitating the task for users. Similarly, Preece et al. (2002:12) describe a user-centred approach involving involve four basic activities:

1. Identifying needs and establishing requirements

2. Developing alternative designs

3. Building interactive version of the designs

4. Evaluating those designs

The major advantage of the user-centred design approach is that there is a deeper understanding of the needs of the user. In this way, users are able to use the product with a minimum of effort to navigate. In particular, users such as language teachers, who are not familiar with technology, should be able to navigate the website and acquire information easily. In the context of my research, the computer assisted language learning application focuses mainly on the use of website resources in listening classes. Therefore, in this discussion of web design, it is important to recognise that students' first impressions of the website will be highly significant. Because of the issue of multimodality that was discussed earlier, the presentation of audio combined with visual material on a website will be the second important feature. Moreover, the application of website resources in class and after class should be considered. Accordingly, the following discussion focuses on web readability, multiple sensory presentation and web resources. The section on multiple entry points (section 2.5) will raise some further issues to be attended to in the selection of websites for this research.

A. Readability

Nielsen (1997) notes that people generally scan web pages, rather than read them, word by word. In other words, the first impression of a website can determine if users will navigate round that website or not. If a website is of a poor quality design, the users will quickly lose the interest or move to another one. Further, it can potentially reduce the effectiveness of web-based reading. In an alternative approach, Burmark (2002) asserts that clear visual elements such as animation, pictures, or tables within a graphical representation, will help the eye to move on quickly. There are many factors that could affect the readability of computer screen, e.g., the font used for the text, the formatting of the screen, and the colour contrast between text and background. Morton's (2001) study points out that colour is the most powerful building material in visual imagery on the World Wide Web. Accordingly, this examination of readability focuses on colour combination on a website.

The findings of a recent study provide evidence to show that colour combinations have important effects on visual search performance (Ling and Schaik, 2002). Ling and Schaik found that *'higher contrasts between text and background colour lead to faster searching and are rated more favourably'* by readers (Ling and Schaik , 2002:223). Their findings show that this apparently low-level issue of different choices of colour combinations can actually influence both the accuracy and speed of visual searches. It is inferred that background textures and colours can affect the readability of text. Similarly, Shieh and Lin (2000) found colour combination was the most influential factor in subjective preference by investigating the effects of twelve background colour combinations on visual performance. The findings show that blue letters on a yellow background resulted in the best performance. In contrast, purple letters on a red background led to the worst visual performance.

B. Multimodal Presentations

As might be expected from the literature discussed in section 2.2.6, several studies have shown that instruction employing more than one modality, e.g., visual and auditory, produced more positive effects on learning than the single modality format (Tindall-Ford et al., 1997). The study showed that a combination of audio text and visual graphics enhanced learners' comprehension more than a single visual format. Similarly, the use of auditory and visual modalities increased the capacity of working memory to handle the information. Researchers found that second language learners understood a story in the German language better when they were able to select both visual and verbal annotations (Plass et al., 1998).

Mayer and Moreno (2002) noted that animation is one of the most exciting forms of pictorial presentation. They proposed seven principles for the use of animation in multimedia instruction:

(1) Students learn more deeply from animation and narration than from narration alone.

(2) Students learn more deeply when on-screen text is presented next to the portion of the animation.

(3) Students learn more deeply when corresponding portions of the narration and animation are presented at the same time.

(4) Students learn more deeply from animation and narration when

extraneous words, sounds (including music), and video are excluded rather than included.

(5) Students learn more deeply from animation and narration than from animation and on-screen text.

(6) Students learn more deeply from animation and narration than from animation, narration, and on-screen text.

(7) Students learn more deeply from animation and narration when the narration is in conversational rather than formal style.
(Mayer & Moreno, 2002:93-96)

Mayer and Moreno's principles indicate clearly that related visual and verbal information should be presented as closely as possible.

C. Source Evaluation

Salaberry (2001:51) claims that the success of 'a technology-driven activity' is based more on pre- and post-activities than on the technology activity itself. This point was discussed in section 2.4.1 in which it was stressed that the computer is only a tool and it is up to the teacher to provide an overall context of communicative activity. Similarly, websites provide a diversity of information and teachers need to decide what kind of source would be the most appropriate for providing second language learning. There is no single website which is able to provide four language skills (listening, reading, writing and speaking) at the same time. The importance of its features should depend on the particular domain a user is working in. If websites are used as an integrated resource in the curriculum, the criteria of website selection should be based on its potential possibilities for further language learning activities.

For the purposes of this research project, our use of websites focuses on listening classes for university students. Therefore, the criteria should be similar to those needed when selecting a listening coursebook as outlined in Cunningsworth's checklist for listening (1995:68). In Cunningsworth's checklist for a listening course, the coursebook should meet the following criteria.

1. What kind of listening material is contained in the course?
2. What kinds of activities are based on the listening passages?
3. Is the listening material set in a meaningful context?
4. What is the effect of the recorded material?
5. Is there any video material for listening?

In the context of the selection of a website for my listening course, these criteria can be adapted as follows:

1. Does the website give a summary of the information it provides, including a summary of the listening tasks available?

    A good summary should introduce the purpose of the creation of the website. In other words, the website introduction should provide information for teachers to identify how the website can be used in the class.

2. Can the website provide listening activities suitable for use in class and after class?

    For example, good websites should provide different ranges of listening activities which help teachers teach listening skills.

Many listening exercises on the website give students the textual transcripts of the audio recording. In a class setting, teachers can make intelligent use of these transcripts. After class, students may enhance their listening comprehension with the support of a printed text.

3. Is the listening material on the website related to daily life issues?

One of the reasons for using daily life issues as learning material is to make lessons more interesting. Also, on a broader level, English in a daily life context helps students base their use of the target language on reality. So a good website will include daily life issues.

4. What is the quality of the recorded material provided on the website?

On a good website, listening recordings are expected to sound as clear as possible. However, speaking is not the same as reading, word by word. In other words, features of normal speech should be taken into account such as repetition, hesitation, and unfinished sentences.

5. Does the website make good use of the visual medium to provide a meaningful context or show facial expression or gesture?

On a good website, visual information, e.g., gesture or facial expression can aid students' understanding of a listening task.

Apart from the importance of colour combination and multimodal presentation, the above guidelines provide strategies for selecting and/or evaluating Internet resources used in listening applications. These criteria are also reviewed with the three chosen websites in the current study in the later chapters so that they can help in understanding the findings that emerged in relation to each website.

2.5 Applying the Entry Point Approach in a CALL Setting

The pursuit of understanding is the primary goal of education, according to Gardner (1991). How to make students understand a concept, skill, theory, or domain of knowledge is therefore a major consideration. As mentioned in Section 2.3.3, Gardner states that any topic can be presented in at least five ways which he calls entry points. Gardner describes these in different ways on different occasions but always emphases four entry points: aesthetic, narrative, logical and experiential. As will be evident from Sections 2.5.1 to 2.5.4, it is clear that these four entry points could be applied in practice in the classroom setting in which I was working as they seemed to be the most directly relevant. Therefore, I used these four entry points in my own study. The other entry points, e.g., musical, foundation or interpersonal mentioned by Gardner (1999) would have been difficult to use in the context of my research. In the sections that follow, I will outline why each of the four entry points I chose might be expected to be useful in language learning in my teaching context. After that, an indication of why a website offers a powerful means of exploiting each of these entry points will be given. This section will therefore explore the use of four entry points in

CALL classes: aesthetic, narrative, logical and experiential entry points.

2.5.1 Applying an Aesthetic Entry Point to present the Topic

The aesthetic entry point is the use of images in the learning process in order to enhance understanding. Images are considered to *'illustrate, clarify, and reinforce oral and printed communication – quantitative relationships, specific details, abstract concepts, and spatial relationships'* (Dwyer, cited in Moore, 2003:95). These effects of images are likely to be of increasing significance because according to LeLoup and Ponterio's observations (1996), students are becoming more and more visually-orientated. They argue that this is clear from the fact that students often notice heavily illustrated reading material first, in comparison with normal discursive black and white text. Kress & van Leeuwen (1996:2-3) also state that *'visual communication is coming to be less and less the domain of specialists, and more and more crucial in the domains of public communication'*.

Hanson-Smith (1999) discusses some multimedia programmes which can provide greater comprehensibility of input. In other words, using computer technology means that as well as still pictures, video and animation can be available as relevant features in aesthetic entry point activities. The World Wide Web contains a vast array of visually supported content that catches learners' attention. In my setting, each lesson was displayed on a full screen for the whole class. In this style of use, images rather than simply text were likely to be especially import. Careful selection, presentation and development of material containing pictures, video and animation can therefore be expected to make classroom learning easier. Moreover, students will have a much better chance of making progress in the class.

2.5.2 Applying a Narrative Entry Point to describe the Topic

A narrative entry point involves introducing a new concept through telling a story (Dara-Abrams, 2005). Wright (2003:7) explains that '*stories are descriptions of dramatic events in fiction or in fact*'. The reason for using stories in the language classroom setting is that they can engage students with '*the deeper resources of the mind*' of students and can be related to '*the new language*' for learners to learn on '*a rich and enduring level*' (Wright, 2003:8). Baker and Greene (1987:18) point out that the purposes of storytelling are to share and '*create a common experience*'. When the storytelling is through speech as well as the text, learners can '*associate the symbols on the printed page with the words they are hearing*' so as to be familiar with oral language patterns and develop listening skills (Baker & Greene, 1987:21). This is also why Wright (1995:7) mentions that stories help learners notice the '*sound of the foreign language*' and '*build up a reservoir of language in this way*'.

The story can be in textual or audio form to describe what is happening. Audio presentation of a narrative can be especially powerful. Learners can be stimulated via audio elements including sound effects, music or different kinds of characters. The narrator usually mediates the story for listeners by selecting what tone to take, what types of voice to give to characters, and what to emphasise to engage listeners. In this way, listeners can experience how the text is read and imagine the characters in the story. This suggests that stories presented orally may have an even more powerful impact than stories in written presentation. It also emphasises that audio is much more than just an alternative presentation of the language when used in the context of a story. Use of audio and text in a narrative context therefore goes further than simply a dual mode presentation of non-narrative material.

An advantage of the Internet is the availability of authentic material consisting of both audio and visual material telling a story (Collins et al., 1997). The authentic materials imply real life conversation or speech spoken by various native speakers that may be relevant to the learners' life and interests. As Field (1998: 114) states, an additional advantage of authentic listening material can *afford examples of the hesitations, false starts, filled and empty pauses* and help learners *become familiar with the real cadences of the target language*. As for audio in multimedia presentations, it provides *a useful venue* for learners to experience *a dual-processing model* of learning (Moreno & Mayer, 2000:117). In other words, the use of the Internet can provide aesthetic and narrative entry points at the same time.

2.5.3 Applying a Logical Entry Point to involve the Topic

A logical entry point approaches the concept by involving thinking or a problem-solving process. To use this entry point, comprehension exercises or activities are included in the different phases of a lesson. These ranges from short answer questions to a multiple-choice test. The problem solving activities help teach new language and can be focused so that they involve different degrees of complexity. The practice can go from activities related to the acquisition of a single word to those related to the comprehension of the whole topic.

The increasing availability of ready-made quizzes on the Internet such as comprehension questions or crosswords offers the teacher instant access to problem solving activities for students to check their understanding. A logical entry point based on such quizzes might therefore be especially motivating as they support initial learning and provide immediate feedback. Except for computer-made exercises, teachers may wish to use some related tasks involving decision making, effective reasoning or logical thinking to assure that the target skill will re-occur and persist.

2.5.4 Applying an Experiential Entry Point to represent the Topic

The experiential entry point refers to the actual experience of participating in different activities and allows learners to deal with the material that embody the concept. In other words, experiential learning is involved with an experience which is real and meaningful

(Kolb, 1984). Kolb (1984) defines experiential learning as a process whereby knowledge is created through the combination of understanding and transforming experiences. Accordingly, learning approaches can include negotiation, planning, engaging, experiencing, reflecting, evaluating, sharing and publishing.

Online discussion boards may be regarded as one means of applying experiential learning. Although computers mostly rely on keyboarding and the use of the mouse, the point is that various discussion boards make learners active participants in the learning process. Teachers can create a class discussion board for students to place their work, receive feedback from their peers and give similar feedback to others. Alternatively, teachers can ask students to participate in a specific group drawn from the existing discussion list. They are actively engaged in exploring their understanding. Students can post their work, read others' ideas and respond to what their classmates have written. Also, the students' writing is not only read by one person (the teacher) but also by their classmates and by people they do not know. In other words, students see the purpose of what they are doing, they usually become more productive learners (Baum et al. 2005). Hands-on activity is actually similar to a problem solving activity but is far more open ended. From constructing the idea to expressing the message explicitly in written form, students encounter situations which they cannot predict. In the process of revisiting data and revising their thinking, academic skills are practised repeatedly.

The multimedia environment, with its combinations of text, images and sound, enable teachers to find and construct multiple entry point activities. The capability of website resources and multimedia help teachers bridge the gap between the printed text and a concrete idea. In other words, the World Wide Web may be regarded as a means of constructing learning material incorporating multiple entry points. While incorporating multiple entry point instruction, teachers can effectively present website material.

2.6 Summary

This literature review attempts to apply both second language acquisition and multiple intelligences theory to the implementation of computer assisted language learning courses. The characteristics of language input and student/teacher interaction, in computer assisted language learning, are of concern to researchers. The main reason is because technology is able to provide multiple modalities to help comprehension and respond to learning differences. Although there is a variety of input theories, the notion of multiple entry points derived from the theory of multiple intelligences, seems particularly powerful. Accordingly, specific entry points are introduced and justified where they have been adopted in my research.

The practical problem is how teachers choose an appropriate website for a computer assisted language learning course. Hence, the review briefly introduces the development of computer assisted language learning and draws on the criteria of web design and source application. A research proposal is then outlined showing how to take advantage of the opportunities of multimodal presentations offered by the Internet and the practical idea of multiple entry points to refine class teaching. Therefore, the research project explained in later chapters consists of the design, implementation and evaluation of these approaches to professional teacher practice. Finally, this research project attempts to explore ways in which the World Wide Web may strengthen English teaching with multiple entry point approaches.

CHAPTER 3

THE RESEARCH APPROACH

3.1 Introduction

This chapter explains the research approach used in this study. The purpose of this research is an attempt to explore how English teaching can benefit from the Internet, in the classroom and to what extent, World Wide Web links, used to access authentic real-life teaching materials, may facilitate students' interest in English learning. Accordingly, this methodology is designed around a core strand of action research, which supports new action and reflection for all involved.

The content of this chapter summarises, first, three potential research paradigms. A paradigm is then chosen, and the reason for the choice, outlined. The research design indicates that the study would best be guided and informed by an approach of action research, under the rubric of the interpretative paradigm. A brief introduction of action research and the reasons for locating that action research, within an interpretative paradigm, are next explained. The chapter goes on to explain how the research is organised and then details the processes used in the main study, including a description of data collection and research procedures.

3.2 Research Paradigms

The researchers' choice of methodology should depend on the nature of the study and its research inquiry. Husén (1997:17) claims that a paradigm determines how the researcher '*selects and defines problems for inquiry*' and how the research '*approaches them theoretically and methodologically*'. Similarly, Rossman and Rallis (1998:28) argue that researchers use '*the concept of paradigm to capture the idea that definitions are the products of shared understanding of reality*'. Further, Crotty distinguishes four basic elements of any research process, generally addressed within a paradigm:

Table 3.1 Four Elements of the Research Process

epistemology	the theory of knowledge
theoretical perspective	the philosophical stance
methodology	the strategy, action plan, process or design
methods	the techniques or procedures used to gather data

Adapted from Crotty (1998:3-5)

In other words, the paradigm, within which researchers work, influences what they look for, and the way in which they understand and construct what they find.

My methodological journey reports a brief discussion of three educational research paradigms. In seeking to identify and clarify their most salient characteristics, the next section outlines each paradigm with a set of concepts or ideas, and preferred techniques that frame the conduct of a piece of research. The characteristics of the three paradigms are summarised below as: the positivist paradigm, the interpretative paradigm and the critical paradigm.

3.2.1 The Positivist Paradigm

Both the positivist and the interpretivist stance carry a set of assumptions with specific implications for social science research, including educational investigations. The positivist paradigm assumes an objectivist epistemology and implies '*that reality is fact based*' (Rossman & Rallis, 1998:30). In order to find out how knowledge is acquired and put to use, the positivist paradigm implies a '*functional-structural, objective-rational, goal-directed approach*' (Husén, 1997:19). This view is similar in underlying concepts to Bassey's view, as it says: *positivist researchers do not expect that they themselves are significant variables in their research* (Bassey, 1995:12). The role of positivist researchers is designed to avoid any actions creating significant variables in their research. The positivist paradigm assumes an objectivist epistemology which implies:

> *the world is independent of and unaffected by the researcher; facts and values are distinct, thus making it possible to conduct objective, value free inquiry; (Snape & Spencer, 2003:16)*

This means studies under the positivist rationale are supposed to be '*independent, objective and value free*' (Snape & Spencer, 2003:23). Moreover, it is assumed that clear '*cause-and-effect*' relationships exist in the world (Cohen et al., 2000:14).

However, Burns (2000:10) points out that the positivist approach docs not concern '*people's unique ability to interpret their experiences, construct their own meanings and act on these*'. As Cohen et al. (2000:19) point out, positivism regards '*human behaviour as passive, essentially determined and controlled, thereby ignoring intention, individualism and freedom*'. By contrast, interpretative researchers believe that the situation at any given moment is not the same as at the next moment.

3.2.2 The Interpretative Paradigm

The interpretative paradigm subscribes to subjectivist assumptions about epistemology, which maintain '*an understanding of reality is formed through personal experience, interaction, and discussion*' (Rossman & Rallis, 1998:31). Moreover, Ritchie and Lewis (2003: 21) give a similar explanation, saying that the interpretative stance emphasises '*the importance of understanding people's perspectives in the context of the conditions and circumstances of their lives*'. Interpretative researchers believe that human behaviour is meaningful, so they reject the positivists' view that the '*social world can be understood in terms of general statements about human actions*' (Bassey, 1995:13). From the interpretative standpoint, understanding cannot be defined by mere scientific investigation, but by asking questions or observing the situation. They not only want the answer, but also the reasons for this answer. They want to discover the meaning behind peoples' actions.

In order to understand the questions being raised in educational research, Erickson (1999:121) suggests an appropriate method is *'using participant observational fieldwork'*. Interpretivists assume that researchers are themselves regarded as *'potential variables'* who are intimately involved in their research projects (Bassey, 1995:13). Hence, interpretative researchers necessarily need to engage with their subjects in a field setting, and record what happens in that setting. Thus, they generally use qualitative methods such as *'fieldwork notes, diaries and transcripts and reports of conversations'* (Bassey, 1995:13). These approaches enable them to gain a deep understanding about the subjects under the study and their actions. In this way, researchers can have a close up understanding of why people think and act the way they do as participants and as observers.

3.2.3 The Critical Paradigm

As mentioned above, positivist views of knowledge links tend to emphasise *'determinacy'*, *'rationality'*, *'impersonality'* and *'prediction'* while interpretative knowledge tends to be associated with meaning making, understanding and inter-personal communication (Scott and Usher, 1999:13). Cohen et al. (2000:28) state that *'an emerging approach to educational research is the paradigm of critical educational research'*. Generally, critical researchers hold a range of beliefs in common. Kincheloe and McLaren (1998:264) state that critical research is '*best understood in the context of the empowerment of individuals*' and tries to '*confront the injustice of a particular society or sphere within the society*'. Thus, critical researchers try to investigate the research situation with their assumptions on the table. Kinchcloc and McLaren (1998:265) state that these assumptions may change, particularly if critical researchers recognise '*that such assumptions are not leading to emancipatory actions*'.

In an education setting, Carr and Kemmis (1986) mention that the task of a critical educational science is to be located in concrete practice. In particular, these scholars argue that a critical educational stance requires that teachers become active researchers, in order to increase their understanding of the situation in which their practice is embedded, so they can change it (Carr and Kemmis, 1986:12). In other words, teachers' self-understanding of their practices constitutes a source of critical self-reflective action (Elliott, 1991). These views agree with Comstock's definition of critical research, which begins from the '*practical problem*' of everyday life (Comstock, 1982:378). He suggests that critical researchers should '*participate in a program of education with the subjects*', which gives these critical researchers a view point that creates new perspectives on their particular situation (Comstock, 1982:388).

With critical researchers, the research itself is posed as a set of ideological practices. Cohen et al. (2000:30) cite Habermas' four stages of critical research approaches:

Stage 1- A description and interpretation of the existing situation

Stage 2- A penetration of the reasons that brought the existing situation to the form that it takes

Stage 3- An agenda for altering the situation

Stage 4- An evaluation of the achievement of the situation in practice

The view of researcher participation in a critical study appears to be compatible with the interpretative paradigm. In fact, Crotty (1998:113) distinguishes between critical enquiry and interpretative paradigm, as follows.

Table 3.2 Comparison between Interpretative and Critical Research

Interpretative research	Critical research
seeks merely to understand	challenges
reads the situation in terms of interaction and community	reads the situation in terms of conflict and oppression
reports the status quo	seeks to bring about change

(Adapted from Crotty, 1998:113)

Finally, Kemmis summarises the approach of the critical researcher as being guided by:

An interest in emancipating people from determination by habit, custom, illusion and coercion which sometimes frame and constrain social and educational practice, and which sometimes produce effects contrary to those expected or desired by participants and other parties interested in or affected by particular social or educational practices. (Kemmis, 2001:92)

3.3 Action Research

This section introduces features of action research, types of action research and the approach used when conducting action research.

3.3.1 Features of Action Research

The principle of action research is to help researchers investigate the connections between their own theories of education and practices, in order to bring about improvement and change. In the light of the definition of action research, '*reflection on current practice*' becomes the main issue in action researchers' minds (Macintyre. 2000:2).

In the setting of educational science, Carr and Kemmis (1986:160) comment that the task should be located '*in actual improvements of concrete educational practice*'. These views are echoed by McNiff (1988) in her implementation of action research in classrooms. She mentions that the approach is designed to improve education, through critical reflective practice in teachers, who are '*prepared to change*' their practice (McNiff, 1988:4).

Wallace (1991:56) asserts that action research tends to address '*practical problems and should have practical outcomes*'. This is backed up by Elliott (1991:116) who believes that '*teachers' self-understandings of their practices*' can constitute a source of critical self-reflective action. Elliott (1991:49) emphasises that '*the fundamental aim of action research is to improve practice rather than to produce knowledge*'. In essence, improving practice has to involve '*a continuing process of reflection on the part of practitioners*' (Elliott, 1991:50). In an English teaching setting, Burns also states that '*it is evaluative and reflective as it aims to bring about change and improvement in practice*' (Burns, 1999:30). Moreover, Rainey's (2000) study indicates that English teachers benefited from the potential usefulness of action research.

Viewed this way, action research in an educational setting is a process of research and reflection, whereby teachers take action to improve student learning, while at the same time, gathering data to demonstrate the possible reasons for and usefulness of that action. Underpinning action research, the notion of self-reflection becomes a significant procedural tool for teachers in their attempts to improve teaching and learning.

3.3.2 Types of Action Research

There are a number of different types of action research based on the situation and involvement of the researcher. The discussion here is based on Calhoun and Ferrance's three types of action research: individual teacher action research, collaborative action research, and school-wide research (Calhoun, 1994; Ferrance, 2000).

Individual Teacher Action Research

Individual teacher action research usually focuses on a single issue in the classroom, and is conducted by a single teacher. Teachers themselves identify problems within their classroom, which relate to, for example, classroom management, instructional strategies, or learning materials. They then determine whether a particular teaching approach can improve their individual practice or not. As it is an individual teacher action research plan, teachers may also need critical feedback from their colleagues who may be '*working concurrently on the same problem*' (Ferrance, 2000:4).

Collaborative Action Research

Collaborative action research is carried out by a group of teachers or others who are interested in addressing a certain issue. The purpose of collaborative action research is to focus on problems and changes in a single classroom or on several classrooms, within a school or district or across schools and districts (Calhoun, 1994). The primary audiences for results from collaborative action research are the members of the research team nominated by teachers or administrators.

School-wide Action Research

In school-wide action research, the main focus is the improvement of the organisation. A school faculty which has a particular concern about the curriculum then organises a project to seek a solution. An inquiry, using a school-wide action research plan is often initiated in a school, because of its affiliation with a league or consortium that promotes action research as a major school improvement strategy (Calhoun, 1994). Calhoun points out that school-wide action research is also collaborative, but it is different from what is termed collaborative action research, in that everyone in the school is involved in the inquiry.

To sum up, different types of action research allow educators to investigate different areas of concern and meet the challenges within their classroom settings. Calhoun (1994) reminds us that the use of one type of research does not exclude another. Individual and collaborative research may nest comfortably and productively within school-wide action research.

3.3.3 Action Research Steps

A cyclical process is generally used in conducting action research. Kemmis and McTaggart (1988:22) represent the process of action research as a '*self-reflective spiral*'. The spiral model conveys the nature of action research as an ongoing process, continually repeating the four steps of '*planning, acting, observing and reflecting*', which follows the identification of the initial thematic concern or problem (Kemmis and McTaggart, 1988:25). The purpose of the four action cycles is to identify issues, assumptions and thoughts, so that focused questions can be asked as the process progresses. In this way, action researchers as practitioners can learn consciously from their experiences. Likewise, Arhar et al (2001:30) point to action research as '*a type of applied research*' which '*uses a problem-solving approach to improve social conditions and processes of living in the real world*'. In order to understand the situation that researchers are studying, they often apply '*a continuing cycle of action, observation, and reflection on the consequences of action*' (Arhar et al, 2001:31).

In educational settings, Wallace (1998:12) has proposed a similar '*reflective cycle*' process for teachers to increase their professional competence. His reflective cycle includes the stages of considering problems and issues, asking questions, carrying out '*action research, data collection and analysis*', and applying findings to professional action (Wallace, 1988:14). Each stage represents a way of '*structured reflection*' in order to acquire a solution (Wallace, 1998:14).

3.4 Locating Action Research in the Interpretative Paradigm

The purpose of the research indicates that the study would best be guided and informed by the action research methodology under the rubric of the interpretative paradigm. The form of this research is an individual teacher research plan, which seeks solutions to problems arising when websites are used in the language classroom.

Some researchers identify action research as a critical educational science, because it is regarded as an emancipatory model. Carr and Kemmis classify emancipatory action research under the critical paradigm by saying:

> *the practitioner group takes joint responsibility for the development of practice, understandings and situations, and sees these as socially- constructed in the interactive processes of educational life. (Carr and Kemmis, 1986:203)*

Based on the above principles, practitioners have the power to overcome false awareness, in order to generate change. This is also a key assumption of what is called the critical paradigm, which views educational research in light of conflict and oppression, and sees any resultant change as empowerment of the participants (Postlethwaite, 2004). Carr and Kemmis (1986:144) are of the opinion that researchers of critical theory are concerned about '*the rationality and justice of social action and social institutions*'. They try to pay more attention to the emancipatory purpose of identifying unnecessary constraints. The model sees that the actions of the researcher and other participants are directed outward, towards any institution imposing restrictions and constraints upon a group of practitioners. This is intended to bring about change, that may result in emancipation from these restrictions (Postlethwaite, 2004).

The focus of the inquiry in the present study is to explore how website material can be used in a listening course. More explicitly, this inquiry is working on efforts to improve English teaching practice with the aid of website resources and multiple entry point approaches, a practical framework of multiple intelligences. It does not work under the critical paradigm to emancipate people by challenging the power relationship in the current school system, nor does it seek to change the status quo of the present curriculum or general expectations of this school system.

It is conducted for the express purpose of helping me to understand my own classroom practice of teaching English in a school in Taiwan through that understanding to contribute to broad the development theory in the field. The research is an action research project by me as an individual teacher, concerned with my own understanding about the use of website resources and MI-inspired instructions for language teaching. It is on this basis that this research also tries to draw some conclusions from the reflection on my own practice. As a result of this focus this action research is located within the interpretative paradigm aimed to '*understand the subjective world of human experience*' (Cohen et al., 2000:22).

The conclusions will be based on a reflection of my practice results and will serve to develop a general understanding of how website resources may be integrated with MI-inspired instructions for English learning for other teachers. By choosing action research as the research methodology several additional points are raised: my research stance, the teacher as a researcher, and the teacher's voice, which are as follows.

3.4.1 Research Stance

According to McNiff and Whitehead (2002:17), the action researchers' ontological perspective is to acknowledge people to '*create their own identities*' and to '*allow other people to create theirs*'. Action researchers try to make improvements, both large and small and have a positive view of the future, which means that standards of living and progress may constantly improve. From an action researcher's epistemological view, people acquire knowledge experientially and individually. They remain '*knowledgeable about their own situation, and the fact that they are in their situation, and not detached from it as the scientific researcher is supposed to be'* (Scott & Usher, 1999:37). According to McNiff & Whitehead's (2002:18) view of knowledge,

> *it regards reality as a process of evolution, surprising and unpredictable. There are no fixed answers, because answers would immediately become obsolete in a constantly changing future.*

My own philosophical stance is that people can learn better through identifying and using their strengths. Learners' strengths are, I believe, a key to the ways in which they may best acquire knowledge, through a process of trial and error. Because of the inherent differences within individuals, it seems reasonable that teachers should use their own experience and reflections in formulating a methodology to assist this process. Learning should be described as an on-going process which is never static.

3.4.2 The Teacher as Researcher

Hopkins (1987) argues that traditional educational research has been inadequate in terms of helping classroom teachers to improve their own practice. He points out:

> *teachers often regard educational research as something irrelevant to their lives and see little interaction between the world of the educational researcher and the world of the teacher.* (Hopkins, 1987:14)

He evidently believes that teachers may not benefit from the results of educational research, which does not draw upon their own practice. As Wallace (1991:56) notes, '*the classroom teacher should also become a researcher*'. This means that action research, under a teacher's control, may explore '*real problems*' and be '*more relevant to the classroom*' (Wallace, 1991:56).

The action research approach provided me with an opportunity to be involved in my own research, addressing issues and drawing upon my own experience. My aim was to maximise the learning resources for language learners in the area of computer assisted language learning. As Kemmis mentions:

> *teachers are encouraged to treat their own educational ideas and theories, their own work practices and their own work settings as objects for analysis and critique. (Kemmis, 1997:174)*

Likewise, Carr and Kemmis (1986:165) define the aims of action research as being '*to improve*' and '*to involve*'. They suggest that action research '*aims at improvement in three areas*': the improvement of the practice, the improvement of an understanding of the practice, and an improvement of the situation in which the practice takes place (Carr and Kemmis, 1986:165). Action research can provide opportunities for teachers to re-examine their own knowledge, performance, beliefs and influences, in order to improve their practices. In my view of computer assisted language learning, the Internet and the World Wide Web can provide authentic learning materials, tailored to language learners with different needs. The action research approach encouraged me, as a teacher, to be reflective of my own practice in an attempt to explore the use of websites in English language classroom teaching. This may be beneficial to learners of English as a second language, and may also improve the computer assisted language teaching approaches, currently in use.

3.4.3 Teachers' Voices

According to Winter (1998:55), the theme of action research is to find '*an authentic voice*'; this refers to practitioners' own voices, with which they discuss their own experiences and their ability to learn from those experiences. In this way, student learning is facilitated by teachers' continuous reflections. In my observation, many English teachers still tend to resist integrating the Internet into their English teaching syllabus. This view is demonstrated by Bax's comment (2000:216), '*few modern language teachers are currently at this level of technological understanding and confidence*'. Some language teachers assume that they must adjust their teaching practice, in order to incorporate a new technology into their teaching syllabus. In order to minimize teachers' fear of technology, I have attempted to present a principle that teachers may focus on, regarding this aspect of teaching, by slotting the new technology into their lesson plans. The aim, in using technology, is to support teaching and learning, not to dominate the teaching methodology.

Hence, my hope is that my own practice may be an example of flexible computer assisted language teaching. Through my example,

I wish to inspire my colleagues to try to do things differently. Winter's description of an '*authentic voice*' reminds me to address issues by drawing on my own professional experience and learning (Winter, 1998:55). I present my action research project as evidence of my own professional learning in support of my proposal.

3.5 Research Design

The study took place in a University of Science and Technology class in Taiwan, during the first semester of the 2004 academic year. The process began in September and ended in January, lasting for four months. The research project was formed through a continuous cycle of self-reflection, in order to develop my professional competence. The cyclic nature of my action research methodology is presented in the following diagram, adapted from Kemmis and McTaggart's (1988) original action research cycle, and guided by Wallace's (1998) professional development process.

Figure 3.1 Research Cycle

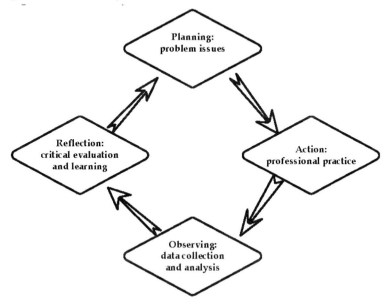

Since this study was the teacher as researcher's individual action research, the whole research process was continually undergoing change, in order to adapt to each particular context. The research procedures were processed through the following steps: identifying the research problem; planning possible actions to solve the problems; taking action; evaluating the experimental process; and going back again, to the beginning in light of the new understanding gained.

3.5.1 Identifying the Research Problem

In the literature review section, it was established that the web abounds in authentic materials that can benefit English teaching.

However, from the literature review and from my own experience in the computer assisted language learning classroom, it is evident that some practical problems exist in the Computer Assisted Language Learning classroom: the speed of web access and students' attitudes toward learning with the World Wide Web. When I implemented 'Computer Assisted Language Learning', a compulsory course for applied English majors at a technology university in Taiwan in 2000, I often encountered slow network server connections to web pages and links. For instance, if the whole class tried, simultaneously, to shift to the next website, it could involve a huge amount of time, which caused a problem in the limited lesson time slots. Further, during practice sessions, some students checked their email or accessed other websites. Sometimes, they casually used the mouse to search the screen for other links. These two situations reduced the efficiency gained by the use of the technology. After identifying the above problems, for which there seems to be no solution at present, one must focus on practical aims.

3.5.2 Formulation of the Research Questions

The entire cognitive process is orientated around the research questions, which should be directed at the research problem and the practical aims. This requires narrowing down the research problems, which can be achieved with the help of specific questions, aimed at how the World Wide Web (WWW) may be used more effectively as a teaching tool, for language classroom students. In particular, the investigation tended to focus on how website material may facilitate or discourage the learning of English. At the same time, it explored how the multiple entry points could be applied to computer assisted language teaching. The initial questions used in this research project are laid out below:

1.How can teachers use website resources more effectively as teaching materials for learners of English in a language classroom? (This question demonstrates how the World Wide Web may be used as a classroom resource as an approach to EFL teaching.)

2.Which sort of web page design appears more likely to engage learners? Audio? Visual? Text? (This question provides insights into learners' perceptions of website features, such as pictures or content, which initially may engage learners of English language in set learning tasks.)

3.How can teachers implement the theory of multiple intelligences in a web-assisted language learning setting? (This question provides reflection on the implementation of MI-based instructions used in a web-assisted language learning class.)

4.How do website materials and MI-inspired instructions shape language learning? (To what extent, do multiple entry point activities facilitate language learning with website resources?)

3.5.3 Planning Possible Actions to Solve Problems

In light of the four research questions: number 1 highlights the teacher as researcher in the study; research questions 2 and 3 explore the extent to which the web may assist learning; and research question number 4 explores how the framework of entry points may be inspired by the theory of multiple intelligences. The research resources included the teacher's journal, colleagues' comments, students' perceptions of websites used in the classroom, and the tasks assigned to students. All of the information from these sources was helpful in determining the course development and improvements to teaching practice. The research process, participants, and instruments used in the gathering of data, are described below.

3.6 The Course Design

The classes met one hour a week for a total of 18 weeks in a listening laboratory. The course setting in this study was a '*listening comprehension practice*', a compulsory subject. This section will introduce the classroom setting, the materials used during the semester and the lesson plan design.

3.6.1 The Classroom Setting

The classroom had a smart board, an overhead projector, one projection screen, a slide projector and a media console, which had one Internet-enabled computer with a touch screen panel, two cassette recorders, two wireless microphones, a video cassette recorder, and a DVD player. The instruments most often used in this study were the teacher's computer with a touch screen, the data projector and the projection screen. The teacher's computer was equipped with a networking system. All functions were operated via this computer when selecting a projection source, e.g., computer, VCR, or DVD. The teacher operated these functions by clicking the mouse or by touching the screen with a finger. The listening laboratory setting is shown below (Figure 3.2).

Figure 3.2 The Classroom Setting

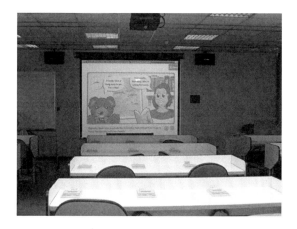

3.6.2 Teaching Materials

Teaching material, available on certain websites, was chosen for listening training. The World Wide Web is suitable for English teaching, because it offers authentic language source options. In this study, the function of the World Wide Web was regarded as an electronic coursebook, with multimedia features: sound, pictures, and text. The computer sent pictures to the projector, which projected a picture onto a big screen, visible to the whole class. The advantage of a large pull-down screen is that it allows the best picture possible, holding the students' attention and supporting whole class teaching. Only one website was demonstrated during each lesson, in order to avoid the slow access problem. The websites were chosen according to the educational and technical criteria. The educational criteria were based on the following questions (Herring, 2004:51):

(1)Is the content of this site related to my purpose?

A website's language use must be taken into account. Although a website indeed offers authentic language, it may not be easily understood by learners. The aim of the course was to train students' listening competence. Thus, the chosen websites had to provide listening-related content; also, the sound effects of the sites had to be clear. The form taken by each listening website could be part of conversation, an article, a story, or a song. The point was to encourage learners to cope with different everyday-life listening situations. In addition, each type of listening could take the form of a lead-in to a discussion or role play. Learners were given the opportunity to practise and reinforce their listening competence.

(2)Is the level of language used suitable for my students?

The language used at some sites may be beyond the learners' current competence. Learning happens when learners are asked to understand messages that are just beyond their current stage of comprehension. This idea echoes Krashen's definition of comprehensive input and addresses the requirement that students must be able to comprehend the input materials and instruction.

As for technical criteria, accessibility and workability must also be taken into account. Some websites may have ceased to exist or their addresses may have changed. Hence, the websites, and links, must be checked before the class convenes, to make sure they are still accessible. Also, the sound quality and speed of access must be satisfactory.

In addition to the use of the website, a coursebook was adopted for the syllabus, to be used when the website was unavailable. The coursebook, *Atlas Video Lab Guide A,* comprises 15 units with different topics, including 15 video tapes. Each video clip features a unit which reflects the way people actually speak, including hesitation, rephrasing and a variety of accents. Each lesson in the coursebook contains three sections for the students: '*Before you watch*', '*As you watch*' and '*After you watch*'. The first section, '*Before you watch*', briefly introduces the content of the video clips, which engage learners in a pre-listening task. This section tries to establish students' understanding of the current lesson. '*As you watch*' is focused on the unit's theme and provides gap-filling exercises for students to show their understanding of the content. Grammar exercises and TOEIC-style multiple choice listening questions are included in the third section, *After you watch*. During teaching sessions, the videotape was usually played at the beginning of each lesson, with the students doing the coursebook exercises as they watched the video. After playing the video, students took turns writing their answers on the board.

3.6.3 Lesson Plans

The idea of writing a detailed lesson plan is to help determine class progress and classroom management. In each section, the lesson procedures were outlined in the order in which they were to be presented, including resources to be used, student activities and specific points to be made. The lesson plan also detailed how the principle of multiple intelligences was to be adopted in the class. Salaberry (2001:51) mentioned a very significant point that is frequently ignored by most language teachers:

The success of a technology-driven activity will likely depend as much, or more, on the successful accomplishment of pre-and post-activities than on the technology activity itself.

The above view indicates that the importance of lesson plans, as WWW technology, is not in itself, interactive, and may not promote interactivity between students. Thus, it is the teacher's job to make the contents of the World Wide Web understood by all students.

In order to motivate students to engage in listening practice and to improve their listening ability, the entry point approach, inspired by the theory of multiple intelligences, was incorporated into each lesson plan of this listening course. A series of activities, based on a given website, were designed as entry points to convey ideas and facilitate the students' learning of English. Each lesson plan, based on multiple intelligences principles and used in this study, is presented in chapter 4.

3.7 Participants

Participants in this study included students from four different programmes of a university, as well as two colleagues. Although there were four distinct groups participating in this study, with some comparison being made between groups, the primary purpose for reviewing these differences was to acquire a better understanding of these particular participants. There was no intention to generalise any population from which these perhaps might have been drawn. Although inferential statistics were used, they were interpreted non-inferentially (Backhouse, 1984). In this approach, *'the $p<0.05$ level of significance is used, not to indicate that generalisation to a population is acceptable, but simply as a consistent yardstick'*, for the particular group of students currently being investigated, in order to *'separate findings worthy of further investigation and discussion from the rest'* (Postlethwaite & Maull, 2003:451). This use of statistics is particularly appropriate in the current project, *'where the quantitative data serves to support and extend the findings from the qualitative strand'* (Postlethwaite & Maull, 2003:451).

3.7.1 Students

The participants in the study were students in the first semester of their first year in a four-year programme of a national science and technology university. These students were from four different programmes: Business Administration, Information Management, Industrial Management, and Textile Engineering (Table 3.4).

Table 3.3 Departments Attended by Students

Student numbers Departments	Female	Male	Total
Business Administration	20	6	26
Information Management	17	10	27
Industrial Management	7	19	26
Textile Engineering	1	26	27
Total	45	61	106

According to Table 3.3, it can be seen that the Departments of Business Administration and Information Managements were female-based groups, while Industrial Management and Textile Engineering were mainly male-based. The reason for choosing these students from this school was because the school is equipped with a well-structured networking system and the listening lab is equipped with multi-technology tools. These advantages are listed below:

First, the school provides an excellent networking system on campus. Students can access the Internet from their desktop or laptop computers, from any corner of the campus. Meanwhile, there are two computer rooms with 60 seats each for self study, which open at 8:00 AM and close at 11:00 PM every day. In other words, this environment provides teachers, who want to adopt website materials for language learning, a flexible approach. Teachers can specify a website for students to access, where they may practise their language skills.

Second, the labs are equipped with a data projector and projection screen and connected to the Internet. Teachers are able to take advantage of website resources in the class, such as providing authentic materials. Meanwhile, with the aid of the data projector and projection screen, teachers can present website materials visually, thus holding learners' attention.

In brief, the choice of research participants revolved around whether they had access to full technological support. If participants are able to take advantage of website materials to practise English skills, under a well-constructed networking environment, the study is then focused on exploring whether or not the website materials facilitate language learning, and is not tied up with solving problems with the technology itself, during the language lesson.

3.7.2 Colleagues

As Ferrance (2000: 23) notes,

One of the basic principles of action research is that researchers need each other's ideas for stimulation and depend on other people's perspective to enrich their own.

For this reason, I invited two colleagues to participate in this study, filling the role of *'critical friends'* (McNiff et al., 1996:30). The first colleague is a teacher of English language, who has taught college students for five years. In order to promote learning, she sometimes uses website resources as supplementary materials. Accordingly, she was willing to discuss website applications of computer assisted language teaching in the classroom, based on my practice. The other colleague is a researcher and advocate of how the multiple intelligences theory may help the learning disabled. Hence, she was interested in observing how MI theory can facilitate teaching. Each of them came to my class at different sessions. After the classes, we discussed my classroom teaching practice, students' performances and future possible development.

3.8 Choice of Instrumentation

A variety of methods of enquiry were used to explore the research questions, including the collection of both qualitative and quantitative data. McKernan (1996:57) introduced both qualitative and quantitative research techniques such as *'observational and narrative techniques*, *'questionnaires'*, *'interview'*, *'checklist'*, *'rating scales'*, and *'self-report techniques of projective methods'*. In the current study, a type of action research is employed, and changes are expected to occur. Therefore, the information that is collected must include both quantitative techniques and qualitative data. Using quantitative data provides a more general understanding of how website materials can assist learners with practising their language skills, and, then allows qualitative data to pinpoint it more precisely. Both quantitative and qualitative data are employed to address the difference between groups. This relationship between quantitative and qualitative enquiry provides a different perspective from the understanding that qualitative work is only useful for providing examples of generalisable relationships arrived at by statistical methods (Postlethwaite & Maull, 2003).

The collection and analysis of data is a significant factor in action research, because the progress involves analysing and evaluating data during the whole research period, rather than at the end. As the research progresses, the additional techniques may be added for more understanding. This study was explored from the following sources:

1. MI Inventory (Appendix 1)

 Purpose: The use of an MI inventory aims to help students identify their preferred intelligences and to value their own strengths

 Mode: The inventory is based on Armstrong's 'An MI Inventory for Adults'

2. The GEPT

 Purpose: Two tests were used to determine to what extent students' listening ability was improved or not improved.

 Mode: The General English Proficiency Test conducted by the Ministry of Education in Taiwan

3. Students' evaluation of each website for each cycle (Appendix 2)

 Purpose: to acquire information about student perceptions of each website used during the semester, in order to improve teaching practice

 Mode: An open-ended questionnaire with three sections

 The *'Randall's ESL Cyber Listening Lab'* website (20-25 December, 2004)

4. Learners' perspectives of the three websites (Appendix 3)

 Purpose: to gather learners' perceptions, comparing the three websites

 Mode: a closed questionnaire

5. Interviews

Purpose: to acquire in-depth information and to clear up any remaining questions from learners as well as from colleagues

Mode: face to face interview in Mandarin Chinese

6. Class Homepage

Purpose: to collect learners' written work

Mode: student written tasks posted on the discussion board

7. Research Journal

Purpose: to understand the limitations and strengths influencing teaching practice

Mode: research journal

Each instrument, which had a unique focus for data collection, is described in detail, as follows.

3.8.1 MI Inventory

The multiple intelligences inventory, *An MI Inventory for Adults*, developed by Thomas Armstrong, appears in Multiple Intelligences in the Classroom (2000) (See Appendix 1). There are 80 statements, 10 for each of Gardner's 8 intelligence categories. Students rated each statement as 0, 1 or 2 to distinguish how each statement best described them. This inventory had already been translated into Chinese, so students were given the Chinese version.

The participants chose the most appropriate statement for themselves. I explained to participants that the inventory was, in no way, an IQ test. They were informed that it was helpful for discovering their potential strengths and may help them realise their learning preference.

3.8.2 The General English Proficiency Test

The General English Proficiency Test (GEPT) was established by the Ministry of Education in 1999. The design of the test was designed by the Language Training and Testing Centre (LTTC), which is a government sponsored organization. Based on the education system in Taiwan, the test is divided into five levels: elementary, intermediate, high-intermediate, advanced and superior.

Table 3.4 GEPT Level vs Educational Degree

GEPT level	Educational degree
Elementary level	Junior high school
Intermediate level	Senior high school
High intermediate level	University
Advanced level	English university major
Superior	Native speaker

The test at each level includes listening, reading, writing, and speaking. Each level of the test is administered in two stages. After candidates pass the listening and reading tests as the first stage, they then go on to take the writing and speaking tests.

The General English Proficiency Test certificate can be used by individuals to indicate their level of proficiency, to public and private institutions, such as the Ministry of the Interior for use by the National Police Administration, the Ministry of Education for applicants for government scholarships for study overseas and so on. In addition, more and more universities require students to have passed a certain level of the test before graduation.

Thus, General English Proficiency Tests were used in this study, in order to measure the increase or decrease scores in listening comprehension. Students in this study took pre- and post- General English Proficiency Tests at the intermediate level, at the beginning and the end of the semester; this level was chosen as the students in this study had just finished senior high school and had just entered university. As they were first-grade undergraduates with different majors, the intermediate level test was most appropriate. Further, the course observed in the research study was in a listening comprehension setting. As a result, students only took the listening section test, which consisted of three parts: pictures, dialogue, and long conversation. The content of the first part is based on pictures. Candidates hear a question, with four possible answers; they are asked to choose the appropriate answer, related to the picture. In the second part, candidates hear a question and simultaneously read the four choices in their test books; they must determine the best answer, after they hear the question. The last part includes 15 short conversations between two people. After each conversation, candidates hear a question about the conversation and must choose an answer from the four choices in their test books. Samples of the pre and post tests can be found in Appendix 1. The pre and post versions of both tests were downloaded from the website of the Language Training and Testing Centre (LTTC):

http://www.gept.org.tw/download-index.htm

3.8.3 Students' Evaluation of Each Website for Each Cycle

An open-ended questionnaire on students' opinions of each website was used in the classroom (Appendix 2). A total of three websites were used for the entire semester. Each website had unique feature, e.g., travelling topics, news articles, and daily life issues. Hence, the questionnaire was divided into three sections, according to the content of the three websites and the activities used in the classes. The questionnaire items were mostly open-ended questions. After each website had been applied in the class, students were given the section of the questionnaire, appropriate for that website.

3.8.4 Questionnaire for Comparing the Three Websites

At the end of semester, students were given a questionnaire to evaluate the three websites used in the class (Appendix 3). The questionnaire comprised 10 questions, which focused on students' opinions toward website resources for learning English, comparing the three websites, website features related to English learning and learning preferences toward website materials. Apart from question 10, the questions were close-ended and based on a single choice, with a Likert-type scale, having five possible scores, ranging from *'Not at all important'* to *'Extremely important'*. There was also space for participants to explain their reasons for choosing specific answers.

Participants answered each statement of this questionnaire without translation. Based on previous experience, participants still misunderstood the meaning of some sentences, even though they were written in Chinese. This may have been caused by the wording or a translation problem. Therefore, each statement was explained to each of the participants, with clarification if necessary. The questionnaire design process, involved advice and discussion with relevant experts, e.g. supervisors and colleagues. These experts provided feedback on the validity of all questions. Their suggestions improved the validity of the content, after which both content and language were deemed appropriate. This support for the validity of the revised questionnaires gave us more confidence in the results.

3.8.5 Interviews

Interviews were carried out after each questionnaire had been completed. Formal and informal interviews attempted to clarify any unclear information in the participants' questionnaires, in order to further understand some of the participants' feedback. The interview questions took the form of statements and sought participants' explanations for their answers. Credits were added to each questionnaire, based on the interview data.

3.8.6 Class Homepage

In order to provide a place for students to post their writing tasks on the Internet, a class homepage was set up. On the class web page, updated announcements, and a discussion board were built for students to complete writing tasks and collect feedback. There were four main web pages, based on four departments: Business Administration, Information Management, Industrial Management, and Textile Engineering. Each web page was simply created, to provide a comfortable visual presentation. As well, a simple page meant faster downloading, making an immediate impression on the reader. This is extremely important on the web, where students may leave the website if the web page does not appear fast enough. Accordingly, students have to post their writing to a certain discussion board based on their department.

3.8.7 Research Journal

In order to understand the constraints and strengths influencing teaching practice, a research journal was kept to record reflections, an important element in the action research process. This reflective process, '*recognise and transform the constraints implicit in the research process*' resulted in ongoing changes being made (Shacklock & Smyth, 1998:6). Kermis and McTaggart point out the reason for keeping a personal journal for action researchers is so that:

> *we can record our progress and our reflections about two parallel sets of learning: our learnings about the practices we are studying ... and our learning about the process (the practice) of studying them (Kemmis & McTaggart 1988: 22-25).*

Within the research journal, I gathered information needed to evaluate my own working practices. Through reflection, I was then able to identify positive and negative aspects of teaching material. Moreover, my teaching approach could be examined and improved.

3.8.8 Data Analysis

The data underwent three major stages of analysis. The first task I undertook was to annotate the data. During this initial stage, participants' comments were delineated in descriptive categories. Following annotation, I found comments that provided insights into areas which overlapped. Having assessed points raised, I was sometimes able to integrate two categories into one. In this way, additions to the overall framework were created, revised, and discarded. Finally, participants' comments were used for both analysis and presentation in order to confirm or disconfirm the theories mentioned in the chapter of literature review and to add new insights into how these theories might be combined.

3.9 Ethical Considerations

As Cohen et al. (2000:229) mention, '*action research involves people in making critical analyses of the situations (classrooms, schools, systems) in which they work*'. Accordingly, researchers must pay close attention to ethical considerations as they conduct their work. Cohen et al. (2000:245) listed a number of principles when inviting research participants to respond to questionnaires.

1. *their informed consent;*
2. *their rights to withdraw at any stage or not to complete a particular item in the questionnaire;*
3. *the potential of the research to improve their situation;*
4. *the guarantee that the research will not harm them;*

5. *the guarantees of confidentiality, anonymity and non-traceability in the research;*

6. *the degree of threat or sensitivity of the questions;*

7. *factors in the questionnaire itself;*

8. *the reactions of the respondent,*

In order to fulfil the above points, I initially explained my research project to the whole class. Moreover, I informed them that our discussions would help me to understand the application of website materials for learning English. Meanwhile, their opinions were also shaped by my teaching practice, with the idea of the entry point approach framework, inspired by the theory of multiple intelligences. As Rossman and Rallis' (1998:50) stated, '*gaining the informed consent of participants is crucial for the ethical conduct of research*'. Therefore, I acquired all participants' informed consent to use their contributions and also confirmed their anonymity. Students themselves could decide to withdraw, if any difficulties arose at any time.

Apart from the questionnaires, channels of communication were kept open with participants. Hence, participants were able to express any concerns during private talks after class or via emails. In order to proceed with the follow-up interviews, student questionnaires were identified by number instead of name. This ensured greater validity, as the students were not as afraid to give their opinions and provided clues for follow-up questions. In addition, student numbers within the data were not shown in the study. Apart from student information, colleagues' names were replaced by codes and all such data, including questionnaires and interviews were stored electronically in a secure file.

3.10 Summary

This chapter has explored the basic assumptions and principles involved in selecting a research method. It provides an overview of competing paradigms and perspectives and the various theoretical positions that have informed the methodology. The research target was used as a starting point to design an appropriate methodology, which in turn indicated the methods most appropriate for data collection and generation. As a consequence, the inquiry drew on an action research approach as the appropriate stance for the study. The latter sections of the chapter describe the participants and the instruments used.

Several concerns arose during the study. First, an attempt was made to explore how teachers could make use of Internet resources in the class. A computer assisted language learning lesson can be applied in a classroom with a computer connected with network instead of a computer classroom. Second, an expansion of more learning opportunities for students, via the principle of multiple intelligences, was investigated. Third, website resources were explored in relation to learners' experiences in English learning. The action research stand informed these concerns.

CHAPTER $\boxed{4}$

ACTION RESEARCH CYCLE 1

4.1 Introduction

As noted in Chapter 3, this project was designed to explore how website resources, when integrated with MI-inspired instruction, can help English learning from the perspective of the students. Therefore, three websites were used over the course of the entire academic term in addition to the use of the coursebook. Each website used during the course was covered in from two to five lessons depending upon their usefulness and their complexity. At the same time, the framework of an 'entry point approach' was adopted in the teaching instruction.

The action research cycle for each website is explained in an individual chapter. This present chapter reports on the first action research cycle which was undertaken as part of the whole project. Moreover, since this study was a teacher-as-researcher's individual action research, the whole research process was applied in a continuous cycle: plan, action, observation and reflection. The action research project was divided into three stages, based on the three websites used in the classroom. At the investigation level, quantitative methods were applied to acquire general concepts, while qualitative methods were used to inquire further into the changes that I was initiating and facilitating in my classes.

Therefore, the structure of this chapter is based on the first action research cycle in order to gain a student's perspective on the initial use of website resources in an English class for the purpose of learners to practise their listening and speaking skills. In addition, a parallel discussion focuses on the approach taken to integrate the website, and the related intelligences that inspired each approach. An investigation of the learners' perceptions of the first website and pilot discussions of research questions are included.

4.2 Introduction of the Barnaby Bear Website

The *Barnaby Bear* website was the first site used during the course (URL – http://www.bbc.co.uk/schools/barnabybear/stories/) and two lessons were to be spent studying it. This section introduces the contents of the website and explains the reason for choosing it as the first website used in the listening class.

4.2.1 Description of the Barnaby Bear Website

The Barnaby Bear website includes two stories: '*Barnaby Down Under*' and '*Barnaby's Day Trip to Paris*'. The main character is

Barnaby Bear, a cartoon bear who travels to a number of different locations within two countries, France and Australia. The screen layout of this website is shown in Figure 4.1.

Figure 4.1 The Barnaby Bear Web Page

There are several instructional web pages to enable users to set up user defaults for story presentation. For example, if users click on '*Barnaby's Day Trip to Paris*', the following web page will appear (Figure 4.2).

Figure 4.2 Web Page Instructions

At the bottom of the screen, there is an icon, '*Full screen*' for users to enlarge the web page to whole screen mode. With this function, audiences can see the content more clearly.

In addition, two small graphic icons, '*Sound on*' and '*Sound off*' represent the different functions: '*with audio clips*' and '*without audio clips*' (Figure 4.3). The story with audio clips was used in the class.

Figure 4.3 Two Instruction Icons: 'sound on' and 'sound off'

Moreover, each story is presented over several web pages using a sequence of pictures. Each web page contains a picture, as shown in Figure 4.4.

Figure 4.4 Text and Dialogue Displayed in Story Presentation

The *Barnaby Bear* story is narrated by a man. On each web page, the words are shown as the man reads them. After the narration, a short dialogue is read by the same man with voice variation to represent *Barnaby Bear* and his friend, Liz. Users can see the words while listening to the dialogue.

4.2.2 Review of the Barnaby Bear Website

The criteria for this review of the *Barnaby Bear* website are based on the issues discussed in Chapter 2, section 2.4.3. For the purpose of this research project, listening application is the main focus for the use of the website and the criteria are discussed with this focus in mind. Accordingly, readability of the website is only considered to determine if the website is able to make a good first impression on users, and to determine if animation helps narration. The discussion of the criteria concentrates mainly on the application of a website in a listening class. One of the aims of this review is to confirm the suitability of this particular website for the project. Another aim is to provide a framework for analysing students' comments in the result sections of the book.

A.Readability

As mentioned by some researchers, the degree of contrast of the web colours between text and background generally improves readability (Hall & Hanna, 2004). On the *Barnaby Bear* Website, the background colour is yellow and the text is printed in dark blue. Therefore, the design is compatible with Shieh and Lin's (2000) study that showed that blue and yellow combinations are rated, in order of preference, the highest. In other words, the readability of the *Barnaby Bear* website can be evaluated as being well-designed to attract readers' initial attention.

B.Multimodal Presentations

The stories are designed with a combination of static pictures, animations and audio clips. The text is written at the bottom of each web page and is read with a British accent simultaneously. This website therefore consists of multimodal presentations which could be expected to enhance instruction when used with a whole class via a projection facility. Students might be expected to understand the story better through the optimal use of their preferred modality, and by the way in which each modality supports the others. Although there is some animation, users have to click on the icon themselves to see the animation. Mayer and Moreno's (2002) study indicates that narration and animation should be presented at the same time to help learning. According to their criteria, the animation on the *Barnaby Bear* website may not be sufficiently integrated with the narration.

C.Evaluation of Website Content

Criteria for evaluation of the *Barnaby Bear* website, which were developed in Section 2.4.3 are listed below for the convenience of the reader.

1. Does the website give a summary of information?
2. Can the website provide listening activities for use in class and after class?
3. Is the listening material on the website related to daily life issues?
4. What is the quality of the recorded material provided on the website?

5. Does the website make good use of the visual medium to provide a meaningful context or show facial expression or gesture?

The *Barnaby Bear* Website is about travelling and is produced by the British Broadcasting Corporation (BBC). The stories are based on travelling to well-known countries, which is potentially attractive to students. This website introduces related information about Barnaby Bear under the rubric of 'Teachers & Parents' and it can be accessed from the following web address (criterion 1):

http://www.bbc.co.uk/schools/barnabybear/teachers/credits.shtml

Although this website is marketed for children aged 4 to 11, the level of language used is useful as introductory support for students, as it provides them with experience of a daily life context. As for the follow-up activity, the theme, travelling, is suitable as a speaking and listening task about a planned journey (criteria 2 and 3).

The recorded material consists of the narration and a dialogue which attempts to portray genuine emotive reactions. There are different actors but the voices are used in very much the same way. Basically, the effect of the voice is clear and the speed is regular (criterion 4). The visual design on this website is based on static pictures which show the story context. Each picture is linked to the descriptive information. For example, the picture shows a Eurostar train when the printed text is about Barnaby and his friend going to take a train. These pictures are presented in a meaningful context (criterion 5).

4.3 Planning

An action plan outlining the way in which the *Barnaby Bear* website helps English learners in the language classroom was necessary. Accordingly, a lesson plan was designed for enhancing classroom management through a multiple intelligences framework, which helped the teacher monitor the teaching practice.

4.3.1 The Lesson Plan

The lesson plan listed the title used in class, website URL, features of the website, website contents, and the need for teaching aids. Following the introduction of the theme, the plan was divided into three sections: classroom activity, entry point activity, and related intelligences. The lesson plan for the *Barnaby Bear* website is shown below.

Table 4.1 Lesson Plan for Barnaby Bear's Story

Title	Barnaby Bear's Day Trip to Paris
Website	http://www.bbc.co.uk/schools/barnabybear/stories/
Web features	Audio, Animation, Text
Theme	Travel and tourism, impressions of places
Website content	Barnaby is a Bear. He goes to Paris for a day trip with his friend Liz and her family. They visit many famous locations in Paris by train, metro and boat. This is a picture story with animated links to further information.
Listening content	Describing tourist destinations and giving personal impressions. A traveller's view of France and French culture

Teaching Aids	A multimedia computer with Internet access, data projector, full-size screen, broadcast system for full surround-sound
Setting up	Photocopy one complete dialogue (Appendix 5) for each group of 4. Cut it into strips and keep each set of paper in a separate envelope. Photocopy a handout (Appendix 5) for each student. Test the computer network in advance.

Lesson Possibilities and Entry Point Activities

Classroom Activity	Entry point activity	Related intelligences
(Class 1)		
Present topics through listening	Aesthetic and Narrative: demonstrate the story on this section of the website.	spatial intelligence (through watching pictures) linguistic intelligence (through listening)
Reporting	Experiential: build a representation of jigsaw results Experiential: conveying the concept by working with the materials	linguistic intelligence (through informal speaking)

Follow-up Tasks

(Class 2)

Brief review of previous lesson

Writing task - - Ask students to work in groups and design a one day trip introducing a tourist destination or location in Taiwan.	Experiential: design a day tour in Taiwan Narrative: highlight some vocabulary and phrases for students to use in their speaking task role play conversation.	linguistic intelligence (through writing exercises) logical-mathematical intelligence (through arranging sequential itinerary)

Speaking task - (1) Students prepare an itinerary and report a detail of a journey in front of the class next lesson. (2) role play – tour guide and tourists	Experiential: report a day tour in Taiwan	linguistic intelligence (through listening to someone expound on their ideas)

4.3.2 The Framework of the Entry Point Approach

The entry point approach, proposed by Gardner (1999), describes different aspects of learners and demonstrates how to use different pathways to help them make meaning of a subject. As he claims,

One begins by finding a way to engage the student and to place her centrally within the topic. I have identified at least seven discrete entry points, which can be roughly aligned with specific intelligences (Gardner, 1999:169).

Gardner indicates that the MI theory offers a framework to use students' strengths as entry points to bridge areas that may be more problematic for them. In this study, a problematic area can be defined as English learning. Hence, this study tried to introduce students to a website with different entry points, in order to help them develop more understanding of the subject matter. As Gardner (1999:168) notes,

When teachers are able to use different pedagogical approaches, they can reach more students in more effective ways.

In other words, when a concept can be approached in several different ways, with some of them particularly accessible to different groups of students, then teachers should provide their students with these different ways to explore and gain knowledge. Based on the above consideration, as indicated above, the lesson plan design includes a variety of activities as entry points.

The first approach, at the aesthetic entry point, engages the senses of visual properties and attempts to draw learners' attention through the display of the website (Dara-Abrams, 2005). The website content is presented in both pictorial and textual renderings because *'several perspectives can help to dissolve single-dimensional perspectives'* (Veeneman & Gardner, 1996). The main idea is to get the students interested in the learning materials. Then, once they are interested, the goal is to have them remember the information gained from the lessons better than if it had been first introduced through verbal instruction. Students with preferred linguistic intelligence could listen to the audio clips, while others with preferred visual-spatial intelligence, could appreciate the animation or picture presentation. As Lyman notes, a website with the *'incorporation of images and sounds has the potential to involve students who are strong in the non-verbal intelligences'* (Lyman,1998:58). When students are encouraged to use their particular spectrum of intelligences to involve learning, they usually make the effort to satisfy their own interests.

A subsequent approach is a narrative entry point which helps learners understand the story through listening to the narrator and understand the language through the structure and interest of the story. Moreover, a story *'jigsaw'* is used as a building activity bridge to assist learners' comprehension of the story. Through the jigsaw activity, learners are expected to know what the main theme is about, where the story takes place, and who the characters are.

The function of the jigsaw is to provide a problem for learners to solve by cooperating with other classmates. The potential of problem-based learning with groups is to provide prompt feedback and allows a student-centred learning environment. When learners had completed the jigsaw task, one member of each group was chosen to read out the written answers in front of the whole class. Moreover, when one student did the presentation in front the class, the others had to check if their answers were same as the speaker's. This approach attempted to help learners to listen and practise oral more or less. As Gardner claims (1999:172),

Many people learn more effectively, however, in a group setting, where they can assume different roles, observe others' perspectives, interact regularly, and complement one another.

The experiential entry point activity involves students in the design of a day tour inspired by the website story. Students can select how their ideas are represented such as through the medium of role play or group presentation. The pedagogical aim is to create a real life situation for groups of students so that they can apply what they have learned about vocabulary or sentence structures. In this way, basic academic skills are integrated into the creative process.

Moreover, students may be encouraged by the different assessment approach and feel motivated to use their particular strengths to achieve higher quality (Baum et al. 2005). The underlying research principle in the above lesson plan was that website materials, with a combination of visuals and sound, could assist teachers by facilitating the design of a series of entry point activities.

4.4 Acting

The action proceeded in three steps, which are explained below.

4.4.1 Step 1

I began the lesson by showing the first web page of the story, *Barnaby Bear's Day Trip to Paris*, via the projection screen. I chose '*sound on*' mode for students to listen to the audio version. Students were told that they were going to watch a story in which a bear goes on a trip to Paris with his friends. Students focused on listening to the audio clips and watched the animations in the first display.

4.4.2 Step 2

After the video had finished, I gave each group an envelope containing a cut-up conversation. Each group was requested to put the dialogue into the correct sequence. Then, I replayed the story one more time for students to check their work. Once the students had finished the task, I asked a student from each group to go to the front of the class, in turn, and read a section of dialogue, so that the other students could check their answers.

4.4.3 Step 3

I gave each student a handout (shown in Appendix 5) and asked them to discuss the questions on the handout with their partners. Then, I replayed the whole story again for students to answer the questions. When most students had finished the handout, I again played the video clips and went through the details of each web page.

I did not immediately proceed with the follow-up activity for two reasons. The main reason was that the class time of only one hour per week was not sufficient to participate in so many activities. The other reason was that I was not familiar with students' learning preferences and was not confident about managing the process of follow-up activities. Thus, I decided to proceed with follow-up activities only after I had a better understanding of the students' abilities.

I returned to the first website when I had finished all the lessons related to the third website. As shown in the lesson plan, the follow-up activities included an itinerary and a presentation. The students had to plan an itinerary for a day trip for tourists in Taiwan as an assignment. Then, they had to present their itinerary in presentation style or as a role play in class. When learners can work out their own learning processes, they become responsible for their learning (Hopper and Hurry, 2000).

4.5 Observing

This section discusses students' perceptions of the *Barnaby Bear* website, which was used as English learning material. All of the information was documented and collated for my subsequent self-reflection.

4.5.1 Data Collection

In order to understand the effect of using website resources on teaching practice, data was collected from colleagues' critical comments, student responses and my research journal. A colleague, Kimberly, who teaches in another college and also occasionally adopts website resources in her English class, came to observe my classes and provided critical comments; this helped me to reflect on my own teaching practice when using website materials. Our discussions are given in section 4.6. Students' perceptions of the *Barnaby Bear* website were collected via a questionnaire with six open-ended questions, and follow-up interviews. Students, within four different majors, were given 106 questionnaires; of these, 96 completed questionnaires were returned, indicating a 90% rate of return. The discussion surrounding the data gathered focused on the open-ended questions and interview information. The six open-ended questions, laid out below, covered several themes:

Table 4.2 Questions Investigating Students' Perceptions of the Barnaby Bear Website

Question	Theme
1. What do you think you have learned or now understand better from this website?	Checking students' understanding of website materials
2. Is there anything on this website that you did not understand? Please explain.	
3. What did you like or dislike about this website?	Comments on website design
4. Did you find listening to this website easy or difficult? Please explain your reasons.	Listening level of website contents
5. Which element of this website drew your attention first? Please explain your reasons.	Website features arousing attention
6. Which one element on this website most helped you to understand the content? Please explain your reasons.	Website features best suited for learning

Questions 1, 2 and 4 were designed to elucidate understanding of students' comprehension of website material. Students' perceptions then became a guide to teaching practice in the next stage. Questions 3, 5, and 6 were designed to investigate which website features best facilitated learning.

4.5.2 Data Coding

Collating students' comments mainly consisting of words, phrases, and short sentences, involved a repeated process of coding, categorising, and sorting the data in a search for patterns (Miles & Huberman, 1994). Therefore, categories were established initially, based on students' comments in the questionnaires and follow-up interviews. The categories were derived, usually in basic terms such as element (type of content), and degree (level of material). The data were consulted many times in order to simplify and merge categories. For example, the first question was about what the learners thought they had learned from the *Barnaby Bear* website. Some students mentioned that they knew some places in Paris and this was coded as 'geography'. Some people stated that they knew some French food items which was identified as 'culture'. Later, these two categories were merged as 'context' to include participants' statements about French life. The coding categories, derived from data and data examples that fitted each category, are explained in Table 4.3.

Table 4.3 Categories Derived from Students Comments

Q1 - What do you think you have learned or now understand better from this website?		
Categories	Indicators	Examples from data
Context (60%)	Knowing more about Paris and its famous tourist locations	I learned something special about another country. I feel that I now know how to take the metro.
Vocabulary (19%)	Feedback related to learning lots of words	Some vocabulary, new words
Listening (6%)	Description of listening skills	I can understand a bit of conversation.
Text (15%)	Learning how to describe a place or an event	I learned every day conversation.
Q2 – Is there anything on this website that you did not understand?		
Vocabulary (34%)	Response related to the context of certain words	I still did not understand some vocabulary.
Pictures (3%)	Students did not understand some of the pictures	I could not connect the pictures to the story.
None (63%)	Direct quotes from students	No

Q3 - What did you like or dislike about this website?		
Visuals (33%)	Items included pictures, animation and clickable items	*The animation design is great.*
Story (42%)	Comments about the text or the story	*The story is interesting.*
Character (17%)	Opinions about the character, *Barnaby bear*	*I liked Barnaby bear. He is so cute.*
All (8%)	Some students simply wrote '*all*' to question 3. (Direct quotes from students)	*No*
Q3- b (dislike)		
None (45%)	Some students simply wrote '*no*' to this question. (Direct quotes from students)	*No*
Screen (21%)	Opinions about unclear images, or small fonts	*The screen is too dark. I could not see it clearly.*
Voice (15%)	Opinions about the audio clips	*The voice of Barnaby bear is a fake. It sounds like a machine speaking.*
Speed (8%)	Comments about the speaking speed	*The speed is too fast to keep up.*
Others (11%)	Answers did not fit into discrete categories	*I did not like pictures. It was too childish.*
Q4 - Do you think that listening to this website was easy or difficult?		
Easy (22%)	The theme of question 4 concerned the level of learning materials. Thus, a coding scheme was devised: *easy, medium, difficult*, and *very difficult*	*It was easy, because I knew most of the vocabulary.*
Medium (61%)		*I still did not understand some parts*
Difficult (14%)		*The speaking speed was too fast sometimes.*
Very difficult (3%)		*I still did not understand the content.*
Q5 - Which element in this website drew your attention first?		
Pictures (58%)	Comments about visuals used in the story	*cute pictures; pictures are authentic; cute cartoon features*

Story (17%)	Notes about the content of the story	*I like the story. It is very interesting.*
Design (12.5%)	Statements about the design of the link	*I was attracted by the flashing icon that appeared in the story sometimes.*
Sound (12.5%)	Opinions about voice, audio, clear tones, or music	*I was curious about how the bear was able to speak.*

Q6 - Which one element on this website most helped you to understand the content?

Pictures (41%)	Comments about pictures or animation.	*These pictures convey ideas and feelings in a simple way.*
Text (21%)	Statements about the text shown on the screen	*I understood the story by reading the text.*
Sound (36%)	Notes about the audio clips or speaking	*The audio clips helped me to understand how people speak English.*
Teacher's explanation (3%)	Opinions about teachers' explanation	*I understood the contents after the teacher went through each web page.*
Mix (9%)	Comments about how pictures and words or words and audio clips help understanding	*The pictures and text helped me learn more vocabulary.*

Finally, the qualitative coding analysis was represented within the quantitative tables based on the students' four different majors: Business Administration, Information Management, Industrial Management, and Textile Engineering. As shown in Table 3.4 in Chapter 3, the Departments of Business Administration and Information Management could be regarded as female-based classes, while the Departments of Industrial Management and Textile Engineering were male-based. The numbers or percentages mentioned in the analyses were marked with different colours.

Nevertheless, the following issues were generally discussed from an overall standpoint. Data drawn from the questionnaires and follow-up interview transcripts, as given below, identified which features of a website, such as the one with the *Barnaby Bear* story, held learners' attention and raised their motivation for learning. This actually is the focus of research question 2: '*which sort of web page design appears more likely to engage learners?*' The features were categorised into visuals, sounds, text, story context, and instructions, each of which is discussed below.

4.5.3 Finding 1 - Visuals

As can be seen from Table 4.4, the most significant feature that drew the attention of learners and helped learning was the pictures (58%).

Table 4.4 What Drew Students' Attention in the Barnaby Bear Website

Question 5 - Which element in this website drew your attention first?									
N=number, %=percentage									
Categories	Departments								
	Business Administration		Information Management		Industrial Management		Textile Engineering		Total	
	N	%	N	%	N	%	N	%	N	%
Pictures	15	63	10	40	15	65	16	67	56	**58**
Design	2	8	6	24	2	9	2	8	12	**12.5**
Story	2	8	5	20	5	22	4	17	16	17
Sounds	5	21	4	16	1	4	2	8	12	**12.5**
Total	24	100	25	100	23	100	24	100	96	100

In the data illustrated in Table 4.4, 58% of the students chose '*pictures*' as the element which drew their attention first. For the majority of students, this was the first time they had been asked to learn English from this type of website with colourful pictures and animation. It was not surprising that a large number of students chose '*pictures*' because they were attracted by the main character, *Barnaby Bear*, who was considered cute and interesting. Examples were noted below.

The bear is so cute that I would like to know what happened to him.

(Business Administration)

This cartoon website was so colourful that I really would like to visit Paris soon.

(Information Management)

Apart from the element of '*pictures*', 13% of the students reported the '*design*' of the website drew their attention first (Table 4.4). The design here means the mouse-like icon from the screen animation on several of the web pages. One of the sample web pages is presented in Figure 4.5.

Figure 4.5 The Web Page 'Mouse' Icon

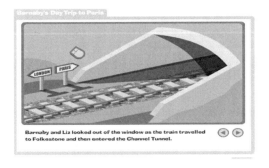

The students indicated that they were curious about the animation and wanted to click on the mouse to see what would happen. Their comments about animations in the *Barnaby Bear* website were stated below.

I was attracted by the flashing icon that sometimes appeared in the story.

(Business Administration)

I felt excited after the mouse icon had been clicked on, and the animation was running.

(Information Management)

I first noticed that there was a mouse icon on several of the web pages. I wanted to see what kind of animation would be shown.

(Information Management)

Animation actually shows me a way of learning, so I can better understand the action described in the story.

(Industrial Management)

Students' opinions seemed to agree that the animation had a direct functional value. For example, many students did not know the word '*lift*', but made the correct association when the link to an animation of the family in the lift was clicked. The two versions of '*before clicking*' and '*after clicking*' are shown in Figures 4.6 and 4.7.

Figure 4.6 Before Clicking on the Link

They decided to travel to the top in the lift.

Students saw the above picture first. After clicking on the mouse icon, an animation appeared. The door of the lift was closed and there was an arrow showing that the lift was climbing.

Figure 4.7 After Clicking on the Link

They decided to travel to the top in the lift.

The animations presented above may help generate ideas and make sense of the accompanying text. From learners' perspective, the pictures and animations conveyed ideas, raised learners' interests and helped them make connections with the vocabulary. As can be seen in Table 4.5, 41% of the students reported that *'pictures'* helped them to understand the story better.

Table 4.5 Which Elements on the Barnaby Bear Website Helped Students Learn

Question 6 - Which one element on this website helped you to understand the content most?									
N=number, %=percentage									
	Departments								
Categories	Business Administration		Information Management		Industrial Management		Textile Engineering		Total	
	N	%	N	%	N	%	N	%	N	%
Pictures	7	29	9	36	13	57	10	42	39	*41*
Text	5	21	3	12	5	22	7	29	20	21
Sounds	10	42	9	36	4	17	2	8	25	*26*
T's explanation	1	4	0	0	0	0	2	8	3	3
Mix	1	4	4	16	1	4	3	13	9	9
Total	24	100	25	100	23	100	24	100	96	100

The comments from the students of how pictures have helped them with learning are listed below.

I was attracted by Barnaby the talking bear, as well as the places he introduced. That way I could get a sense what the famous sightseeing places look like.

(Business Administration)

The pictures help me to build a mental image. Then, I can follow the story when I do not understand all of the dialogue.

(Industrial Management)

According to the comments from learners, learning benefits are incurred when pictures and text provide supporting information. This issue reflected Herron et al.' (1995) finding on the principles of using pictures to facilitate understanding. The students in their study *'acknowledged the helpful contextual support afforded by the pictures'* (Herron et al., 1995:393). However, the notion should be raised whether this *'visual'* effect benefits all readers. As Collins et al. state:

> *animations may help a concept to 'come alive' or gain meaning for a learner. But are there also difficulties in the use of images for learning? (Collins et al., 1997:63)*

For example, three students said that they could not make any sense of the pictures on the *Barnaby Bear* website. Subsequently, when asked *'is there anything on this website that you do not understand'* (question 2), 3% of the students wrote *'pictures'* (Table 4.6).

Table 4.6 Points that were Unclear to Learners' on the Barnaby Bear Website

Question 2 - Is there anything on this website that you did not understand?									
N=number, %=percentage									
	Departments								
Categories	Business Administration		Information Management		Industrial Management		Textile Engineering		Total	
	N	%	N	%	N	%	N	%	N	%
Vocabulary	15	63	13	52	3	13	2	8	33	34
Pictures	0	0	0	0	1	4	2	8	3	**3**

None	9	38	12	48	19	83	20	83	60	**63**
Total	24	100	25	100	23	100	24	100	96	100

The above data implies that certain students, although in a small minority, were not impressed by the colourful pictures and vivid animations.

4.5.4 Finding 2 - Text

As can be seen in Table 4.4, 9% of the students answered that a combination of both '*pictures*' and '*text*' helped them to understand the story. Their comments were stated below.

The pictures with subtitles helped me understand the story completely.

(Information Management)

The pictures helped me to recognise the museum, the cathedral, or the food the bear ate. However, if I had seen the pictures without the text, I would not have known what the cathedral was.

(Textile Engineering)

It appears that the students only fully understood the whole story after both listening to the narration and reading the text. These students seemed to benefit from the advantages of multimodal presentations. Students who wrote '*text*' felt only that it had helped them learn how to describe a day trip to Paris. They wondered whether they really understood what the word '*Euros*' meant or what boat cruising was like.

Sometimes the speaking was not clear enough, so I had to rely on the text.

(Industrial Management)

I understood the content based on the words shown on the screen.

(Textile Engineering)

In reality, the sound setting of the classroom was equipped with a broad-casting system. In other words, students were able to listen to the dialogue from any location in the room. The students found some of the narration to be unclear because of a problem with the technology. When I clicked 'sound on' to begin the story, sometimes the narration function did not work smoothly. As a result, the screen occasionally presented the pictures with no sound and students had to rely on reading by themselves. This situation caused the students to depend more on the text. Overall, students stated that the words and dialogue, associated with every day life contexts, were very realistic. Once learners had been introduced to the vocabulary, they felt a sense of achievement.

4.5.5 Finding 3 – Sound Features

From Table 4.4, it can be seen that 13% of the respondents thought '*sound*' attracted their attention first (question 5). There were two possible reasons for this. First, the main character in the story, a bear, could speak; second, the *Barnaby Bear* website is designed by the British Broadcasting Corporation (BBC) and the characters speak with an '*English accent*', which is not often heard by Taiwanese learners who are used to listening to American accents. There were two reactions when students first noticed that the accent was different from what they were used to hearing. Some students felt that they did not understand what the bear was talking about, because of the unfamiliar accent. Others were very interested and wanted to imitate the English accent.

Apart from the English vs. American accent issue, 26% of the students wrote that '*sound*' helped them learn, because they could imitate aural intonation clues in order to practise the pronunciation of the vocabulary (question 6).

I learned how to pronounce some new vocabulary including some French words.

(Business Administration)

Audio clips helped me to hear English in authentic context. Moreover, I can connect what I read with what I heard to understand the story.

(Information Management)

The audio clips helped me understand how people speak English.

(Industrial Management)

The respondents' opinions showed that the *Barnaby Bear* story could be regarded as audio text, which added value to the learning. In contrast, about 15% of the students answered '*voice*' as the item they did not like (Table 4.7-3b). From the follow-up interviews, they expressed the opinion that the voices had no gender identification.

Liz is a girl. Why did she speak like an adult male? It was so weird.

(Business Administration)

There are four characters in this story, but I heard the same voice talking all the time. The voice of the narrator was the same as the voices

of the four characters, too. I think the website designer should use
different voice effects to distinguish the characters.

(Information Management)

It is odd that a man pretended to be a little girl. The sound effects were
so unnatural that I did not want to listen to the story a second time.

(Industrial Management)

The sound design was poor. There was only one voice to present all
characters in the story.

(Textile Engineering)

These voice design critiques can be summarised by saying that
the female character's voice was depicted by an adult male speaker;
this masculine voice was deemed to be too masculine and
inappropriate. As a result, these students did not perceive the voice
to be genuine.

4.5.6 Finding 4 – Instruction Issues

Except for the picture and text features, three students answered
'teacher's explanation' in reply to question 6 (Table 4.5). These three
students expressed:

Although you have played the audio/video clips many times, I did not
have a clue as to what the story was all about. After you explained the
story page by page, I finally understood what Barnaby Bear was doing.

(Business Administration)

Honestly, at first I did not understand the story at all, and I could not
answer any questions in the handout, either. However, you explained
some of the things in the story, such as what it meant to take the

underground train or the bullet train. Then, I became very much interested and wanted to know more about what was happening.

(Textile Engineering)

According to these students, although the pictures attracted their attention, and they heard the text being read aloud, neither helped them make sense of the context. Probably, because of their weak listening and reading skills, they were unable to process the written content on the screen. As a result, in the initial stages, the story was unclear; only after hearing the teacher's explanation of the story, in its entirety, did they finally understand. This indicates that the teachers' explanation was necessary, even though the learning material seemed to be fairly easy.

4.5.7 Finding 5 - Story Context

According to the data in Table 4.7, 42% of the students stated that they liked the *Barnaby Bear* story very much.

Table 4.7 Learners' Comments about Website Design

Question 3.a - What did you like about this website?									
N=number, %=percentage									
	Departments								
Categories	Business Administration		Information Management		Industrial Management		Textile Engineering		Total
	N	%	N	%	N	%	N	%	N	%
Visuals	6	25	11	44	6	26	9	38	32	33
Story	15	63	7	28	9	39	9	38	40	42
Character	2	8	4	16	6	26	4	17	16	17

All	1	4	3	12	2	9	2	8	8	8
Total	24	100	25	100	23	100	24	100	96	100
Question 3.b - What did you dislike about this website?										
	N	%	N	%	N	%	N	%	N	%
None	7	29	12	48	13	57	11	46	43	45
Screen	12	50	2	8	3	13	3	13	20	21
Voice	0	0	3	12	5	22	6	25	14	**15**
Speed	3	13	5	20	0	0	0	0	8	8
Others	2	8	3	12	2	9	4	17	11	11
Total	24	100	25	100	23	100	24	100	96	100

The main reason for them liking the story was that it involved a trip to Paris. They showed great interest in perhaps visiting Paris one day, to see the places and do the things mentioned in the story; such as taking a boat cruise along the River Seine or visiting Notre Dame Cathedral. Most of the students had never been to Paris, a famous city, which all of them had heard about. They said that they were curious about French food, mentioned by *Barnaby Bear*. For example, *Barnaby Bear* exclaims that he dare not try frog' legs. Some students were intrigued by this and said that they would like to try them, if they ever visited Paris. One student mentioned that this plot reminded him of another French delicacy: snails. As well, some students asked how to make an omelette, which was mentioned in the dialogue between *Barnaby Bear* and his friend, Liz.

In addition, it was evident that the *Barnaby Bear* website facilitated students' understanding of the Paris experience, more than it helped their listening practice. When students were asked what they had learned from this website, 60% of the students wrote that they now knew something about Paris, such as the art galleries, categorised as '*context*' (question 1) in Table 4.8.

Table 4.8 Learners' Understanding of Website Materials

Question 1 - What do you think you learned or now understand better from this website?									
N=number, %=percentage									
	Departments								
Categories	Business Administration		Information Management		Industrial Management		Textile Engineering		Total	
	N	%	N	%	N	%	N	%	N	%
Context	9	38	17	68	16	70	16	67	58	**60**
Vocabulary	3	13	3	12	5	22	7	29	18	19
Listening	3	13	2	8	1	4	0	0	**6**	**6**
Text	9	38	3	12	1	33	1	50	14	15
Total	24	100	25	100	23	100	24	100	96	100

Actually, question 1 was designed to check students' understanding of the story content, as well as linguistic issues, such as grammar and vocabulary. Surprising, only 6% of the students stated that they had benefited from the audio clips for listening practice. A large number of students mentioned that they had known about Paris and its famous tourist locations such as the Louvre and the Eiffel Tower after reviewing the website. More interestingly, 70% of Industrial Management students expressed that they had a general idea about the story context. Students' comments about their understanding Paris were:

It seemed that I had actually been to Paris after viewing this website.

(Business Administration)

I may need to change platforms when I want to take the metro.

(Information Management)

I was amazed that a train can cross the sea from London to Paris. In addition, I didn't know that Paris had so many rivers.

(Textile Engineering)

Students also expressed the reasons why they wanted to go to Paris one day.

Now, I know which sites to see, if I visit Paris one day.

(Business Administration).

I now know what Paris looks like. I wished that I had a chance to visit Paris by Euro Star.

(Information Management)

The responses of the students, related to understanding the context, may be looked at from two perspectives. First, students said that they now knew what Paris looked like, because of the pictures. Second, after reading the text and listening to the narration, they had a better understanding of the whole story.

Basically, the data shows that the *Barnaby Bear* website, indeed, aroused learners' interests and motivated them to read the whole story. They wanted to know what happened to the characters, regardless of their lexical comprehension. Besides the language structure, learners were helped by the visual and audio communicative aids. Student opinions indicated that the design of this website satisfied the criteria of being attractive for users, enabling them to experience authentic situations without physically being there. In addition to a combination of sound and vision in the website presentations, the story itself caught the learners' attention (Kang, 2004). Visual and audio features helped learners capture the meaning and context, showing that multimedia websites may help students' comprehension, which was evident from the answers to question 2. Sixty three percent of the students simply wrote '*no*' to this question (Table 4.6). In the follow-up interviews, these students said that they completely understood the content of the website after watching the video clips, listening to the audio clips and reading the text from the screen. Moreover, a handout with simple questions helped them comprehend the story.

This indicates that similar websites, which are picture and sound orientated, may be able to enhance viewers' overall understanding of a story. However, the context of the story is the key to attracting readers' attention, by keeping them alert to watching what happens next, on the screen. With the aid of animation, language learners can readily identify the characters in the story and the relationships between them.

4.6 Discussion and Reflection

Initial discussions were about my teaching processes with a colleague, Kimberly, who is a lecturer in the Applied English Department of a College. She has been teaching for five years at this college and often uses website materials in her class. For example, she has used a website which introduces grammar in an animated mode. Our discussion focused on

(1) the implementation of the Barnaby bear website in class;

(2) the limitations of using the Barnaby Bear website in an English listening class; and

(3) the multiple entry points for the Barnaby Bear website.

Each of these is addressed in turn below.

4.6.1 Implementation of the Barnaby Bear Website in Class

The *Barnaby Bear* website was used as an electronic coursebook. The contents were presented via a data projector and projection screen. Students listened to the audio clips and watched the pictures simultaneously. After finishing one page, I clicked on the '*next*' arrow to go to the next web page. Students were not involved in operating the computer or using the mouse to click on items. In this way, students were expected to pay more attention to the content, by comparing it to a coursebook-based class. Based on my previous teaching experience, listening practice, based on a coursebook plus a tape, usually got a negative response. Students often said they could make no sense of a tape. When they did not understand what was being talked about, they simply ignored the exercises. Some students even fell asleep in the class. In contrast, the application of the *Barnaby Bear* website indeed attracted most students' attention. As the story was being recited by a bear, most students paid attention to the projection screen.

I noticed that some students stood up and moved their chairs to the front. This may have been because they wanted to know the story or to try to complete the handout. They were unable to see the text because it was masked by their classmates sitting in the front seats. The learning situation was much more engaging than in a traditional class based on a teacher lecturing. In the traditional lesson, the students would either have copied another classmates' answer or have waited for the answers to be read out.

The *Barnaby Bear* website is just like a living storybook, which is acted out page by page, and initially arouses learners' curiosity. Its presentation gives readers a clearer understanding of the way native language used and described different cultures. The main feature, reading with a bear, makes the story very interesting and offers students a vivid learning experience. Overall, it can be stated that this type of website presentation, which includes audio, visuals and text, is intrinsically interesting for language learners. This is consistent with Chisholm and Beckett's ideas on integration of TESOL standards, MI theory and technology. Learners can get help to develop language skills through '*exposure to authentic text*' and '*digital voice recording*' (Chisholm & Beckett, 2003:259).

Apart from multimedia effects, my colleague Kimberly mentioned the other positive aspects of using a networking computer with a data projector in the language lab, in preference to individual students using individual computers in a computer classroom. Generally speaking, there are a multitude of computer classrooms in the many colleges and universities throughout Taiwan; these computer classrooms are usually used by computer majors, however. Few English Departments are equipped with computer classrooms. If teachers want to use the computer classroom, they have to schedule it, in advance. Alternatively, there are generally three or four lab classrooms in each English Department, some of which are equipped with a computer connected to the Internet, a data projector, and a projection screen. If teachers are interested in using website resources in an English class, they can use such a lab, equipped with an Internet connection, as I did with the *Barnaby Bear* website.

This type of situation, where there are an insufficient number of computer classrooms, exists in the college in which my colleague, Kimberly. In that college, there is only one computer classroom for the entire English Department. If she wants to use the computer classroom for her students, she must reserve it during the first week of the semester, as it is in high demand. As a result, she only used the computer classroom twice in the previous semester. Further, she has experienced difficulty in managing students, when they are in the computer classroom, as some students check their emails instead of doing the assigned tasks. After observing my class, she acknowledged that in future, she would consider using the type of language lab used in this study, for her class. This approach of one computer with networking system can be reference for teachers who '*commented on a lack of available computers for their departmental use*' (Murray, 1998:21).

4.6.2 Limitations of Using the Barnaby Bear Website in English Listening Class

The *Barnaby Bear* website was regarded as attractive and interesting by the students, but my colleague, Kimberly, claimed it was too visual, and thus influenced the progress of students' listening training. The *Barnaby Bear* website is very colourful, incorporating visual humour, both of which hold the students' attention. Consequently, students tended to watch the pictures or read the text provided at the bottom of the screen, instead of listening to the audio clips. For many of my students, it was the first time they had listened to English on a website. They explained that their listening skills were not good enough. Without the aid of the text, they could not understand what *Barnaby Bear* was talking about. This is clearly shown in Table 4.8. The majority of students did not appreciate the function of the audio clips. Based on Table 4.8, only 6 students felt that their listening skills had progressed (question 1). In the follow-up interviews, many students said that their reading speed was not sufficient to keep up, so they were unable to follow along while the audio clips were playing. Unable to read the text, they were also unable to understand the story. This indicated that learners only understood the content through their reading strategies, because the text appeared on the screen. In other words, listening class had turned into reading practice.

A crucial point raised here, is that a word for word spoken version may help a poor reader, but this feature in no way facilitates the improvement of listening skills. Also, the website itself does not provide any listening comprehension exercises. After my colleague's reminder learners' comments and my reflection, I was aware that the *Barnaby Bear* website may be useful for catching learners' attention, but it is not sufficient for a listening lesson.

4.6.3 Multiple Entry points in the Barnaby Bear Website

According to Armstrong (2000:75), gaining students' attention at the beginning of a class may be *'the best illustration of MI theory's utility in the area of classroom management'*. In order to get students' attention focused on the teaching material, the aesthetic and narrative entry points were used simultaneously. From my observations, the *Barnaby Bear* website indeed was able to attract the class attention.

Compared to traditional teaching methods, the World Wide Web adds additional value. When I demonstrated the website, the whole class was very quiet, being attracted by either the pictures or the content. Students were eager to know what the story was about because the main character was a talking bear. Moreover, students almost felt that they had actually been in Paris, after reviewing the story. I believe that traditional textbooks are unable to provide this kind of enriched experience.

(Research Journal, September)

During this first research cycle, I became increasingly convinced that by projecting the website content on a screen attracted the learners' attention and helped comprehension to some degree. When I used the coursebook, students often could not find where the text was, even though I had mentioned several times the page number and which section. Students often asked the classmates next to them about the section and started chatting. Therefore, teaching with website materials by using a data projector and a projection screen can not only attract learners' attention but can also contribute to a more effective presentation of a lesson which emphasises the need for visuals to support the introduction of learners to new materials. As Moore (2003:94) notes, '*images in an educational setting are thought to increase learner interest, motivation, and curiosity*'. Displaying the website materials through a data projector in front of the whole class tends to offer learners a more concrete idea of what they are going to learn. At the same time, audio clips and text assist the learners in their understanding of the whole context.

As an experiential entry point it was planned to ask students to design a one-day tour itinerary, but the plan was not realised immediately during the first stage. The reason is explained in section 4.4.3 in detail. Although the experiential entry point had not been used at this stage, the idea of tour-design activity was envisaged for future lessons. The proposals included a group presentation giving learners the opportunity to participate in a problem-solving task. How do they design the visual contents and manage visual aids while other members are doing the presentation? If members of the audience ask a question, how does the team respond? According to my past experience, students normally felt dissatisfaction with their first performance because they were nervous in front of the whole class. However, many of them stated that the presentation was a positive challenge and helped them gain more confidence. This is accordance with one of the principles of multiple intelligences: i.e., using learners' strength to solve a problem and create a new product (Baum et al. 2005).

4.7 Learning Outcomes and Changes

The overall goal of this research is aimed at improving teaching practices using an action research approach. Therefore, changes are expected at the next stage in order to facilitate the next objective. During the first action research cycle, the data gathered showed that learners agreed that multimedia websites do increase learner interest, so that such an approach, using websites to foster successful learning, can be cultivated. Moreover, the *Barnaby Bear* website experiment provided a clue to explaining research question 2: *Which sort of web page* design *appears more likely to engage learners? Audio? Visual? Text?*

According to Table 4.5, 41% of the students answered that '*pictures*' helped them understand the content. The opinions of these students indicated that my primary object, proving that website resources with large visual images are able to initially attract learners and enhances learning, had been met for a substantial proportion of the class. In addition, other elements such as text, sound and the explanations offered by the teacher also helped their comprehension.

Learners' observations confirmed that for many, the visual approach was useful. Furthermore, the narrative effect attracted learners' attention to a greater or lesser extent even though there were some technical problems. One problem identified in the first research cycle was the insufficient content of the *Barnaby Bear* website. The limitations of using the *Barnaby Bear* website for teaching English arose from the insufficient number of stories and exercises. Although the level of complexity on this website was appropriate for the first lesson with our students, the insufficient number of stories made it difficult to draw the maximum advantage from the website.

The other problem was that learners did not have a chance to practise their language skill through different tasks. I had been aware that the teaching process had not fully achieved the goal of multiple intelligences, i.e. students being asked to solve problems using authentic methods of inquiry. I was so conscious of effectively presenting the website, via a projection screen, that I lost sight of the fact that I should have designed some activities for them to demonstrate their learning in different ways. Therefore the following adjustments, as outlined below, were suggested in order to improve future teaching.

1.A potential World Wide Web site should contain the following features: daily-life topics for young learners or adults, short stories of one to two pages, audio and video clips, and after-class exercises.

2.Teaching instructions should be carried out in as broad a range of methods as possible, in order to reach students with different strengths. Therefore, the course is designed so that it becomes a small-scale project for learners to inspire their strengths, and allows them to contribute their experiences. Through the processes of completing a project, learners are expected to form new understandings and take responsibility for their own learning.

Teaching English using the Internet and the Multiple Intelligences Approach

CHAPTER **5**

ACTION RESEARCH CYCLE 2

5.1 Introduction

This chapter explores the second website and the associated MI-inspired pedagogy in the context of listening courses. Based on the reflection on the first action research cycle, the first website did not provide efficient information for listening practice. The other problem was that there were no sequencing activities to support learning. In other words, one of the MI principles, e.g., providing learners a chance to demonstrate their understanding did not work out well. Thus, in the second stage, I tried to overcome these problems.

5.2 Introducing the Adult Learning Activities Website

The second website used in the classroom was the *Adult Learning Activities* (http://www.cdlponline.org). There were five lessons devoted to the study of this website. This section outlines how the website was used in class.

5.2.1 Description of the Adult Learning Activities Website

This website contains a collection of 11 topics, which are '*Working, Law and Government, Family, School, Health and Safety, Housing, Money, Science and Technology, Services, Going Places and Nature*' (see Figure 5.1).

Figure 5.1 Topics on the Adult Learning Activities Website

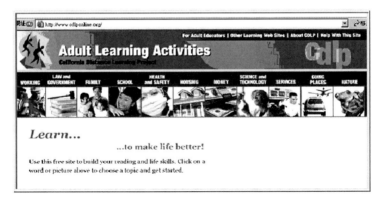

Each topic includes several articles combined with audio clips. Some articles also have video clips provided. The topic, *School*, for example, provides video clips for four stories: *Free Food for Kids, Fun Reading Show, Money Helps Teachers*, and *School Nurse* (see Figure 5.2).

Figure 5.2 Stories on the Topic, 'School'

Story List

*Click on the name of the story you want to read, or
pick another topic. Stories with a 📹 have a video to
watch.*

- Computers in the Classroom
- Free Food for Kids   📹
- Fun Reading Show   📹
- Kids' Cafe
- Money Helps Teachers   📹
- Police Arrest Parents
- School Deal
- School Nurse   📹
- Students and Satellites
- Teen Drinking
- Threatened at School

After clicking on a topic, users see a list of articles. The sample article used here, *Free Food for Kids*, is based on school meal times. Users can listen to the audio and simultaneously read the contents by clicking on the icon, *Listen*, or alternatively, they may click on the video link to watch the video clip, which is presented with a different audio track (Figure 5.3).

Figure 5.3 An Example of a Story: 'Free Food for Kids'

Basic Story | Full Story | Video | Activities

Free Food for Kids

(before 2003)

*Read the story. Click the "LISTEN" button at the bottom
of the page to hear the story. When you are done, click
the "NEXT" button.*

Some children are sent to school with empty stomachs.
It can be hard to concentrate and work when you are
hungry. One school district has taken steps to make
sure all of their kids are fed.

Anyone under 18 years of age can get a free breakfast
and lunch in this school district. It is only served at
some of the schools. Parents can call their school to ask
where their kids can get these free meals.

Children can now get breakfast and lunch during the summer too. In the past the meals were
only served during the school year. Many families are very happy to get this extra help for their
children.

Moreover, each of the stories contains several activities, designed to interactively help learner comprehension (Figure 5.4).

Figure 5.4 Activities List Provided for Each Article

Activities/Scores

Go to a story activity by clicking on the activity name below, or choose a new story. When you are done for the day, you can print your scores or email them to someone.

Free Food for Kids

Activity	Score
Basic Story	Completed
Full Story	
Video	
Learn New Words	
Spell a Word	
Matching Game	
Pick an Answer	
Write an Answer	
Learn More At Other Web Sites	

'*Learn New Words*' and '*Spell a Word*' are vocabulary tasks; '*Matching Game*' and '*Pick an Answer*' are comprehension tasks; and '*Write an Answer*' is a writing task. The item, '*Learn More at Other Web Sites*', provides links to related information, found on other websites.

5.2.2 Review of the Adult Learning Activities Website

The evaluation of the *Adult Learning Activities* website is based on Chapter 2, Section 2.4.3.

A. Readability

The *Adult Learning Activities* homepage lists eleven categories which are written in white on a background colour of dark blue. Each story title is marked in dark blue and the background of the web page is white. As for each story, the web page is created with black text on a white background. The design of the colour combination on this website is in accordance with the principle that greater contrasts between text and background colour are more efficient and likely to help readers search specific information on the website faster (Ling & Schaik, 2002). It does not, however, use the yellow/blue combination that was found to be most effective (see Section 4.2.2)

B. Multimodal Presentations

All the stories on this website consist of an audio description and a small picture related to the story context which is presented on the righthand side. The narration is presented at the same time as the text. As a large of amount research about listening points out, presenting visual content related to the listening situation results in better learning capabilities (Vandergrift, 2004). This kind of presentation is designed to help those learners who would like to know the pronunciation of some of the words. Brett (1995) states that text can make input more comprehensible and provide a way into accents and dialects.

C. Source Evaluation

Criteria for evaluation of the *Adult Learning Activities* website, which were developed in Section 2.4.3 are listed below for the convenience of the reader.

1. Does the website give a summary of information?
2. Can the website provide listening activities for use in class and after class?
3. Is the listening material on the website related to daily life issues?
4. What is the quality of the recorded material provided on the website?
5. Does the website make good use of the visual medium to provide a meaningful context or show facial expression or gesture?

The *Adult Learning Activities* website was created as a project for basic education for adults. The purpose of this website and the source of the stories on it are described in 'Help with this site'. It can be accessed from the URL:

http://www.cdlponline.org/index.cfm?fuseaction=help
(retrieved May 9, 2006)

There are eleven categories with eleven pictures, each presenting a specific topic. Readers can consult immediately a summary of the information concerning either a picture or a text provided on this website. In brief, this website introduces background design and resource content clearly (criterion 1).

All stories are narrated by audio clips and some stories also have video clips provided. At the same time, there are a series of activities including comprehension questions, vocabulary quizzes and writing task. The main strength of this website lies in its rich context. Further, the length of each article is about one or two pages. Thereby, the story is suitable for low level intermediate learners and caters for their different interests or needs. The news broadcasts provide an insight into 'real stories' which stimulate learners' curiosity. Because of the diversity of the news broadcasts, some stories can be regarded as potential materials for speaking tasks, e.g., role play, debate, or group presentation. A minor disadvantage of this website is that the reading comprehension questions are too simple. Sometimes, students can answer the question correctly without taking the trouble to read the story. Thus, teachers need to add some questions to make sure students complete effectively the exercise in comprehension. In other words, this website provides not only various activities for listening practice but also useful news about daily life (criteria 2 and 3).

Each story is clearly narrated and the tone is even, both of which are helpful for learners to understand the story while they are looking at the comprehension questions. Apart from the narration, some stories are represented in a news format. Therefore, learners can listen to how the people present the news and react to a given situation (criterion 4). Apart from audio clips, some stories are supplemented with video clips based on news broadcasts. Each news broadcast runs approximately two minute. The news broadcasts increase the level of difficulty for listening because subtitles are not provided. If students' listening is at the beginners' stage, they can read the whole story first. In this way, they can guess the context of the news broadcast and the interview. On the other hand, students at the intermediate level can watch the news broadcast first to understand the context. The various topics enable teachers to make good use of a valuable resource in a listening class (criterion 5).

5.3 Planning

This section outlines a lesson plan incorporating the *Adult Learning Activities* website, both during class and after class. It also describes how the entry point approach may be engaged in learning.

5.3.1 The Lesson Plan

The lesson plan, incorporating the *Adult Learning Activities* website, outlines the context within which computer assisted language learning lessons may be designed. Similarly, teaching instruction was inspired by the entry point approach, a term which refers to utilising student strengths to learn and understand academic content. Each entry point activity, connected to related intelligences, is illustrated.

Table 5.1 The Adult Learning Activities Website Lesson Plan

Title	Free Food for Kids
Website	http://www.cdlponline.org/
Web features	Audio, Video, Interactive exercises
Theme	The school provides a government-sponsored free meal program for students under 18 years old.
Teaching Aids	A multimedia computer with Internet access, data projector, projection screen, broadcast system with full-surround sound

Lesson Possibilities and Entry Point Activities		
Language Skills	Entry point activity	Related intelligences
(Class 1)		
Vocabulary Students learn vocabulary by listening to the audio clips and reading the text via a project screen.	Aesthetic: the presentation of the story in this section of the website. Narrative: presenting vocabulary through reading and listening	spatial intelligence linguistic intelligence
Listening Students watch and listen to the article on the projection screen.	Aesthetic: demonstrating materials by visuals Narrative: presenting topics through listening Logical-quantitative: students practise taking notes of significant points.	logical-mathematical intelligence
(Class 2)		
Speaking Students work in groups and participate in a role play consisting of a short conversation to express their opinions.	Experiential: design a dialogue related to the topic	bodily-kinesthetic intelligence interpersonal intelligence
Follow-up Tasks		
Reading Students choose their favourite topic to read after class.	Foundational: examines the viewpoints and vocabulary that support the topic or concept	linguistic intelligence logical-mathematical intelligence
(Class 3-4)		
Writing Students express their opinions about the topic they have chosen through writing. Students raised the questions or difficulties they encountered during the writing process.	Logical: using deductive thinking about a topic	linguistic intelligence logical intelligence interpersonal intelligence
(Class 5)		
Presentation	Experiential: conveying	interpersonal intelligence

| After students finish writing, they have to post their work on a discussion board. Therefore, students can review their classmates' work on a class homepage from a data projector. | concepts by working with website materials and sharing their work with others | linguistic intelligence |
| | | interpersonal intelligence |

5.3.2 Explanation of Entry Point Activities

The lesson plan above shows that an aesthetic entry point and a narrative entry point were used as first and second activities. The reason for using an aesthetic entry point as the first activity to engage students was because, on the basis of the Barney Bear investigation, it was expected that a visual presentation would draw many learners' attention. Meanwhile, a narrative entry point involved the introduction of the topic by reading a news article with a strong story line and listening to a dialogue about people being interviewed about it. The reason for using aesthetic and narrative entry points simultaneously was that we found many of the participants in this study did not have strong linguistic skills, according to the MI inventory. Such students may not have been motivated to learn, if we had tried to introduce the concept through speech only, for example in a lecture format.

Role play was actually regarded as a combination of the logical and experiential entry points. Students were put in an imaginary situation where they had to adopt the role of someone different from themselves. Further, they had to speak from the characters' point of view and use personal feelings to engage in role play preparation. This was a hands-on activity for learners to experience the target language use. Gardner (1993:23) notes that role-playing is '*an effective teaching mode for students with potential interpersonal intelligence*'. The group members had to negotiate how to present their performance. Moreover, they tried to build an appropriate communicative discourse to convince the audience - a process which involved logical thinking.

In the second stage, the role play topic was the same for all four groups: *Free Food for Kids*. Students were encouraged to present their opinions by various means. For example: in a debate between the food supplier and the parents; as an announcement by the principal; or in an interview by a journalist. The idea of role play aimed to tap into students' problem solving and interpersonal ability to develop language ability, such as speaking or listening.

In addition, the other logical and experiment entry points were writing and posting tasks. The principle was to create opportunities for students to solve problems and develop new products. Students accessed a story on the Internet and responded to a specific question, based on the story they had chosen. Then, they were asked to share their work with unknown readers by posting it on a discussion board on the Internet. This unique learning situation provided opportunities to assess a variety of skills in authentic ways. First, the writing task required learners to use linguistic and logical intelligences to write a piece of work. Second, when encountering difficulties, learners had to use their particular strengths to accomplish their goals. Some consulted with others, which was categorised as using interpersonal intelligence. The writing and posting tasks may be regarded as an experiential entry point to enhance students' ability to understand (linguistic intelligence), organise (logical intelligence) and complete a task (intrapersonal intelligence).

5.4 Acting

In the second stage, the *Adult Learning Activities* website addressed student-centred learning, which had not been sufficiently identified during action cycle one. The practices covered included listening, reading, speaking and writing activities.

5.4.1 Listening Activities

The listening activities involved three stages: pre-listening, listening, and post-listening tasks. At the pre-listening stage, students viewed the vocabulary in the *Free Food for Kids* theme. Students were told that they would hear the pronunciation of each vocabulary item and read that vocabulary item from the full-size screen. I clicked on the icon, *Learn New Words*, shown in Figure 5.4 and accessed the web page shown in Figure 5.5.

Figure 5.5 Vocabulary List

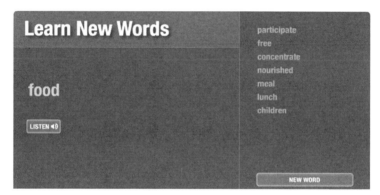

After clicking on the icon, *Listen*, each word was shown as it was spoken. We went through all of the vocabulary once, and then to the '*Spell a Word*' web page which provided a vocabulary test (Figure 5.6).

Figure 5.6 Vocabulary Test

I clicked on the icon, '*Listen*', for students to listen to the word which they then had to spell out. A student was nominated at random to come to the teacher's computer and type in the word they had heard from the audio clip. After completing this word spelling task, the first student nominated another classmate to continue the vocabulary activity, and so on.

The aim of the typing task was to retain students' attention. Students usually were willing to take up the challenge during this activity. Each student had a chance to spell out a word in front of the class, so the other classmates had to pay attention, because they might be the next one chosen to key in the next word. This strategy not only made classroom management easier but also gave students a much better opportunity to progress.

5.4.2 Listening Comprehension Questions

The listening task consisted of two modes. In the first mode, students listened to the audio clips and read the text simultaneously, while in the second task, students listened to the audio clips alone, without reading the text. Before listening to the article, a link, '*Basic Story*' was clicked onto and a web page, '*Free Food for Kids*' was shown (Figure 5.2). After the audio had finished playing, a web page, '*Pick an Answer*' was clicked onto and a question with four possible answers was shown to test students' comprehension (Figure 5.7).

Figure 5.7 Comprehension Tasks

Each web page presented a question and multiple choice answers. After answering a question, students checked their responses by clicking the '*Check My Answer*' icon at the bottom of each question. If the question had been answered correctly, the screen would show the next question. Again, a student was nominated at random to answer the question. I explained to students that they could choose the answer by touching the teacher's computer screen. Several students still felt more comfortable using the mouse to click on the appropriate answer, however. After answering all the questions on comprehension, a score, presenting students' answer rates was shown. The post listening task was designed as a speaking activity and is explained in the next section.

5.4.3 Speaking Activities

A speaking task should relate to a specific situation which will be '*more challenging, more interesting and more realistic*'

(Scrivener, 1994:60). Scrivener (1994:69) points out that role play *'essentially involves using the imagination to make oneself into another character'*. Based on this concept, I placed students into groups of four or five to discuss their opinions of the free meal programme, via role play. The students had to set up a situation describing 'how the free meal is beneficial to school members or vice versa', and then had to decide who would play each of the roles, such as a school principal, food company boss, teachers, parents and students. Students could use a variety of performance styles. For example, using an interview between the journalist and the principle, a discussion between the principal and the parents, or a talk at breakfast between parents and children.

After a group had finished the role play, other classmates questioned them about issues pertaining to their roles. For example, some students questioned the principal about the effectiveness of the free meal programme or interrogated the boss about the nutritional value of the food or the daily menu. The speaking task was aimed at bringing the outside world into the classroom, in order to provide useful and effective practice.

5.4.4 Homework

Students were told to choose one article listed on the *Adult Learning Activities* website and to write a short paragraph on the question provided by the topic. In order to explain this clearly, I displayed the main web page with all 11 topics via projection screen to the whole class (Figure 5.1). Then I clicked on *'school'*, chose an article, and displayed the writing task web page (Figure 5.8).

Figure 5.8 Writing Tasks

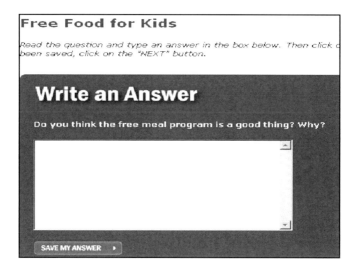

After students had written their assignments, they had to post their work on a website, which had been designed for students to display their work. The website address is (http://home.kimo.com.tw/cla_ss4/). Because the students would be reviewing each other's work, I reminded them that Microsoft Word software has a spell check function, which they should use. In addition, students were required to write a brief reflection on website materials and homework feedback, and post it on the classroom website discussion board. The idea here is to use students' strengths to learn English skills, use language and share their experiences with others. In other words, the homework could be regarded as a small-scale project, designed to achieve multiple intelligences-inspired instruction and to provide students opportunities to use their strengths to comprehend an English text and complete a written task.

The *Adult Learning Activities* website, with various topics, was able to provide students with a broad range of writing topics which related to their own experiences. When students wrote about a topic, they had to think about it carefully. Moreover, publishing their work on a class website made writing assignments become meaningful, because the students had a real audience: themselves.

In order to achieve a fair evaluation, students' writing tasks were assessed by an English teacher who is an IELTS examiner in Taipei. Their writing was graded out of 10 points and was based on the three criteria, shown in Table 5.2.

Table 5.2 Writing Task Criteria

Task fulfilment Did students follow the instructions?	Coherence: Does the writing hang together?	Vocabulary, sentence structure, grammar	Total scores

Students had not received any prior writing training, as no writing courses are available for non-English majors. Consequently, they did not know how to write a cohesive paragraph or how to organise it into understandable text. Many of the students simply wrote sentences which were in no way related to the questions. In order to encourage and motivate students, their grades were negotiable, if they had made some effort. Students received more points, if they corrected their errors or wrote a short reflection on the task. In order to help students write better, I devoted part of each lesson to discussing the students' work.

5.5 Observations

The observation data comprises one of my colleague's comments, my analysis of student perceptions and my research journal. My colleague, Kimberly, came to observe my classes and offered critical advice about classroom management and the use of website materials in class. For example, she suggested that the story should be played section by section. After listening to the first section of the story, the teacher should stop the audio clips and check students' understanding before going on to the next section. However, I thought the story was not that long, so students should be able take it all in, in one session. If they had not understood the story, I played it a second time. I explained my listening practice approach to her, by saying I preferred no interruptions, while listening to a short story. As will become obvious, the analysis of student responses, my colleague's comments, and my research journal deepened my awareness of the students' attitudes towards their learning experiences with website materials. The perceptions of students towards the *Adult Learning Activities* website were collected, using seven open-ended questions in the questionnaire (Appendix 3) and follow-up interviews. In the second stage of my investigation, 106 questionnaires were handed out to the students from the four different groups. Of these, 90 completed questionnaires were returned, indicating an acceptable 85% rate of return. The seven open-ended questions, covering several themes, are given below:

Table 5.3 Questions Investigating Students' Perceptions of the Adult Learning Activities Website

Question	Theme
7. Which topic and article did you choose?	website materials
8. Did you (a) read the text (b) listen to the audio (c) watch the video? 9. Did you get most benefit from reading, listening or watching the video? 10. Did you use a dictionary to look up words?	Approaches to story comprehension
11. What did you like or dislike about the writing tasks? State whether it was too easy, okay, or too difficult? 12. How do you evaluate performance on your writing task? 13. How did you feel about posting your writing task? What did you learn from posting your writing and looking at others' writing?	Comments about task-based learning

Questions 8, 9, and 10 tried to understand students' comprehension approaches during their self-study of website materials. Questions 11, 12, and 13 attempted to elicit students' perceptions of task writing and posting.

The discussion of the data gathered focused on the open-ended questions, interview information and student reflections, posted on the classroom website. The main issues discussed during the second stage were:

(1) Learners' approaches in comprehending articles on the website

(2) Website resources for English learning

(3) Whether writing tasks facilitate English learning with website resources

(4) Did posting tasks add value to entry point activities

Each issue is discussed below.

5.5.1 Learners' Approaches in Comprehending Articles on the Website

An examination of the data indicated that students used a range of approaches to understand the article. The categories within question 8 are based on approaches taken by students to facilitate their understanding of website materials. Accordingly, the following five situations are categorised as *'reading first'*: read only, read → listen, read→watch, read→listen→watch, and read→watch→listen. On the other hand, five approaches based on listening first are listed: listen first, listen→read, listen→watch→read, listen→read→watch, and listen→read→watch→listen. Moreover, answers given as watch→read→listen or watch→listen→read are categorised as *'watch first'*. Each of these question categories is shown in Table 5.4.

Table 5.4 Students' Approaches to Story Comprehension

Question 8 - Did you (a) read the text (b) listen to the audio (c) watch the video? In which order did you do these activities?									
N=number, %=percentage									
	Departments								
Categories	Business Administration		Information Management		Industrial Management		Textile Engineering		Total	
	N	%	N	%	N	%	N	%	N	%
Read and listen	10	45	10	42	19	76	12	63	51	**57**
Listen first	10	45	12	50	6	24	7	37	35	**39**
Watch first	2	9	2	8	0	0	0	0	**4**	4
Total	22	100	24	100	25	100	19	100	90	100

A review of the study data presented in Table 4.8 showed that 57% of the students read the articles first and then listened to the audio clips or watched the video clips (question 8). In contrast, the data reported in Table 5.4 also revealed that 39% of the students listened to the audio clips first (question 8). Feedback from question 8 indicated that over half the students understood the content by reading the text. From the interviews, I found out that the reason they read the text first was because their listening comprehension was not good. They felt that they would not have understood the audio text if they had not first read the text. The students' approaches to understanding the article via reading is also reflected in the feedback shown in Table 5.5.

Table 5.5 The Approaches Most Beneficial for Learners

Question 9 - Did you get most benefit from reading, listening or watching the video?									
N=number, %=percentage									
	Departments								
Categories	Business Administration		Information Management		Industrial Management		Textile Engineering		Total	
	N	%	N	%	N	%	N	%	N	%
Read the text	13	59	12	50	16	64	13	68	54	**60**
Listen	8	36	8	33	8	32	6	32	30	33
Read & listen	1	5	2	8	0	0	0	0	3	3
Watch the video	0	0	2	8	1	4	0	0	3	3
Total	22	100	24	100	25	100	19	100	90	100

According to the data from question 9, the four groups agreed that the most benefit was gained from '*reading the text*'. Overall, 60% of the students wrote that '*reading the text*' was the element which most helped their learning. Their reasons were stated below.

I thought that reading helped me to learn more vocabulary. When I saw a word I did not recognise, I would look it up in the dictionary, and so learn some words.

(Business Administration)

I got most benefit from reading because my listening ability is poor. I understood the content of the article through reading.

(Industrial Management)

From the statements quoted above, the students indicated their weaknesses in English listening. This was why they depended so much on reading to understand the story content. Only three students stated that they simultaneously read and listened to the audio clips, to get the idea. Another three students said that they watched the video first, to get a general idea of the article. They noted that they really did not understand what the speaker was talking about, but they could guess what the articles were about by watching the video clips. When they were faced with vocabulary they did not understand, 88% of the students generally looked up the words, using either the on-line dictionary or an electronic dictionary (question 10), as illustrated in Table 5.6.

Table 5.6 Approaches to Understanding Vocabulary

Question 10 - Did you use a dictionary to look up words?									
N=number, %=percentage									
	Departments								
Categories	Business Administration		Information Management		Industrial Management		Textile Engineering		Total	
	N	%	N	%	N	%	N	%	N	%
Yes	21	95	21	88	22	88	15	79	79	*88*
No	1	5	3	13	3	12	4	21	11	*12*
Total	22	100	24	100	25	100	19	100	90	100

According to the above data, most students were used to looking up words in the dictionary when they were faced with unknown vocabulary. The dictionaries used by the students were either an on-line dictionary or an electronic dictionary. Some students expressed that they were used to open another window with an on-line Chinese English dictionary when they read the website materials. When they met a new word, they could type the word into a blank and got its Chinese translation immediately.

When I met vocabulary I did not understand, I looked up the words. I used an on-line dictionary. It was very convenient. I could immediately know the Chinese meaning of those words. Then, I wrote it down in my notebook.

(Industrial Management)

The others just used an electronic dictionary to check the meaning of the word. Interestingly, no one used a paper-based dictionary. The proportions of dictionary use by students indicated that they depended on the Chinese translation to recognise lexical meanings when they did their homework. Regarding the 12% of students who did not look words up in a dictionary, their reasons were:

I was too lazy to look up words in the dictionary. Also, I thought the article was not too difficult. I still can understand part of the content.

(Information Management)

The comprehension questions actually were quite easy even when I did not completely understand the whole story. So, I did not bother using a dictionary.

(Textile Engineering)

Actually, I noticed that many of them had an electronic dictionary with them in class. They often used it to check the Chinese meaning of the vocabulary, while we were listening to a story. Some of them explained that if they did not know a word in the story, they found it difficult to go on to the next section. This indicates that students depended a lot on the translation approach, to understand a story with English text. This also accords with Secules et al.'s (1992) study:

Many second language learners believe they must understand every word, even though they do not do this to comprehend their native language. (Secules et al., 1992:487)

When learners met new vocabulary, they invariably wanted to check the meaning by use of a dictionary.

5.5.2 Website Resources for English Learning

The *Adult Learning Activities* website provided 11 topics, each of which included at least 10 stories. In other words, a variety of stories were available for students to choose from. The rich information found on the *Adult Learning Activities* website was an important factor in encouraging students to explore information related to their lives or their interests. Table 5.7 shows that the topics students chose were quite varied (question 7).

Table 5.7 Topics Chosen by the Learners

Question 7 - Which topic and article did you choose?									
N=number, %=percentage									
	Departments								
Categories	Business Administration		Information Management		Industrial Management		Textile Engineering		Total	
	N	%	N	%	N	%	N	%	N	%
School	6	27	10	**42**	5	20	2	11	26	**29**
Family	4	18	6	25	0	0	1	5	13	14
Money	3	14	2	8	5	20	3	16	13	14
Going places	2	9	1	4	1	4	1	5	5	6
Health	1	5	0	0	4	16	2	11	7	8
Working	0	0	1	4	0	0	2	11	3	3
Service	1	5	0	0	0	0	1	5	2	2
Nature	4	18	4	17	3	12	4	**21**	15	**17**
Housing	0	0	0	0	5	20	2	11	6	7
Science	1	5	0	0	2	8	1	5	4	4
Total	22	100	24	100	25	100	19	100	90	100

According to the data collected from the questionnaire, the top-ranked topic was '*school*' (29%). Interestingly, 42% of the majors of Information Management chose stories from this category. The reasons students chose different topics as their favourites can be identified by two factors: authenticity, personal experience, and levels of content.

Authenticity

I chose this story, 'Red Light Runner', from the topic, 'Going Places', because traffic is a big problem in Taiwan. More and more car accidents occur all the time. The main reason for this is that people do not obey the law. They are just concerned with their own convenience, which is terrible.

(Business Administration)

I chose 'Teen drinking', one story in the topic of Family. I felt that the alcohol problems of teenagers were getting serious. I would like to know more this kind of news.

(Business Administration)

I wanted to know whether computers were popular in the other country. That was the reason I chose this story, Computers in the Classroom, under the category of 'School'.

(Information Management)

I liked to choose a story which was related to our daily life. That is the reason I chose Health Insurance.

(Textile Engineering)

I chose Team Player, a topic of Working. I thought this issue was very important when we needed to complete a project.

(Textile Engineering)

Personal Experience

This website is written in English, but the articles are not too difficult. I was interested in the 'school' topic, because it is related to the context of our daily lives. The content of the 'school' topic has also become a topic between my classmates and me.

(Business Administration)

I chose this article, 'Family', because I love my family very much. I hope that they continue to be healthy and are able to do what they want.

(Business Administration)

I chose the 'school' topic because I am a student. This topic relates to my current situation.

(Information Management)

This topic was about animals that had been saved. I chose this topic because I like having pets. I felt sad when I saw a stray dog on the street. I really wanted to give it some food. So, the saved animals attracted me a lot; I think it is an important thing to do.

(Information Management)

I like airplane. That's why I chose Air Rage, one story in the category of Going Places.

(Industrial Management)

I chose Wind Worries, a story about firefighter. My father is a honorary firefighter. I usually saw him go to fight fire hardly. And I am so proud of being his son. In my dream, I want to be a good firefighter, too. I can save people and their home just like what my father did.

(Textile Engineering)

Students' feedback implied that they were interested in their familiar context of learning materials. This issue is in agreement with Good and Brophy's (1978) opinions about that task should be matched to interest. Learners' interest will help them to *'focus attention and persist in learning even complex material'* (Good & Brophy, 1978:344).

Levels of the Content

I chose 'smoking', one story in the topic of 'Family'. The content was quite simple so I can understand most of it.

(Industrial Management)

I chose the article, pollution fight, because it looked simpler than the others.

(Textile Engineering)

The above comments revealed that students engaged with the web material because the topics were close to their personal experience or related to their interests. Accordingly, the web is regarded as an enormously valuable learning tool (Owston, 1997; Peterson, 1997).

As mentioned in Section 5.5.5, students were required to write a brief reflection on website materials and homework feedback in addition to answer the question provided by the story. Some students commented about the story they read, while the others commented on the topics of this website. The students' comments proved that they were satisfied with this website as it included the following advantages: rich information and various exercises for language practice.

Rich Information

This website helped me learn a lot. I found many authentic stories about life. Also, the vocabulary in the article was not difficult. I also liked the pronunciation, which I imitated.

(Information Management)

It is a very good website. The articles were all related to current events.

(Industrial Management)

Language Practice

This website provides a good method of learning English. There are many short and practical stories. After study, I can practise the multiple choice questions to check my understanding

(Information Management)

I thought that this website provided a good way to practise listening. I used to listen to an English radio programme. Now, I can use this website to enhance my listening skills.

(Industrial Management)

This website is so great. We can make use of the rich resources to learn English.

I think that this is a nice way to learn English, because the topics and stories are lively and interesting.

(Textile Engineering)

5.5.3 Writing Tasks Facilitating English Learning

On the *Adult Learning Activities* website, a writing exercise is designed with each story. Learners are asked to provide their opinion or solution based on the story. Consequently, I designed a writing task at the second stage of teaching practice. Four groups of students were required to choose a story and write a short essay according to the question provided by the website. After that, they had to post their writing work on a classroom website. With this way, students were able to review other classmates' work. From students' comments, writing was actually a challenging task for most students in the four groups. Students mentioned their frustration at their inability to perform the writing tasks well. In discussions during the course, many of them stated that they did not know how to begin writing the first sentence. They tried using a Chinese-English dictionary to look up the English words they were looking for. Alternatively, they asked senior classmates how to write a piece of work. In the beginning, some of the students did not take the writing task seriously. Then, I reminded them that their writing work would be posted on the classroom website, with the four-classes of students I was teaching reviewing each other's work. After this announcement, students asked lots of questions about the details of writing and posting their work on the classroom website. Also, some students started to take notes about how to post an article to the assigned website discussion board. In general, students took writing much more seriously and acquired a sense of achievement after they learned that their writing work was going to be posted on the classroom website. In total, 79% of the students stated that the writing task was quite difficult, but that they had learned a lot.

Table 5.8 Learners' Comments about Writing Tasks

Question 11 - What did you like or dislike about the writing tasks?									
N=number, %=percentage									
	Departments								
Categories	Business Administration		Information Management		Industrial Management		Textile Engineering		Total	
	N	%	N	%	N	%	N	%	N	%
Difficult	2	9	9	38	6	24	2	11	19	21
Positive	20	91	15	63	19	76	17	89	71	79
Total	22	100	24	100	25	100	19	100	90	100

Two positive descriptive categories were identified by analysing the interviews: problem solving and a sense of achievement.

Problem Solving

I generally wrote down some phrases which related to the questions. Then, I organised the statement order. Also, I used an on-line dictionary to help me with the words I wanted to use.

(Business Administration)

I took a lot of time to think of how to write a paragraph with 50 words. It was very difficult to organise my opinions. However, it was good practice to think in English.

(Industrial Management)

A Sense of Achievement

I felt the writing task was a bit difficult. I graduated from a vocational high school, so I had not had any writing lessons. However, I was very glad that I could finish a piece of work at last.

(Information Management)

Twenty-one percent of the students mentioned that they did not like the writing task because it was too difficult. They also suggested that writing should not be a component of the course.

I spent a lot of time on thinking how to write. I did not know how to write a paragraph with 50 words.

(Industrial Management)

Honestly, I did not like the writing task, because it was too difficult. Writing 50 words was too much for me.

(Information Management)

In fact, 9 students did not submit their writing task. 7 of them were from the Textile Engineering group. The other two students were from the Industrial Management group. These students expressed that the writing task was too difficult to complete it. On the other hand, it also showed that those students may have had weaker intrapersonal intelligence and thus, have been unable to display the strong will needed to finish a difficult task. According to Armstrong's (2000) definition of intrapersonal intelligence, learners with high intrapersonal intelligence should be able to display a sense of independence or a strong will. As to student perceptions of their own writing work, 58% of the students said '*okay*', '*not too bad*', or '*so so*', which were categorised as '*medium*' (Table 5.9).

Table 5.9 Learners' Comments about their Writing Performance

Question 12 - How do you evaluate performance on your writing task?									
N=number, %=percentage									
	Departments								
Categories	Business Administration		Information Management		Industrial Management		Textile Engineering		Total	
	N	%	N	%	N	%	N	%	N	%
Poor	3	14	2	8	7	28	0	0	12	**13**
Medium	15	68	14	58	17	68	6	32	52	**58**
Good	4	18	8	33	1	4	13	**68**	26	29
Total	22	100	24	100	25	100	19	100	90	100

From the responses to question 12, it can be seen that 13% of the students said that they did not do well in their writing, while 58% regarded their writing as being at the intermediate level. Interestingly, 68% of Textile Engineering students marked their writing work as 'good', because they emphasised, in the follow-up interviews, that they had made great effort in the writing task.

I don't think I did well on my writing task. However, I did read over the articles many times in order to get some ideas and to answer the questions logically.

(Textile Engineering)

I spent a lot of time on writing. Although there were a lot of mistakes, this was my first time writing English. Therefore, I felt that my writing was good. At least, I finally completed a piece of work.

(Textile Engineering)

5.5.4 Posting Tasks Adding Value to Entry Point Activities

In order to provide an opportunity for students to share their written work, I designed a simple homepage on which they could post their work. There were links for the four different classes and three websites were used during the course. All the instructions on the sites were written in Chinese, in order to clarify the task. Students were required to post their homework to a discussion board, based on their majors.

Originally, I thought that students' computer skills would not be a problem. Surprisingly, some of them had never used the Internet. Although I explained the instructions for posting their writing on the discussion board, many of them still asked me the same questions after class. Some of them just sent their writing to my email account. Initially, I questioned whether I should ask students to print out their writing instead of posting it on the discussion board. The reason for this was that I had encountered technical problems with using a class homepage. Moreover, students were not familiar with the use of Internet functions, such as posting something to an assigned discussion board on the class homepage.

However, I still insisted that all students had to post their work on the discussion board. My purpose was to deliver a message to students that their work would be reviewed by other classmates in addition to me and the other marker. In this way, they would hopefully be willing to take more responsibility for the quality of their writing. Students were provided with real audiences which were themselves and some unknown people. After collecting the data from the questionnaire concerning students' perceptions of the *Adult Learning Activities* website used in the classroom, I was pleased that I kept my original plan of posting the writing task on the class homepage. I realised that posting the writing task had a positive value even though the students and I encountered some difficulties initially.

According to Table 5.10, 56% of the participants provided positive comments. For example, the posting task increased their knowledge of the Internet. They received a sense of achievement, because they had posted their '*own*' work on a discussion board, especially as this work had been written in English, a subject they often felt was difficult. Most of them expressed a feeling of being generally excited, challenged, and embarrassed, but at the same time, proud of their work.

Table 5.10 Learners' Comments about Posting Writing Tasks on the Internet

Question 13 - How did you feel about posting your writing task?									
N=number, %=percentage									
	Departments								
Categories	Business Administration		Information Management		Industrial Management		Textile Engineering		Total	
	N	%	N	%	N	%	N	%	N	%
Embarrassed	4	18	1	4	7	28	6	32	18	**20**
Positive comments	17	77	17	71	13	52	3	16	50	**56**
No opinion	1	5	6	25	5	20	10	53	22	**24**
Total	22	*100*	24	*100*	25	*100*	19	*100*	90	100

Most participants' positive comments about writing and posting were about writing for real audiences or that their work would be reviewed by other classmates. Their statements were presented as below.

Due to the fact that people may read my work, I tried to pay attention to my writing. I asked people to proofread my paper before I posted it.

(Industrial Management)

I felt great, because other classmates were able to appreciate my work.

(Information Management)

I was able to compare my writing with other classmates. I also learned more about grammatical structures and vocabulary.

(Information Management)

It was very interesting for me to post my work on the Internet, because my classmates may review my work. It was my first time doing this kind of task. I hope we can do it again, some time.

(Textile Engineering)

The above comments actually touched upon Rollinson's opinion on writing for real audiences (2005:25):

Peer response operates on a more informal level than teacher response. This may encourage or motivate writers, or at least provide a change from (and a complement to) the more one-way interaction between the teacher and the student.

In brief, students felt that the writing task was interesting or challenging because they knew that someone would read their work. Moreover, they also had a chance to read others' work which encouraged them to provide feedback for each other. In contrast, some students provided negative comments. 20% of the participants felt so embarrassed at having to post their work on the Internet that they did not want to show their writing to anyone. In addition, 24% of them said that they did not care about their work being posted on the classroom website because they would not access that website again. One student gave a very honest answer: *I am just too lazy to do it*.

5.6 Reflections on the Application of Entry Points

The review of teaching instruction focuses on a review of the logical and experiential entry points that were applied at the second cycle of my action research. The discussion is based on three activities: role play, writing task, and posting activity.

5.6.1 Reflection on Role Play Activity

When participating in role play, the first problem was that the classroom was much noisier than the teacher-centred approach, in which the students sit quietly listening to the teacher. When a group was acting out a story, I noticed that some students did not pay attention to the group presenting the role play. They were either chatting or doing something else. I tried to get the student audience to ask questions to the acting group. However, most of them did not do so. Some of them did not even know what the acting group's topic was or who the characters were. The main reason seemed to be because the acting group did not perform well and was unable to keep the audience's attention. Some students did not memorise their lines, and instead, read notes. In this way, the meaning of the role play activities was lost. To improve the situation, my colleague suggested including a role play performance as part of their final exam grade, to encourage students to take it seriously. Meanwhile, other students could participate in the evaluation, by writing down their comments about each acting group. As a result, I added peer evaluation, in line with her suggestion, as discussed in cycle 3.

5.6.2 Reflection on the Writing Task

As mentioned in the interview data, many students did not receive any formal writing training. Their writing experience was merely about making sentences or translating some sentences from Chinese to English. Therefore, I was not surprised when learners stated that they did not know how to start.

However, an interesting issue was raised, which was related to the attitude of learners to their writing task. In the beginning, some students did not submit the writing task. They assumed that I might not find out that they had missed doing their assignment. I did not point out who did not submit the assignment. Instead, I emphasised that the writing task was a part of the academic evaluation. If they submitted it and followed the basic rules listed on the class website, they would get 50% of points in total. Afterwards, some students asked me for an extension and others asked for guidelines. This situation implied that some students were used to a formative assessment. If they were not informed that their work would be evaluated by scores, they would not bother to make the extra effort. This attitude prompted me to adopt a score-oriented approach for the practice in the third stage.

5.6.3 Reflection on the Posting Activity

Regarding the posting activity of students' work, I experienced several difficulties during the experimental period. These difficulties included: designing a homepage where students could post their work; maintaining the homepage to keep students' work updated; and encouraging the students to post their work on the Internet.

The first difficulty was that I had to design a homepage on which four classes of students could post their writing tasks. This was a challenge for me, as I did not understand HTML code, (hypertext markup language). I merely applied to a free website with step-by-step instruction for novices to create their own sites. I tried to design my homepage in a simple style, which offered students clear writing task instructions. Nevertheless, I was often unable to manage the image setting or to separate the title and the text. As a result, I lost the document and had to start the whole process over again. Eventually, through trial and error and experimentation, I learned the skill of using Microsoft FontPage software to design four websites, for the use of the four groups, and how to post information on the Internet.

The second difficulty I encountered was homepage maintenance. The problem was compounded because several students from each of the majors posted their tasks to the wrong discussion board. For example, the Information Management majors should have posted their writing tasks to the discussion board built specifically for them, entitled 'Information Management'. Some posted their writing to other discussion boards. Students were reminded that they had to post their tasks to the correct discussion board, based on their major; many students simply posted their essay, without checking the discussion board link. One example is stated below.

I saw there was a discussion board link, so I posted my writing directly to it.

(Information Management)

Because of the carelessness of some students, I had to keep cutting and pasting their work into the correct sections of the homepage I had designed. In relocating their tasks, I also ran the risk of losing their work.

When I started the experiment of posting writing tasks on the discussion board, I really wondered whether it was a wise decision. Was the posting of student writing tasks on the Internet in keeping with the principle of computer assisted language learning? I was particularly inconvenienced by constantly having to move student postings to the correct location, especially as I had a heavy teaching and research load. If I made an error, the writing could have been lost.(Research Journal, 16 November, 2004)

The third difficulty I encountered was how to encourage students to post their work on the Internet. Some students were unable to post their tasks to the discussion board because they encountered problems in accessing the Internet.

I spent a long time trying to access the website for posting my work, but it did not work. Consequently, I posted it to your email box instead.

(Textile Engineering)

However, some students thought posting their writing on the Internet was too much trouble. They had to access the Internet and followed the instructions. Some of them just brought a disc with them to the class and gave it to me.

I felt posting my writing work on the Internet was too much trouble; why not just print out our writing?

(Information Management)

It was easier for me to save my writing to a file on a disc and give it directly to you to copy and paste it to the correct discussion board. I was worried that you might think I had not submitted my writing if I posted it to the wrong discussion board.

(Textile Engineering)

At the beginning of the posting experiment, my thoughts were similar to those of the students above. I wondered whether posting a piece of writing was helpful in motivating learning. After reviewing the students' reflections about the writing and posting tasks, I had more confidence in the application of Internet activities. Some students reflected that they finally became somewhat familiar with the posting task and wanted to spend time modifying their writing. Their reflections indicated that they were immersing themselves in the task, having fun, understanding an alternative perspective and gaining a sense of achievement. Their comments encouraged me to consider retaining the posting activity in future English lessons, as it seemed to support the principle of computer assisted language learning.

5.7 Learning Outcomes and Changes Adopted Subsequent to Observation of Cycle 2

This website, *Adult Learning Activities* can be regarded as a useful aid in attaining both the multiple intelligences objective and the goal of teaching English. First, the wide variety of topics, available on this website, may appeal to students' multiple intelligences. Second, the combination of text, sound, and visuals can accommodate a variety of learning approaches. Finally, small-scale projects, from choosing a topic to posting students' opinions on the classroom discussion board, may provide a bridge between students' areas of strength and preferences to the course topics. In other words, '*this shared decision-making made the classroom more learner-centered*' (Kallenbach & Viens, 2002:68). Allowing my students to have more control was the most important thing I attempted, in order to improve my teaching practice. Specifically, these small-scale tasks were designed to validate students' potential strengths, to help build their self-confidence and to enable them to take control over their own learning. This approach is the most common MI-inspired practice, which provides a variety of entry points for students to engage in language learning. This is in line with Kallenbach and Vien's study:

as students began to express preferences through choice-based activities, they also became more assertive in other ways, slightly shifting the balance of power in the classroom.

(Kallenbach & Vien, 2002:68)

One of the distinctive strengths of MI theory is allowing students' learning processes to be accessible to them, through personalisation of the course material. This concept inspired me to design a task for students to make content connections through a range of activities, which included listening, reading, writing, and posting the work on the classroom website, which may be regarded as a form of problem solving. Students' comments highlighted how they became involved in the small-scale projects.

However, many of them still tried to understand an article's content by reading the text. In other words, reading was the main approach taken by students to understand website contents. Consequently, it was necessary to find a website which focused on listening exercises for learners, in order to enhance their listening skills in the next stage of teaching.

The other problem mentioned in the second stage was the task of posting on the class homepage. Although some students did not agree with this activity, most of them regarded it as an interesting and challenging learning experience. An alternative approach in future practice could be the designation of one student from each class to take responsibility for the class homepage. I noticed that there are always some students who are good at computer skills. This procedure can be adopted in future lessons related to computer assisted language learning courses.

The last problem stated in the second action research cycle concerned the attitude of the students regarding peer-presentation. Some of them did not take it seriously when another group was doing role play. Therefore, a peer evaluation approach was adopted for the next practice with the expectation that learners would participate more in the class activities.

ACTION RESEARCH CYCLE 3

6.1 Introduction

In this chapter, the process of the third action research stage will be described, as will be my reflections on my attempts to improve the problem identified in the second action research cycle.

6.2 Introduction of the Randall's ESL Cyber Listening Lab Website

The third website used by the class was *Randall's ESL Cyber Listening Lab* (http://www.esl-lab.com). Four lessons were used with the third website. This website offers a range of audio and video-based listening quizzes, designed for three levels: easy, medium, and difficult. A screen shot of this website is reproduced below (Figure 6.1).

Figure 6.1 Screen Shot of the Randall's ESL Cyber Listening Lab Website

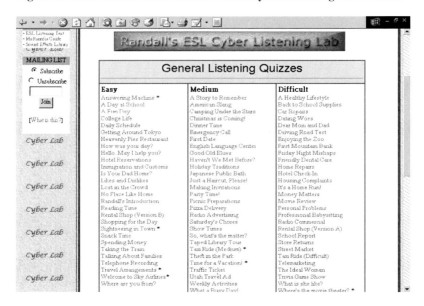

Each of the levels has at least 20 daily life topics for learners of English to navigate. After selecting a topic, learners are given a brief introduction to that topic, including the level of the quiz, the types of language, the speakers and the length of the audio clip. Each topic includes several components, such as listening exercises, quiz script, text completion quiz, and vocabulary list. As an example, the listening quiz, *Christmas is Coming* is shown in Figure 6.2.

Figure 6.2 The Components of 'Christmas is Coming'

6.2.1 Listening Exercises

Listening exercises comprise pre-listening, listening and post-listening exercises. Users can click on the icon, *Play Audio*, which accesses Real Player to listen to the conversation or the narration. After the conversations end, the site provides a quiz for learners. Each quiz asks questions about the conversations heard and contains multiple-choice questions, so that learners can select the most appropriate answers. After completing the quiz, users can click on the icon, *Final Score* to check the answers; a summary of the comprehension score is then provided.

6.2.2 Quiz Script

A script is provided and key vocabulary words are underlined and highlighted in pink. When users click on a word, a vocabulary definition box pops up (Figure 6.3).

Figure 6.3 Vocabulary Definition Box from the Quiz Script

Man: Well, Christmas is almost here. So, what do you want from Santa this year?

Micky: A toy car and walkie-talkies.

Man: Really? Well, a[DEFINITION: walkie-talkies]t do you want for Christmas?

Emily: If I can't have [small portable radio receiver-transmitters used for communicating with others]e some fragile dolls. And if I can't have some fragile dolls, it doesn

Man: Wow. Well, I'm ... And how is Santa going to get inside the house, Micky?

Micky: Um, go down ...

Man: Okay, so he's going to go down the chimney, and should we prepare anything for Santa?

Micky: Yeah!

Following the script, a listing of vocabulary and explanations are given (Figure 6.4)

Figure 6.4 Vocabulary Listing

Key Vocabulary[Top]

- **walkie-talkies** *(verb)*: small portable radio receiver-transmitters used for communicating with others
  - We always take walkie-talkies when we go hiking in case of emergencies.

- **barbie** *(noun)*: the name of a brand doll
  - My daughter wants a barbie doll house for Christmas.

- **fragile** *(verb)*: easily broken or damaged, delicate
  - Handle this vase with care. It's very fragile.

- **chimney** *(noun)*: the place in a house where smoke from a fire goes up and out of the roof
  - You should clean out the chimney before we use it this winter.

- **Rudolph** *(pronoun)*: the name of Santa's reindeer with the shiny red nose
  - According to the story, Santa needed Rudolph to guide his sleigh on one stormy, Christmas Eve.

6.2.3 Text Completion Quizzes

Most topics on this website also provide *Text Completion Quizzes* which are based on completion exercises (Figure 6.5). Users can click on the icon, *Play Audio* to listen to the conversation and fill in the answers.

Figure 6.5 Text Completion Quizzes

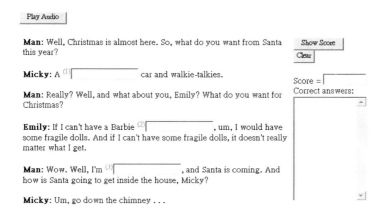

6.2.4 Review of the Randall's ESL Cyber Listening Lab Website

The *Randall's ESL Cyber Listening Lab* website is well known and fairly popular. Hence, the website has been reviewed by several CALL researchers (LeLoup & Ponterio, 2005). The review here still follows the guideline in Chapter 2, section 2.4.3.

A. Readability

This website lists five sections on the homepage: general listening quizzes, listening quizzes for academic purposes, 20-minute ESL vocabulary lessons, language learning and life tips, and a long conversation with RealVideo. Each section is divided into easy, medium and difficult and new stories are added constantly. Accordingly, the first impression of this website is presented as a multitude to users. This kind of design may have different impact on both holistic and serial learners. According to Pask (1976), serial learners concentrate on one aspect at a time while holistic learners look for an overall framework. In other words, serial learners may encounter difficulties when they navigate this website because they may be unable to make use of broad context.

Apart from the way in which the information is presented, the design follows the principle of greater contrasts leading to better readability (Hall & Hanna, 2004). The colours used on the homepage are a black text on a light purple background. As for each web page, a purple text is on a light yellow background.

B. Multimodal Presentations

Some topics on the website are presented in different multimedia modes, such as audio, video, audio caption or slide shows, which assist learners in choosing their favourite approaches to complete a listening exercise. Some guidelines noted in Mayer and Moreno's (2002) study can be applied to this website because a variety of multimodalities, e.g., static slide, video caption or audio caption, are incorporated into it. For example, the story, 'our family roots: genealogy', provides audio, text, and slides. Hence, students are expected to learn more readily by watching the slides and listening to the narration simultaneously (Mayer & Moreno, 2002).

C. Source Evaluation

Criteria for evaluation of the *Randall's ESL Cyber Listening Lab* website, which were developed in Section 2.4.3 are listed below for the convenience of the reader.

1. Does the website give a summary of information?
2. Can the website provide listening activities for use in class and after class?
3. Is the listening material on the website related to daily life issues?
4. What is the quality of the recorded material provided on the website?
5. Does the website make good use of the visual medium to provide a meaningful context or show facial expression or gesture?

The website was designed by Randall Davis with the help of his friends and family. Some of stories are actually about his family. The website focuses on listening activities, so there are a variety of topics for listening, including movies, family, schools, hotel reservations, business and the campus. The explanation in detail for first-time users can be accessed from the URL:

http://www.esl-lab.com/handouts/index.htm (retrieved May 9, 2006)

The website offers audio files and how teachers or students can make good use of them is explained in detail at the above URL.

The website can be useful for a listening class and self-study (criterion 1).

This website includes a series of listening tasks such as comprehension question and gap filling exercises. Each story is accompanied by pre-listening, while-listening and after-listening activities. If teachers want to exploit this website to the full, some stories can be used for dictation or pronunciation. Moreover, the level of difficulty is clearly determinable, so students can practise their listening after class. There are three levels of exercises and each level has at least 15 daily life topics. The vocabulary is provided below the activity. This website indeed offers daily life issues (criteria 2 and 3).

The sound is recorded by native speakers including adults or children, which allows students to experience the normal pronunciation of the target language (criterion 4). Students can send email to the author and listen to the answer recorded by Randall from the Internet. The questions for authors are not limited to his website. The questions can include any topics. Listening to the answer required by students is good motivation for students to practise listening skills.

Some articles in the column, 'Long conversation with Real Video', can be watched with a video device. However, the lectures or news reports do not seem interesting. The reporter simply talks in front of the video which does not provide a meaningful context (criterion 5).

6.3 Planning

The lesson plan for *Randall's ESL Cyber Listening Lab* website was based on the framework of the entry point approach and website materials. At the same time, each entry point was associated with different intelligences, presented in the '*related intelligences*' column.

6.3.1 The Lesson Plan

The lesson plan for the *Randall's ESL Cyber Listening Lab* website is shown below.

Table 6.1 Lesson Plan of ESL Cyber Listening

Title	Randall's ESL Cyber Listening Lab	
Website	http://www.esl-lab.com/	
Web features	Audio, Audio Captioned, Video, Slide Show	
Theme	A site designed for the development of listening and comprehension skills for learners of English	
Website content	There is a wide selection of daily life topics with easy, medium and difficult exercises. Computers must have RealAudio Players. A quiz follows each lesson. An automatic message window appears with the results.	
Teaching Aids	A white board, a multimedia computer with Internet access, data projector, projection screen, broadcast system for full-surround sound	
Lesson Possibilities and Entry Point Activities		
Language Practice	Entry point activity	Related intelligences
(Class 1 & 3)		

Listening Students read the comprehension questions and listen to the topic simultaneously.	Aesthetic: Presenting quizzes by visuals Narrative: presenting topics through listening	spatial intelligence linguistic intelligence logical-mathematical intelligence
Listening competition game Students answer listening comprehension questions provided by the website.	Experiential: Set a competition for students to enhance language skills	bodily-kinesthetic intelligence
(Class 2)		
Speaking - Role play Students develop and revise their understanding by exploring the characters' thoughts in the website topics.	Experiential: Organise a dialogue related to the topic	linguistic intelligence logical-mathematical intelligence bodily-kinesthetic intelligence interpersonal intelligence
(Class 4)		
Writing – peer evaluation Students comment on the performances of fellow classmates.	Experiential: Provide a chance for students to evaluate the performances of their peers	linguistic intelligence

6.3.2 Framework of Entry Point Activities

In grappling with how best to explore the use of website materials in the class, the entry point approach was adopted to provide multiple ways of helping learners understand content. Believing that visual display would attract most learners, the aesthetic entry point was again used as the first step. A topic was introduced, using a combination of visuals and sound as a multi-dimensional approach to capture learners' attention. Visual presentations are believed to attract attention, especially in learners who '*favour an artistic stance to the experience of living*' (Gardner, 1993:204). The narrative entry point of the topic was presented via computer sound effects. Narration tends to more deeply engage learners with preferred linguistic intelligence, in the subject matter.

On this website, each level provides a series of listening comprehension quizzes to check students' understanding. In order to practise these listening materials, an experiential entry point was used to navigate students through a competitive game design. According to Gardner's definition of the experiential entry point, people are easily involved in learning through 'an activity in which they become actively engaged' (Gardner, 2006). The experiential entry point approach here was that of a competitive game, which was on vocabulary practice. The idea of a competitive game was to encourage students to participate in class activities more willingly. Their reluctance to do so was a problem detected during the second stage of teaching practice. The students were not enthusiastic enough to volunteer to answer the question, but they probably wanted to get more points. Therefore, an approach was adopted based on the principle of a score-oriented reward.

Students first listened to the whole article, while reading the quizzes on the website. After that, they had to write the answer on a white board. There are two modes of listening exercises on this website, a multiple-choice mode and a fill-in-blank mode. The fill-in-the blank mode is an exercise in text completion. The reason for choosing the exercise for text completion was to encourage students to listen to specific information which normally provided a clue. Students not only needed to know the word but also had to be able to spell it. In this way, students had to listen carefully in order to be able to write a correct answer for more points. If the answer was correct, the student earned points. To encourage students' participation, they were allowed to use a cooperative learning approach to improve their scores. It means that students can seek the help from their classmates.

Another typical experiential entry point was role play, which was again applied at this stage. The idea of role play is to offer students an opportunity to use the target language which is one of the principles of the experiential approach, i.e., manipulate materials and carry out an experiment. Moreover, a peer evaluation task was added as part of the role play assessment at the third stage. Peer evaluation offered students the chance to reflect on their speaking practice and listening comprehension.

All the entry point activities were aimed at helping bridge the gap between learning experience and language skills. Sequential activities, within each lesson, made quite an impact on learners by allowing them to build up their own understanding at their own pace. The entry point approach used a mixture of both verbal and nonverbal teaching skills to engage learners, thus, responding to their own preferred learning methods.

6.4 Acting

In the third stage, the approaches for adopting *Randall's ESL Cyber Listening Lab* website in the English class addressed listening practice, which was identified as being insufficient during the second stage. A similar role play procedure was set up, to help improve my teaching practice using website materials. The focus was on listening and speaking activities.

6.4.1 Listening Exercises

Several topics and listening exercises were adopted in the lessons of the four classes of students. Below, the topic, *Our Family Roots* is used as an example. First, I accessed the homepage of the *Randall's ESL Cyber Listening Lab* website and clicked on the topic. Second, I went through each question in the listening exercises by scrolling down the computer screen (Figure 6.6).

Figure 6.6 Listening Comprehension Questions in Our Family Roots

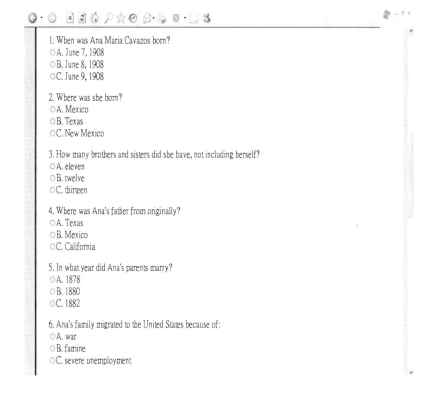

1. When was Ana Maria Cavazos born?
   ○ A. June 7, 1908
   ○ B. June 8, 1908
   ○ C. June 9, 1908

2. Where was she born?
   ○ A. Mexico
   ○ B. Texas
   ○ C. New Mexico

3. How many brothers and sisters did she have, not including herself?
   ○ A. eleven
   ○ B. twelve
   ○ C. thirteen

4. Where was Ana's father from originally?
   ○ A. Texas
   ○ B. Mexico
   ○ C. California

5. In what year did Ana's parents marry?
   ○ A. 1878
   ○ B. 1880
   ○ C. 1882

6. Ana's family migrated to the United States because of:
   ○ A. war
   ○ B. famine
   ○ C. severe unemployment

It was explained to students that they were going to watch a slide show with a narrator, introducing a brief family history of Ana Maria Cavazos. Following this, they had to answer some multiple-choice questions. After the audio had ended, I asked for a volunteer to come to the teacher's computer and to click on an answer. It did not surprise me that no one volunteered. At that moment, the whole class became very quiet. I noticed that students did not participate actively. Therefore, I used a scheme which tried to attract the attention of the whole class. Each student was given a small piece of paper, on which I asked them to write their names. After folding the pieces of paper and placing them on my desk, I randomly nominated one of the students to pick one of them up. At this point, the classroom atmosphere changed. The student who chose the piece of paper often read out the name extremely slowly, to make his or her fellow students nervous. Students began to pay close attention, because any one of them could be the next one to answer a question in front of the whole class.

After the first student had clicked on the answer, he then picked up another piece of paper and read out the next student's name, and so on. If students chose the wrong answer, they were given the chance to try again. As Scrivener (1994:149) suggests, *'don't immediately acknowledge correct answers with words'*. Alternatively, I played the audio clips again for students to confirm their ideas. When the last question had been answered, a student clicked on the icon, *'Final Score'* to check the answers. In order to clarify if any answers had been wrong, I explained that the answer could be found in the *'Text Completion Quiz'* section.

6.4.2 Text Completion Quiz

The *Text Completion Quiz* was actually a fill-in-the-blanks exercise that gave students the opportunity to listen carefully. Again, students were reminded that they would be asked to take turns to answer on the teacher's computer. Sometimes, students volunteered to answer questions, because they did not want to be chosen at random and perhaps be asked to answer a question they did not know the answer to. After volunteering, they were not nominated again. If students did not know the answer, they could click on the icon, *Play*, and listen to the narration once more.

Another technique which encouraged students to participate in activities was earning '*points*'. I wrote the numbers 1 to 8 on the white board to represent the blanks. When the narration had ended, students wrote down the answers next to the relevant number. If the answer was correct, they earned five points. In contrast, if the answer was wrong, they lost five points. The reason for the second part of the rule was to encourage students to think their answer over carefully. So as to not discourage students, I prompted them by asking, *Are you sure? Do you want to ask your classmate again*? In this way, students suspected their answers were perhaps incorrect and chose another answer. Students seemed to thoroughly enjoy this section and some actually '*ran*' to the white board. They did not want another classmate to reach the board first, when they knew the answer.

When all the blanks had been filled in, I clicked on the icon, *Show Score* to check the answers. Then, I accessed the web page,

Quiz Script, to go through the quiz transcript, where I could click on an underlined word to show the definition of that word.

6.4.3 Speaking Activity

In order to improve the role play problem identified in cycle 2, a similar role play activity was set up. Students accessed this website after class and chose a listening topic as the script for a role play which would take place during the next lesson. They did not have to stick in the materials they had read on the website; instead, they could use their own words. Partners were chosen and decisions, on how to act out a role play in front of the class, were made. The length of the role play was unlimited; the only requirement was that they were not allowed to read from their notes. To manage the class, I applied the peer evaluation approach. All students were requested to make notes and to participate in the task of evaluating each group's role play. They had to note the names of the presenters and their topics. Afterwards, fellow students evaluated each group's performance and provided comments. Moreover, students were informed that this evaluation task would be part of their course assessment, which encouraged students to pay close and respected to other presentation which was another problem raised in action research cycle 2.

6.5 Observing

This section presents the results of the perceptions of students towards the *Randall's ESL Cyber Listening Lab* website, used for listening practice. The insight I gained towards my teaching practice, related to this website, was collected from student responses, my colleague's comments, and my research journal. My colleague, Jenny, who is interested in the implications of multiple intelligences in teaching, came to observe my classes.

Students' perceptions of the *Randall's ESL Cyber Listening Lab* website were collected, using seven continuous open-ended questions in the questionnaire, shown in Appendix 2. In addition, I spoke with students to follow up on questions as they arose in the data. A total of 106 questionnaires were given to students from the four different majors. Of these, 90 were completed and returned, indicating an acceptable 85% rate of return. The seven open-ended questions, covering several themes, are laid out below:

Table 6.2 Students' Perceptions of the Website

Question	Theme
14. What did you think of the quiz from this website we did in the class? 15. Which kinds of listening exercises do you like? 16. Did you try the exercises as self-study? If yes, which level did you complete?	Comments about website material
17. Did you answer the questions after the listening or did you find the answer from the quiz script?	Approaches of story comprehension
18. Were any problems encountered while using this website? How did you solve them?	Comments about website function

19. How did you feel about giving answers in front of the whole class? 20. Did you like participating in role play in front of the whole class?	Comments about MI-inspired instruction

In this section, the data results are presented as answers to examine

(A) the use of the *Randall's ESL Cyber Listening Lab* website for listening exercises

(B) the evaluation of the Randall's ESL Cyber Listening Lab website design;

(C) the effect of role play as an entry point activity; and

(D) the approach of peer evaluation.

Each issue is discussed below.

6.5.1 The Randall's ESL Cyber Listening Lab Website for Listening Practice

There are two types of quizzes on this website: multiple choice and gap filling exercises. Table 6.3 shows learners' perceptions of two quizzes.

Table 6.3 Student Comments on Listening Exercises in the Randall's ESL Cyber Listening Lab Website

Question 14 - What did you think of the quiz from this website we did in the class?									
N=number, %=percentage			Departments						
Categories	Business Administration		Information Management		Industrial Management		Textile Engineering		Total	
	N	%	N	%	N	%	N	%	N	%
Multiple choice										
Easy	0	*0*	4	*15*	4	*17*	6	*23*	14	*14*
Medium	21	*88*	20	*77*	18	*75*	20	*77*	79	*77*
Difficult	3	*13*	2	*8*	2	*8*	0	*0*	7	*7*
Total	24	*100*	26	*100*	24	*100*	26	*100*	100	*100*
Gap filling										
(easy)	0	*0*	1	*4*	3	*13*	1	*4*	5	*5*
(medium)	18	*75*	10	*38*	18	*75*	15	*58*	61	*61*
(difficult)	6	*25*	15	*58*	3	*13*	10	*38*	34	*34*
Total	24	*100*	26	*100*	24	*100*	26	*100*	100	*100*

As displayed in Table 6.3, 14% of the students indicated that multiple choice exercises were easy. However, none of the Business Administration group agreed it. The majority of students from the other three groups thought it was at a medium level. In total, 77% of the students identified the multiple choice exercises as being at a medium level, and while 13% of Business Administration students felt that the listening exercises were difficult, no one from the Textile Engineering group thought so.

Table 6.3 also displays students' perceptions of the gap filling quiz. Learners were required to write the words they had heard in the correct blanks. Of the Business Administration students, 75%

identified the text completion quiz as being at a medium level; the Industrial Management students agreed. In total, 61% of the students indicated that the exercises in the gap filling quiz were of medium difficulty, except for 58% of Information Management majors, who thought they were a bit difficult. They said the articles were difficult to understand and also thought the speech was difficult to follow.

Difficult Content

The dialogue was too fast to keep up with, although the exercise was categorised as 'easy'.

Ambiguous Speech

I did not understand the conversation between the girl and the man but I did understand what the father was talking about. I did not have any idea what the daughter was talking about, although her speech was very short. I am not used to listening to English expressed in such an informal way.

The problem with the ambiguous speech, mentioned above, was in the story, *A Fun Day*. The conversation was between a father and his young daughter who sounded about 7 years old. Actually, the words spoken by the young girl were generally brief. The difficulty arose because the students were not used to listening to authentic speech from a child with a naïve voice. Accordingly, students felt that her language was not easy to understand. For example, when she said 'Muppets in Space', students said it sounded like a girl yawning. They did not appreciate the young girl's somewhat petulant voice.

They thought it interfered with their concentration in listening to the story. As spoken by Buck (2001:168-169):

> *This might be an ideal situation for recording live speech events, if it is practically possible. ... However, natural speech is often too difficult for lower-ability listeners to understand.*

Apart from the '*RealAudio*' based stories, two stories using the '*RealVideo*' mode were presented in the classes. Except for the Business Administration majors, students stated that they preferred listening exercises with video clips. As shown in Table 6.4, 54% of the respondents indicated that they now had a better understanding of English, thanks to the video clips.

Table 6.4 Learners' Comments about the Comprehension Approach to Listening Exercises

Question 15 - Which kinds of listening exercises do you prefer?									
N=number, %=percentage									
	Department								
Categories	Business Administration		Information Management		Industrial Management		Textile Engineering		Total	
	N	%	N	%	N	%	N	%	N	%
audio clips	16	**67**	10	38	9	37	10	38	45	45
video clips	8	33	15	58	15	63	16	62	54	**54**
No difference	0	0	1	4	0	0	0	0	1	1
Total	24	100	26	100	24	100	26	100	100	100

In the follow-up interviews, students indicated that the speed of narration in the story, '*My Family Roots*' was slower. The story was presented with slides which were regarded as video clips. There was a short phrase as a summary of each slide. For example, when the narrator read '*Anna's family came to the United States during the Mexican Revolution in 1913. Their family experienced much hardship*', the sentence, *the family moved to the United States*, would show on the slide. Students made use of the short information to comprehend the current listening passage before connecting with the next.

In addition, as can also be seen from Table 6.4, the Business Administration group results were different from the other three groups. 67% of these students preferred to listen to the story via audio clips. Further interviews indicated that some students often read the questions while simultaneously listening to the audio clips. Because of this, they actually did not have time to watch the video clips. It seems that the video clips did not help them focus on the questions and even distracted their attention. Thus, they had to listen to the audio clips once again. The other reason was because the speed of narration in the story was smooth and clear. They felt that they could understand the story better through listening. These were the two reasons why the majority of Business Administration students preferred listening to the audio clips rather than watching video clips.

6.5.2 Evaluation of the Randall's ESL Cyber Listening Lab Website Design

The *Randall's ESL Cyber Listening Lab* website offers students an opportunity to practise listening at different levels of difficulty.

Each story is supported with multimedia extensions such as captioned video. Learners may listen to the audio clips or watch the video clips. Then, they could answer a series of comprehension questions. This website provides learners with a large number of listening exercises. In other words, learners can use this website to practise their listening skills after class. However, two problems, concerning the use of the site for teaching or learning materials, arose.

The first problem is the necessity of having the '*RealPlayer*' software, required to process the '*RealAudio*' or '*RealVideo*' functions; this can be downloaded from the Internet. However, as the answers to question 18 show, learners still did not know how to manage software when they encountered technical problems. According to Table 6.5, 86% of the students did not encounter any difficulty while accessing this website outside the classroom.

Table 6.5 Learner Comments about Website Functions

Question 18 - Were any problems encountered while using this website?									
N=number, %=percentage									
	Departments								
Categories	Business Administration		Information Management		Industrial Management		Textile Engineering		Total	
	N	%	N	%	N	%	N	%	N	%
Yes	5	21	3	12	1	4	5	19	14	*14*
No	19	79	23	88	23	96	21	81	86	*86*
Total	24	100	26	100	24	100	26	100	100	100

However, 14% stated that they could not listen to the dialogue after they had clicked on the icon '*Play Audio*'. When they were unable to access a function, an explanation box popped up to show what the problem was; the main problem was that most of them still had no idea how to install *'Real Player'*. When encountering such technical problems, most of the students simply printed out the whole text and read it.

Second, the text script did not always match the words spoken, which can cause confusion with the teaching instructions. An example of this was the *'Text Completion Quiz'* from the story, *'My Family Roots'*. In this quiz, the second sentence is *'She was the _____ of twelve children'* (Figure 6.7).

Figure 6.7 Text Completion Quiz from the Story, 'My Family Roots'

Ana Maria Cavazos was born on ⁽¹⁾[   ] eighth, 1908, in Reynosa, Mexico. She was the ⁽²⁾[   ] of twelve children.

Her father, Jesus Cavazos, was originally from Victoria, Texas, but his family ⁽³⁾[   ] to Mexico around 1855.

Ana's mother, Juana Castro, was the oldest of six brothers and sisters. Juana and Jesus were married in ⁽⁴⁾[   ]. Ana's family came to the United States ⁽⁵⁾[   ] the Mexican Revolution in 1913. Their family experienced much ⁽⁶⁾[   ].

Ana grew up in Texas and ⁽⁷⁾[   ] her future husband in 1929. Ana and Abel Contreras were married in 1931 and were the parents of eleven children.

Thank you for joining this ⁽⁸⁾[   ] presentation.

0%
Correct Answers:
1. June
2. eleventh
3. moved
4. 1880
5. during
6. hardship
7. met
8. short

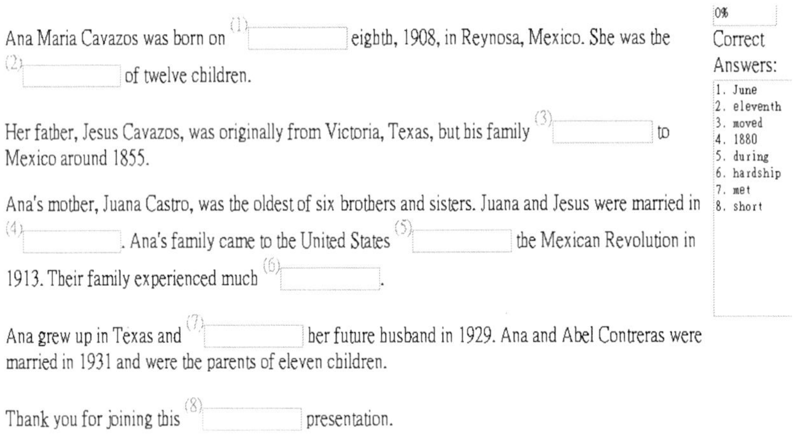

The correct answer here is *'eleventh'* and the text script also shows that *'she was the eleventh of twelve children'* shown in Figure 6.8.

Figure 6.8 Quiz Script of the Story, 'My Family Roots'

II. Listening Exercises

1. Listen to the conversation again by pressing the Play Audio button and read along with the conversation.?

Ana Maria Cavazos was born on June eighth, 1908, in Reynosa, Mexico. She was the eleventh of twelve children.

Her father, Jesus Cavazos, was originally from Victoria, Texas, but his family moved to Mexico around 1855.

Ana's mother, Juana Castro, was the oldest of six brothers and sisters. Juana and Jesus were married in 1880. Ana's family came to the United States during the Mexican Revolution in 1913. Their family experienced much hardship. Ana grew up in Texas and met her future husband in 1929. Ana and Abel Contreras were married in 1931 and were the parents of eleven children.

Thank you for joining this short presentation.

However, what the narrator actually says here is: she was the '*youngest*' of twelve children. It is important to remind teachers that they must check the accuracy of the answers provided by the quizzes, before using the website for listening teaching materials.

According to the above comments, three design criteria about this website are to be noted: multimodal resources, listening tasks and the effect of the recorded materials. The principle of multimodality was applied in a number of ways. First, the modality of visual (slides) and narration (audio) helped certain students get information about the story context (Table 6.4). As for the Business Administration group, audio and text were regarded as a means of listening practice. However, some students did not appreciate the facility of video clips which were regarded as a distraction. Second, this website offered a variety of 'sensory' features, such as Real Audio Player and Real Video Player. These functions were assumed to help listening practice. However, students encountered difficulty in using them for listening because of unfamiliar software. It implies that technical problems are often the main issue affecting the use of the computer to assist learning. Third, the recorded material was regarded as authentic because the dialogue was spoken by native speakers. However, some students did not appreciate some native speakers such as a little girl (Section 6.5.1). Her tone or language confused learners' recognition of sentences.

6.5.3 Effect of Multiple Entry Point Activities

The analyses of entry point activities focused on giving answers in front of the whole class (question 19) and role play (question 20). Table 6.6 shows that 40% of the students felt excited when they had the opportunity to give an answer in front of the whole class.

Table 6.6 Learners' Comments about Bodily-kinesthetic Activity

Question 19 – How did you feel about giving answers in front of the whole class?									
N=number, %=percentage									
	Departments								
Categories	Business Administration		Information Management		Industrial Management		Textile Engineering		Total	
	N	%	N	%	N	%	N	%	N	%
No feeling	2	8	7	27	15	**63**	4	15	28	**28**
Embarrassed	4	17	4	15	0	0	1	4	9	9
Challenge	0	0	7	27	2	8	0	0	8	8
Excited	12	**50**	7	**27**	6	**25**	15	**58**	40	**40**
Nervous	6	25	1	4	1	4	6	23	14	14
Total	24	100	26	100	24	100	26	100	100	100

From Table 6.6, it can be seen that 50% of Business Administration students and 58% of Textile Engineering students felt excited when it was their turn to choose an answer in front of the whole class. In contrast, only 27% of the Information Management students and 25% of the Industrial Management students enjoyed answering the questions. These reasons may be divided into two categories: a sense of achievement and participating in a game-like activity.

A Sense of Achievement

When we were asked a question to which I knew the correct answer, I wanted to rush to the white board in case another classmate reached the board before I did.

(Business Administration)

I felt so excited because I did not believe that I could answer these questions.

(Textile Engineering)

Participating in a Game-like Activity

I found it to be a great way to push me to focus on the listening content, because I wanted to get more points.

(Business Administration)

It was certainly the most fun I've ever had participating in classroom activities. It was very useful in helping me to concentrate on the listening tasks.

(Industrial Management)

I felt very excited. I just tried my best to get a chance to write an answer.

(Textile Engineering)

Apart from feeling excited, challenged, embarrassed, and nervous, 28% of the students expressed that they had no specific feelings about this reward activity (question 19). More surprisingly, 63% of Industrial Management students stated that they had no specific feelings about providing answers in front of the class. Their main reasons were difficult listening context and self-satisfaction.

Difficult Listening Context

Although I wanted to answer the questions, I did not understand the content.

(Industrial Management)

I was unable to understand what the speaker was saying. As a result, I could not go to the front and write down the answer. I felt this activity had nothing to do with me.

(Textile Engineering)

Self-Satisfaction

My score was high enough, so I did not want to get a higher score by giving an answer in front of the whole class. I would like to give the chance to other people.

(Industrial Management)

As to the students' role play feedback, I was very surprised that many seemingly quiet students said they liked this activity very much and hoped to participate in similar activities in the future. The student feedback findings are shown in Table 6.7.

Table 6.7 Learners' Comments about Role Play

Question 20 - Did you like participating in role play in front of the whole class?									
N=number, %=percentage									
	Departments								
Categories	Business Administration		Information Management		Industrial Management		Textile Engineering		Total	
	N	%	N	%	N	%	N	%	N	%
Yes	21	**88**	19	**73**	10	42	16	62	66	**66**
No	3	13	7	27	14	**58**	10	38	34	34
Total	24	100	26	100	24	100	26	100	100	100

In total, 66% of students felt that role play was fun and expressed that they would like to participate in such activity more often (question 20). More interestingly, 88% of Business Administration students and 73% of students from the Information Management group had positive attitudes towards role play and looked forward to more role play activities. In contrast, the two other groups, Industrial Management and Textile Engineering, were not as enthusiastic about role play as the female-based groups. Only 42% of the Industrial Management group said they would like to participate in role play in future English classes, which is very different from the Business Administration group (88%). Both positive and negative feelings towards role play are listed below.

Positive Reason 1- Speaking Practice

Role play increases the opportunities to speak English. In this way, I can be more active in speaking English.

(Business Administration)

There are few opportunities to speak English after class. This was a good chance to practise speaking the target language in class.

(Industrial Management)

I do not have much opportunity to speak English. Role play not only provided me with that chance, but also allowed me to speak in front of the whole English class.

(Textile Engineering)

Positive Reason 2 – Writing and Speaking Practice

I was able to write down what I wanted to say in advance, so I thought role play was good for practising both writing and speaking.

(Business Administration)

Positive Reason 3 – The Chance to Perform

I liked role play because I could become another person. When I imitated a character's tone, I felt I could speak English like a native speaker.

(Information Management)

These student respondents supported Ladousse's statement that the benefit of role play helps shy students, in that '*These students are liberated by role play as they no longer feel that their own personality is implicated* (Ladousse, 1995:7). Role play aroused considerable interest among the students and appeared to give quieter students the chance to express themselves in a more forthright way.

Though most of the students showed an interest in role play, a certain number had negative responses. It is well recognized that students often experience considerable embarrassment in relation to role play (Ladousse, 1995). Hence, it was probably not surprising that 34% of them described their feelings as being embarrassed. Moreover, 58% of Industrial Management students had negative feedback to role play, a rather a high proportion (Table 6.7). Some of them said they did not want to participate in role play activities anymore. The detailed reasons found in the amassed data revealed negative feelings, negative learning attitudes, and even a negative attitude towards English itself.

Negative Feelings

I was too nervous to remember the lines; I do not like this kind of activity.

(Information Management)

I felt so embarrassed when I had to act in front of the whole class. I do not want to participate in the role play task anymore.

(Industrial Management)

I felt embarrassed because I often said the wrong things. I do not like acting in front of the whole class.

(Textile Engineering)

Negative Learning Attitude

I did not like this activity, because it was very difficult for me to remember the lines. I do not want to spend a lot of time memorising lines.

(Business Administration)

I had to spend a lot of time trying to memorise many lines and felt it was too much.

(Industrial Management)

I did not like participating in role play activity, because I was too lazy to memorise the lines.

(Textile Engineering)

Negative Attitude to English

English is too difficult to study. Accordingly, I do not like any activity in English.

(Industrial Management)

The first category of negative comments towards role play was mainly experiencing negative feelings, including being nervous, embarrassed, afraid, and unconfident. These feelings are also mentioned by Ladousse (1995:11): *a related problem is the psychological stress that many people feel when they are asked to be someone else*. Some students thought they were '*totally lacking in dramatic ability*' (Ladousse, 1995:10). Apart from the 'feelings' issue, another factor was that students did not want to make an effort to learn their lines by heart. This was particularly true for the students, in all four groups, who did not like role play. So as not to pressure students too much, they were only asked to memorise at least two sentences. In other words, the students who complained that the lines were too difficult to remember did not want to memorise anything at all. The last category was the students' negative attitude towards English. This indicated that students who did not like English learning did not want to participate in any English related activities.

Although some students did not like participating in role play, a comparison of students' performances, with the previous ones in cycle 2, yielded a significant difference. Many groups did, indeed, make some effort to prepare for the role play activity and commented that both the preparation and the acting were a lot of fun. For example, a group of students chose the topic, *Christmas is Coming* to act out a situation involving gift giving. One student, wearing a green coat, was dressed like a Christmas tree. When one member mentioned the gift she wanted, the Christmas tree suddenly handed it to her. The role of the Christmas tree was actually similar to that of Santa Claus. However, the idea of using a Christmas tree in this way gave an extraordinary effect and impressed the audience.

6.5.4 The Peer Evaluation Task

In stage three, as suggested in action research cycle two, the task of peer evaluation was included in the role play activities. All students were required to give comments about the speaking performances of the other groups. A positive aspect of the evaluation task was evident in students' follow-up interviews. Students felt comfortable about the anonymity of the evaluation form and were prepared to receive comments about their own performance from their fellow students.

I liked being anonymous; I felt free to make sincere comments about those groups who did not take role play seriously.

(Industrial Management)

It was easier to make comments about other players without having to worry about them knowing who was doing the writing, especially as some of them are my friends.

(Textile Engineering)

That the task of peer evaluation can also be a useful tool for strengthening learning was confirmed in the interviews.

I thought the peer evaluation idea was fantastic. When I had to comment on my classmates, I paid more attention to what was happening on stage.

(Information Management)

Through the evaluation task, students were given the responsibility of grading the performances of the other groups. They felt good about being like examiners, with the authority to provide critical comments. Interestingly, their comments were even stricter than those of their teacher. Three descriptive categories were identified through the analysis of their comments, which are preparation, communication, and performance.

Preparation

Group A, was quite fluent, but one member forgot his lines, which affected the whole performance. The performance by Group B was really impressive. I liked their idea of the Christmas tree very much.

(Business Administration)

Group D should have made more effort to prepare for the task. They did not have a complete conversation. Everybody just spoke their own lines without any meaningful connection.

(Industrial Management)

Communication

Group E spoke too quietly. I thought that they should have had their lines better memorised instead of just reading the sentences.

(Information Management)

I had completely no idea what Group C was doing on stage.

(Industrial Management)

Performance

Group C memorised the lines quite well, but their performance could have been more authentic.

(Business Administration)

At the beginning, Group A did quite well. However, they repeated what they had already said, which spoiled the performance.

(Industrial Management)

The role play by Group C was fascinating and authentic.

(Textile Engineering)

The above comments show that students were conscientiously engaged in their examiner roles. Through this process of peer evaluation, students fully participated in classroom activities, achieving a deeper understanding of their own performances and those of others. In other words, the peer evaluation task contributed to learning. Students made the connection between their own practice and the appreciation of others, which probably, will influence their future practice. Considering the students' peer evaluation experiences, in relation to their language learning, encourages its use in future lessons.

6.5.5 Learners' Efforts at Self-Study

In the third stage, students were not asked to do a follow-up task such as writing after class. Sometimes, I told them that there would be a listening test based on several stories on this website. Accordingly, many of the students seemed to review the website just for the preparation of the quiz according to the data in Table 6.8.

Table 6.8 Students' response about the website used as self-study

Question 16 – Did you try the exercises as self-study?									
N=number, %=percentage									
	Departments								
Level	Business Administration		Information Management		Industrial Management		Textile Engineering		Total
	N	%	N	%	N	%	N	%	N	%
Yes-easy	10	42	7	27	6	25	7	27	30	30
Yes-medium	4	16	6	23	4	17	3	11	17	17
No	10	42	13	50	14	58	16	62	53	53
Total	24	100	26	100	24	100	26	100	100	100

Although students stated that they were quite involved in the class activity, it was nothing to do with their willingness to use the website for self-study. In reality, few students accessed this website after class according to the data. If they accessed it, they usually focused on the easy level. In most cases, around half of the students gave a negative response with the Textile Engineering students representing the largest group with 62%. Their reasons for the negative responses were very interesting and practical as shown below.

I knew that the exercises provided on this website were useful. However, I did not have any motivation to review them unless there was going to be a test.

(Business Administration)

I only reviewed it if you said there would be a test next time.

(Information Management)

Although you said that there would be a test next time, I still did not access the website to listen to the story. It was a listening test, so I could not prepare it in advance. I wanted to know my real competence.

(Industrial Management)

If there was no test next time, why did I need to access this website and review these exercises?

(Textile Engineering)

Students' comments indicated that their attitude to English learning was based on an exam-driven goal. If there was no test in the next class, they would not spend time on reviewing, either. However, Dickinson (1987) points out that learners are less likely to develop the motivation to sustain greater autonomy if they are only extrinsically motivated by examination. In this way, it is suggested that teachers design a series of activities used in the class and after class to foster a good learning habit.

6.6 Reflections on Teaching Practice

In order to create opportunities for students to participate in an active way in listening practice, multiple entry point activities were provided. There was also a rich electronic library available for learners to select any information they required. My reflections at this stage focused on the implementation of the entry point approach and classroom management.

6.6.1 Implementation of the Entry Point Approach

The entry point approach may be regarded as a practical application of the multiple intelligences theory (Kallenbach & Viens, 2002). Entry points refer to activities that encourage students to enter into the learning material. Reflections on entry point activities in stage three referred to an aesthetic entry point and an experiential entry point such as role play and peer evaluation. The idea behind this was that the process, from choosing a topic from the assigned website to completing a performance, involved a wide range of intelligences. The opportunity to choose a topic offered students the chance to explore the subjects they preferred. In this way, they became actively engaged in a practical learning experience.

Role play actually involved two entry points: logical and experiential. Students had to create a dialogue for four people. After that, they had to 'recite' it in front of the whole class. Through the topics they selected and the styles, in which they performed, they were able to *'manipulate materials and carry out experiments'* (Gardner, 2006:161). Logical thinking and linguistic practice were taken into account in role play when learners had to organise the sequential dialogue to be spoken. Further, role play involved the negotiation of consensus in order to complete the task.

As for the task of peer evaluation, it offered learners the opportunity of being a meaningful audience. From their evaluation to the other groups, it showed that they participated in the whole class activity more concentration than previously. The application of peer evaluation for role play required learners to take responsibility for their own work.

6.6.2 Classroom Management

Students' comments on classroom activities, such as having to give answers in front of the whole class and role play, were very different. The aim of giving an answer in front of the whole class in cycle 2 was to encourage students to participate in class activity. From observation, some students were not too happy at being selected, especially if they had not paid sufficient attention to the audio clips. Thus, in order to motivate students to participate more in class activities, the listening exercises from the *Randall's ESL Cyber Listening Lab* website were carried out with a 'reward' approach. Students received extra points whenever they answered the comprehension questions or filled in the blanks, correctly. These rewards encouraged the students to concentrate on listening to specific information. Although this reward approach may appear to be a little like bribery, it had the effect of holding the learners' attention.

Using a reward approach, in conjunction with website materials, was a novel way of encouraging students to approach learning with more enthusiasm. In a stereotypical computer-assisted language learning setting, students browse a web page or use software to practise language skills. This is often criticised for the lack of interaction between teacher and student. By connecting website materials via a projection screen in a classroom setting, all students can participate in the task together, which provides a great opportunity for teachers at all levels to be creative and teachers are freed from worrying about which student computer is not working properly. On the other hand, teachers can present their teaching within a rich context, attracting learners' attention with advanced technology. Using such technology, in this practical way, can actually achieve the goals of a technology-enhanced learning environment.

Based on the findings in Table 6.6, the Business Administration and Textile Engineering groups were fond of activities in which they had to give answers, whereas 27% of the Information Management group felt excited by this type of activity, and 27% of them thought it was challenging. After confirming students' opinions, this reward-like task was often repeated in subsequent lessons. In contrast, a quiz was used with the Industrial Management group, because 63% of them stated that they had no specific preference for this activity. In the next English lesson, students listened to a story, read the question from the projection screen and wrote their answers on a piece of paper. Interestingly, many students stated that this was a good way of pushing themselves to practise listening skills, which they did not really want to do after class.

As for role play feedback, the Industrial Management group also had different comments, when compared to the other three groups. As can be seen in Table 6.7, it appears that over one-half of this group wanted no role play activity (58%). Consequently, they did not have any role play activity in class. Instead, I gave students a piece of paper and asked them to write down the answers to the listening exercises. After that, some students were chosen to write answers on the white board. Then, we went through each question and checked the answer on the board. Basically, the teaching approach taken for this group was often more traditional.

Except for the Industrial Management group, the other three groups provided very positive feedback (Table 6.7). Surprisingly, the two female-based groups were more willing to participate in role play in future English lessons. At that time, I was not sure whether role play would work or would decrease students' learning interest. In my research journal, I noted:

> *As I myself do not like to perform in front of people, I hesitated to ask students to participate in role play. I wondered if some of them would also be reluctant to do it. However, I was quite impressed by the fact that many students did much better than I expected, especially the female students. The concept of role play proved to be of interest to creative students at all levels. (12 December, 2004)*

My research journal reflected that my stereotypical image of our students was similar to Young's statement:

Taiwanese students are generally shy and afraid of expressing their own ideas or opinions before the public. They feel less confident particularly in speaking English publicly and are afraid of making mistakes in front of other people (Young, 2003:458).

However, the responses of the students to role play, from these three groups, impressed me and encouraged the belief that everyone has untapped potential.

6.7 Learning Outcomes and Changes for Future Practice

Reflecting on the lessons of the four groups, I recognised the power inherent in peer evaluation. In order to enhance learners' concentration on group presentation, they had to evaluate the performance of each group. Meanwhile, their evaluation was taken into account as a part of their academic evaluation. In this way, they were given a chance to take responsibility for the whole learning process. Also, I recognised that a competition game increased learners' participation in class activities. In addition, I was aware that a certain number of students were probably more used to a behaviourist mode of learning language. Consequently, I adopted different approaches for different groups of the learners. For example, a more passive learning style proved more effective for the Industrial Management group. Therefore, the activities used in the listening lessons for the students in this group were based on the question and answer approach. They listened to a story, read the questions and then answered them.

In viewing role play as a positive way to practise oral skills, I planned to try the speaking activity designed in the first lesson plan. The first website, *Barnaby Bear*, was displayed again after the third website used for four weeks. Students were explained that they had to write an itinerary of one day trip as homework. Students were given the choice of either creating a role play about a one-day trip or writing a report of an itinerary for the next lesson. The idea of an itinerary was inspired by the first website, *Barnaby Bear*, whose character took a one day trip to Paris. Moreover, students were given a slightly different peer evaluation task this time. They had to write down which group they would like to join for the trip and give their reasons, after listening to either the itinerary or the role play. From the students' comments, it was evident that this teaching practice decision motivated the students to participate more fully in classroom activities and become more willing to take responsibility for their own learning.

6.8 Summarising the Three Cycles

The three websites used in a class for undergraduate students were described from Chapter four to Chapter six. Moreover, three continuous action cycles were reported, which focused on classroom instruction initiated by the multiple entry points. Each experiment inspired critical reflection and the implementation offered skilful and thoughtful ways to develop professional teaching experiences. The action research approach helped me increase my capacity to develop teaching skills via application of computer assisted language learning.

Teaching English using the Internet and the Multiple Intelligences Approach

CHAPTER **7**

RESEARCH QUESTIONS AND DATA

7.1 Introduction

In this chapter, the findings from the MI inventory (Appendix 1), the General English Proficiency Test, a questionnaire comparing the three websites (Appendix 3), follow-up interviews and my personal journal are discussed in response to each of the research questions.

The participants were freshmen from four different programmes in the university. The experiment was conducted from September 2004 to January 2005, which was the first academic semester and the total period was four months. A total of 106 final questionnaires were distributed to the four groups of students at the end of the semester; participants responding to the questionnaire numbered 99 for a response rate of 93%.

7.2 Research Question 1

How can teachers use website resources more effectively as teaching materials for learners of English in a language classroom?

In this section, the questionnaire related to learners' perspectives of the website and the interview results are presented in response to research question one. The answers are based on the discussion of

(1) learners' preferences in relation to the materials used in their English lessons and their perceptions of those materials,

(2) learners' positive perceptions of the three websites,

(3) learners' negative perceptions of the three websites,

(4) the discussions surrounding the three websites used in English teaching,

(5) learners' perceptions of using the three websites for self-study,

(6) reflections on website choices, and

(7) technology issues.

7.2.1 Learners' Preferences in Relation to the Materials for English Lessons and their Perceptions of those Materials

The students involved were majoring in four different areas. It was interesting to note that their opinions about their preferred learning materials were quite similar. The majority of students from each of these groups said that they preferred using website materials to the use of the coursebook for working on listening comprehension in English. Students' comments about the different kinds of English materials used for listening practice are discussed below.

According to Table 7.1, it is evident that the students viewed the website materials favourably overall. In total, 86% of them from all majors represented wanted to use website materials for future English listening and speaking courses. In particular, over 90% of the learners from the three groups (if we exclude the Textile Engineering group) would like to use websites as learning. This high percentage, in favour of using websites as teaching materials, indicates that the three websites, used in the 'listening comprehension' course during this semester elicited a positive reaction in these three groups. Nevertheless, there was a significant difference between the Textile Engineering group and the other three groups. Only 73% of the Textile Engineering preferred website materials. The data are presented in Table 7.1.

Table 7.1 Student Preferences in relation to Materials Used in English Class

Department * Q8 the preferred material in English class Crosstabulation

			Q8 the preferred material in English class			
			website	coursebook	both	Total
Department	Business	Count	20	2		22
		% within Department	90.9%	9.1%		100.0%
		% within Q8 the preferred material in English class	23.3%	18.2%		22.2%
	Information	Count	24	2		26
		% within Department	92.3%	7.7%		100.0%
		% within Q8 the preferred material in English class	27.9%	18.2%		26.3%
	Industrial	Count	23	1	1	25
		% within Department	92.0%	4.0%	4.0%	100.0%
		% within Q8 the preferred material in English class	26.7%	9.1%	50.0%	25.3%
	Textile	Count	19	6	1	26
		% within Department	73.1%	23.1%	3.8%	100.0%
		% within Q8 the preferred material in English class	22.1%	54.5%	50.0%	26.3%
Total		Count	86	11	2	99
		% within Department	86.9%	11.1%	2.0%	100.0%
		% within Q8 the preferred material in English class	100.0%	100.0%	100.0%	100.0%

11 students said that they would prefer to use a coursebook as the main teaching material for future English lessons and, of these, 6 were from the Textile Engineering group. It indicates that some students in this group were uncomfortable with website content as

the main learning material. These students' comments about the coursebook as favourite learning material will be discussed later.

To inquire further about students' preferences in learning English from website materials, students were asked some supplementary questions about their perceptions of those materials. For example, '*Why do you like using website contents as learning materials?*' or '*What is the benefit of using website materials in the English class?*' Students' comments were clustered in two main areas: the use of computer to provide '*easy accessibility*' to materials; the *authentic* nature of the website resources. These two categories are discussed below.

Easy Accessibility

I can access the Internet anytime and then choose a website to practise my listening or reading.

(Information Management)

I usually spend a lot of time on the computer. Now, I am pleased to find out about these websites. Then, I can choose some of these articles to practise listening and reading skills.

(Information Management)

I can practise my listening through the audio clips on the Internet, with no need for a 'tape-player'.

(Industrial Management)

The above comments indicate that, for some learners in this study, computer technology is regarded as an easy access tool for searching for resources. Many of them have mentioned that they easily accessed the Internet. As for comments about using those websites to practise listening, it means that some learners in this study have used those resources to practise language skills. In other words, the computer has become a daily life tool for this portion of learners. Further, they are used to accessing the Internet regularly. It indicates that the ease of computer use and its multiple functions as a search tool, storage system and multimedia display system may be helpful to encourage certain learners to participate in listening practice. Moreover, students' comments indicated that some of them did not like websites for listening but rather for other aspects of learning such as reading and writing.

Authenticity

Website materials provide more information, which allows me to enhance my knowledge within a wider context. Compared to the coursebook, the website information is more interesting. Moreover, I can listen to English usage in the real world and learn how to speak the language properly.

(Business Administration)

The coursebook is simple, and the activities' design in each unit, too similar. I found the coursebook boring. In contrast, there is a lot of information on the Internet, which I find authentic and interesting.

(Business Administration)

These three websites have more authenticity than the coursebook. Because of the differences in website content, the teaching approaches were also different.

(Information Management)

The materials on the website are more practical and closer to daily life topics.

(Industrial Management)

The website content is interesting and the range is wider than that found in the coursebooks.

(Textile Engineering)

It is helpful to hear the pronunciation on these websites, as I am trying to improve my English.

(Textile Engineering)

These comments show that the students regarded the websites as helpful in supporting listening, and as interesting and varied resources. Some linked their interest to this variety. One suggested that the variety in the materials encouraged variety in teaching methods and it may be that together these helped to sustain interest. Some linked the interest of the materials to authenticity. Though no one had specifically explained what authenticity meant to them, they linked it to 'real world' material or 'daily life' issues.

At some levels of learning, the website material seemed to bridge the learners' linguistic training and survival needs. Learners had the chance to think about real life problems via website materials and make use of the language. When learners find out that learning materials are close to their personal experiences, on-going learning is expected outside the classroom. The qualitative data revealed that students responded positively to learning with website materials as the authentic experiences. This echoed Felix's (1999:89) opinion of the web as an authentic environment which can bring '*the real world of the target language into the students' experience with the creation of meaningful tasks tailored to their interests and capabilities at different levels of interactivity'*

In addition, authentic website materials also benefit teachers who attempt to design a variety of class activities to motivate learning. My own experience highlighted that potential website resources were able to provide truly interesting topics that raised the attention of the students. It may be important to remember here the role of the teacher. The combination of varied resources and the variety of teaching styles encouraged and generated student interest.

It is important to remember that, 11 students mentioned that they preferred a coursebook as teaching support during the lesson and most of them were from the Textile Engineering group. As shown in Krajka's study, 27% of the learners indicated that coursebooks present grammar in a *'realistic way'*, while 60.26% of them felt it was presented in a *'partly realistic way'* (Krajka, 2001:154). In this study, students' comments about the positive aspects of the coursebook seemed to fall into two categories: *'practicality'* and *'theme-orientated structures'*.

Practicality

I can review the lesson in the coursebook after class, without having to go to the computer classroom.

(Business Administration)

The website materials are indeed interesting and practical, but a computer is required to access Internet information. So, I prefer a coursebook to website resources. The coursebook is easy to carry around.

(Industrial Management)

Theme-orientated Structure

*I wanted to use the coursebook, to know exactly what I had to learn this
semester. Besides, each lesson in the coursebook has certain language
tasks, which guide me in what to focus on and what to remember*

(Business Administration)

*The coursebook provides a concrete point for me to review after class.
At least, I can know whether I understand how much I learn from the
exercises in the book.*

(Industrial Management)

*I am used to using a coursebook, which is the traditional method of
instruction. I have an idea of what I am going to learn next time.*

(Textile Engineering)

These students' views illustrated two advantages of a
coursebook, which cannot be replaced by website materials. A
coursebook is easy to carry and simple to use. It is designed with
organised and sequential structures, which suit learners who like
step-by-step instructions but can also be 'flicked through' to suit
learners who like to have a whole course overview. Interestingly,
there are contrasting views to the definition of 'convenience' being
expressed in the sample. Learners who preferred using website
materials often used a computer at home or school. They had no
trouble using a computer to complete a task or practise a certain
language skill. Consequently, these learners regarded learning
through the Internet as an easy and convenient approach. In contrast,
other learners stated that using a coursebook is convenient, because
it is easy to carry. A coursebook is, of course, much smaller and

lighter than a computer. On the other hand, the coursebook is able to help these students who felt a coursebook as an easy tool and were willing to review what they have learned after class.

In fact, most of the Textile Engineering students paid attention to the exercises in the coursebook based on my observation. Compared to the other three groups, they often finished the exercises provided in the coursebook which was not assigned as homework. Furthermore, they showed more enthusiasm for participating in class activity when we used one unit of the coursebook. For example, they preferred to use one unit of the coursebook as role play script. This suggests that different preferences and perhaps different previous learning circumstances may affect learners' choices and these need to be kept in mind when alternative approaches to teaching and learning are designed.

Moreover, those students who found the coursebook preferable is not surprising given that, in Krajka's study (2001). In that research, 27% of the learners were positive about the coursebook although in this case the key issue was that they felt that the coursebook presented grammar in a realistic way. In other words, a proportion of students in this study were used to using a coursebook to get an overall idea of the contents and learn the linguistic concepts.

In summary, according to Table 7.1 and follow-up interview data, participants' comments on teaching materials may be summarised by stating that website materials were interesting, practical and authentic. Moreover, the variety of the contents was attractive to some learners. However, 11 students preferred a coursebook as the main teaching materials. The reason was that the coursebook was easy to handle and could provide them with a concrete idea of what they were about to learn during the semester. The above excerpts reflect that a coursebook may still be a necessary teaching tool, providing learners with clear instructions and linguistic structure. Website materials may be better used as supplementary materials, to complement the coursebook.

7.2.2 Positive Perceptions of the Three Websites

Table 7.2 shows students' preferences amongst the three websites used in the semester, (*Barnaby Bear*, *Adult Learning Activities,* and *Randall's ESL Cyber Listening Lab*). Students' perceptions of the positive aspects of these website materials are then presented.

Table 7.2 Students' Favourite Websites for Learning English

Department * Q1.a the favourite website for learning English Crosstabulation

			Barnaby Bear	Adult Learning Activities	Randall's ESLCyber Listening Lab	Total
			Q1.a the favourite website for learning English			
Department	Business	Count	9	7	6	22
		% within Department	40.9%	31.8%	27.3%	100.0%
		% of Total	9.1%	7.1%	6.1%	22.2%
	Information	Count	11	12	3	26
		% within Department	42.3%	46.2%	11.5%	100.0%
		% of Total	11.1%	12.1%	3.0%	26.3%
	Industrial	Count	9	15	1	25
		% within Department	36.0%	60.0%	4.0%	100.0%
		% of Total	9.1%	15.2%	1.0%	25.3%
	Textile	Count	5	18	3	26
		% within Department	19.2%	69.2%	11.5%	100.0%
		% of Total	5.1%	18.2%	3.0%	26.3%
Total		Count	34	52	13	99
		% within Department	34.3%	52.5%	13.1%	100.0%
		% of Total	34.3%	52.5%	13.1%	100.0%

Of all the respondents, 52.5% identified the *Adult Learning Activities* website as their favourite for learning English (question 1). However, when the preferences of students from different departments are analysed, some differences emerge. Interestingly, over 40% of the Business Administration students indicated that the *Barnaby Bear* website was their favourite. Similarly, 42% of the Information Management students made the same choice. They regarded this website as cute and attractive. However, only 19% of

the Textile Engineering students chose the *Barnaby Bear* website as their favourite. Over 69% of them identified the *Adult Learning Activities* website as their favourite for learning English. A similar proportion of the Industrial Management students had the same preference. These differences may reflect the nature of the learning cultures of the different departments. For example, the kinds of students they attract, the expectations that these students bring to their studies, the way the departments address learning and the value they attach to different kinds of learning.

One possibly relevant feature was noted in Chapter 3 (Table 3.4): the Departments of Business Administration and Information Management were female-based groups while Industrial Management and Textile Engineering were male-dominated. Therefore, responses related to favourite websites may reflect gender issues, which could perhaps be taken into account when choosing future websites.

In Table 7.3, 55.6% of the students agreed that the *Adult Learning Activities* website offered the best English listening activities (question 2). Over 80% of Textile Engineering students strongly agreed that this website provided the best listening exercises.

Table 7.3 The Best Websites for Listening Activities, Chosen by Learners

Department * Q2.a the website with the best listening activities Crosstabulation

| | | | Q2.a the website with the best listening activities | | | |
			Barnaby Bear	Adult Learning Activities	Randall's ESL Cyber Listening Lab	Total
Department	Business	Count	3	7	12	22
		% within Department	13.6%	31.8%	54.5%	100%
		% of Total	3.0%	7.1%	12.1%	22.2%
	Information	Count	7	11	8	26
		% within Department	26.9%	42.3%	30.8%	100%
		% of Total	7.1%	11.1%	8.1%	26.3%
	Industrial	Count	1	16	8	25
		% within Department	4.0%	64.0%	32.0%	100%
		% of Total	1.0%	16.2%	8.1%	25.3%
	Textile	Count	2	21	3	26
		% within Department	7.7%	80.8%	11.5%	100%
		% of Total	2.0%	21.2%	3.0%	26.3%
Total		Count	13	55	31	99
		% within Department	13.1%	55.6%	31.3%	100%
		% of Total	13.1%	55.6%	31.3%	100%

The participants' comments concerning the *Adult Learning Activities* website could be categorised as follows. Comments about the variety of the content were categorised as '*rich source*'. Comments about the levels of the content were coded as '*levels of difficulty*'. Description about the audio design was labelled as '*clear speech*'. Each category is discussed below.

Rich Source

There are a variety of articles, each of which is quite short, making for easier reading.

(Information Management)

The website is diverse and contains many activities, such as vocabulary pronunciation, vocabulary quizzes, writing exercises, and videos. I can select any topic I choose.

(Industrial Management)

This website is very nice; there are many topics. Hence, I can choose a topic I am interested in, such as 'work', 'money', or 'nature'. I learned a lot from these choices.

(Textile Engineering)

Participants' comments indicated that the issues of variety and real world materials that were raised in relation to students' preferences between different kinds of learning resources appeared again as factors relating to students' preferences amongst the three websites that they experienced. These comments echo at least part of Yumuk's point of view (2002: 143) that learners can select the up-to-date materials and decide '*how best to make use of them for their learning*'. This principle is in accordance with the belief that one of the strengths of multimodal presentations is that they allow learners to become involved in learning using their own preferred approach.

Levels of Difficulty

The stories on the Adult Learning Activities website, are not too difficult to understand. This website is better designed than the other two.

(Information Management)

I liked this website, because I understood the context. Also, the listening tasks were not too difficult.

(Industrial Management)

These comments should be considered alongside the comments below that the *Barnaby Bear* website was regarded by some as 'too childish'. What students seem to prefer is something appropriately matched to their ability.

Clear Speech

On the Adult Learning Activities website, the voice of the speaker is even and clear; I was able to understand what was said.

(Industrial Management)

Each sentence was pronounced very clearly. I was able to learn how to pronounce English sentences..

(Textile Engineering)

Given the focus of the semester on listening, the prominence of this aspect of the sites was easily explicable. In addition to the *Adult Learning Activities* website, 31% of the respondents thought that the listening quizzes on the *Randall's ESL Cyber Listening Lab* website were helpful in enhancing their listening skills. It is interesting to speculate that this could have been related to the value of formative feedback in supporting effective learning (Black & Wiliam, 1998). The reasons the students gave for liking the listening comprehension quizzes seemed mainly to relate to '*exam preparation*'. Students' comments about the contents of the whole website and their comments about the exercises were identified as '*the design of the quizzes*'.

Exam Preparation

This was the first resource where I could practise my listening skills. Now, I can use the school computers to access this website. Also, I can choose a topic, listen to the audio clips, and test my listening comprehension by doing a quiz.

(Business Administration)

There are lots of quizzes on this website. I was able to use it to prepare a listening section for the General English Proficiency Test (GEPT).

(Information Management)

In reality, the listening exercises in the *Randall's ESL Cyber Listening Lab* website contain multiple-choice questions which are similar to the General English Proficiency Test (GEPT) and Test of English as a Foreign Language (TOEFL). As mentioned in Chapter 3, Section 3.8.2, some universities require students to pass a certain level of the General English Proficiency Test and the university highlighted in this study is one of these. Accordingly, the above comments illustrate that the *Randall's ESL Cyber Listening Lab* website helped them prepare for the nationwide tests.

An interesting difference arose between the Business

Administration students and the other three groups. As shown in Table 7.3, the other three groups rated *the Adult Learning Activities* website as the best for practising English listening skills. Nevertheless, a high proportion of the Business Administration students regarded the *Randall's ESL Cyber Listening Lab* website as the best when preparing for exams (54%). Their responses may indicate that this group was more worried about the test. However, their efforts in preparing for the General English Proficiency Test are discussed in the section related to Research Question 4. In addition to the purpose of test preparation, participants' opinions about how the design of the quizzes on this website supported their learning were stated below.

The Design of the Quizzes

The topics were presented in a dialogic style and were easy to understand.

(Information Management)

This website contains numerous topics that are useful for listening practice.

(Industrial Management)

I started at the beginning level and progressed to the intermediate level. When I could answer some of the intermediate topics, I felt a sense of achievement.

(Information Management)

The contents are divided into three levels. I knew which level I was at.

(Industrial Management)

The above statements indicated that students looked favourably upon the part of this website which contained the listening quizzes related to each story. Learners could work at their own level and test their comprehension. This is in accordance with an important volume of CALL research about the potential of technology for second language learners, enabling learners to choose content based on their own linguistic level to practise language skills (Hoven, 1999; Warschauer & Healey, 1998). Moreover, the most important reason why learners preferred the *Randall's ESL Cyber Listening Lab* website was that they could get immediate feedback on the correctness of their response. The value of immediate feedback is to facilitate the learning process involved because feedback is given quickly (Nagata, 1996). In other words, the immediate feedback offered by the website can be regarded as a formative assessment practice and can therefore be expected to raise standards (Black & Wiliam, 1998).

However, one issue about learners' efforts in self-study was necessarily borne in mind as discussed in Chapter 6 (Section 6.5.5). Table 6.8 showed that many of the learners did not actually use the website nor make any effort to engage in self study after class. They only accessed the website and practised listening when they had to take a test based on this website. In other words, quizzes in the *Randall's ESL Cyber Listening Lab* website can be considered as a source for preparing a standardised test on the listening section.

7.2.3 Learners' Negative Perceptions of the Three Websites

In addition to finding which websites were useful for learning English, the respondents were asked which website they felt was *'least useful'* for learning English. Participants' opinions are displayed in Table 7.4.

Table 7.4 Learners' Comments about the Websites they Disliked

Department * Q4 Which website did you dislike most? Crosstabulation

			Q4 Which website did you dislike most?				
			Barnaby Bear	Adult Learning Activities	Randall's ESLCyber Listening Lab	none	Total
Department	Business	Count	5	1	3	13	22
		% within Department	22.7%	4.5%	13.6%	59.1%	100%
		% of Total	5.1%	1.0%	3.0%	13.1%	22.2%
	Information	Count		2	7	17	26
		% within Department		7.7%	26.9%	65.4%	100%
		% of Total		2.0%	7.1%	17.2%	26.3%
	Industrial	Count	10	3	5	7	25
		% within Department	40.0%	12.0%	20.0%	28.0%	100%
		% of Total	10.1%	3.0%	5.1%	7.1%	25.3%
	Textile	Count	12	2	4	8	26
		% within Department	46.2%	7.7%	15.4%	30.8%	100%
		% of Total	12.1%	2.0%	4.0%	8.1%	26.3%
Total		Count	27	8	19	45	99
		% within Department	27.3%	8.1%	19.2%	45.5%	100%
		% of Total	27.3%	8.1%	19.2%	45.5%	100%

Over 27% of participants thought that *Barnaby Bear* website was not that useful. Again, the Industrial Management and Textile Engineering groups took a more negative view of this site than students in other two groups. These two groups strongly disliked the *Barnaby Bear* website; 40% of the respondents from the Department of Industrial Management and 46% from the Department of Textile Engineering. These students were mostly male and stated that the *Barnaby Bear* website appeared to be too childish. Their responses indicated that the teaching websites may need to take gender issues and perhaps broader issues of learning cultures in sites into account. Also, the following comments, provided by the four groups, may be used as a guide for choosing websites. The comments about technical problems have been categorised into '*problematic design*'. The remaining comment is categorised as '*insufficiency*'. Examples are stated below.

Problematic Design

The pronunciation was too electronic.
Barnaby Bear looked funny.

(Industrial Management)

The animation design is poor.
The voice is unnatural and the content too childish.

(Textile Engineering)

Insufficiency

Only two stories are provided by this website. It does not offer sufficient materials for learning.

(Industrial Management)

The respondents' opinions shown above indicate that the voice device was problematic in the *Barnaby's Story* website. It was too electronic-sounding and did not express a natural tone. Moreover, insufficient material was offered for adequate learning, although it was considered visually very attractive, by the female-based group. The issue of insufficiency may be the reverse of '*variety*' which was a feature of resources that were well regarded by the students.

As for the *Randall's ESL Cyber Listening Lab* website, 19% of the students said they did not like it. These students thought that the listening activities were very difficult, even when the exercises were presented in '*easy*' mode. Consequently, participants' feeling about the website content and their opinions about the speed of the audio clips were categorised as '*difficulty*'.

Difficulty

There are many stories and a great deal of listening exercises provided by the *Randall's ESL Cyber Listening Lab* website*. I felt that they were too complicated and difficult to choose from.*

(Industrial Management)

The speed of the speech was too fast to pick up. I was quite frustrated when this website was used for listening practice.

(Industrial Management)

The listening exercises on this website are too difficult. I could not answer any of the questions without first reading the text.

(Information Management)

This suggests again that good matching of difficulty to student competence is a critical issue in website selection or design.

Interestingly, the original questionnaire only provided an opportunity for participants to tick the website they thought not useful. At this item, there was no extra blank for learners to tick '*no*'. However, 45.5% of the respondents did not choose to name a website instead wrote '*none*' in response to this item. Therefore, they took trouble to make it clear that there was no website they actually disliked. Moreover, Table 7.5 shows that 42% of the respondents thought all of the websites were useful, to some extent (question 5). Hence, they replied '*none*' to the question: Which website did you think was least useful for your English learning.

Table 7.5 Learners' Comments about the Least Useful Website

Department * Q5 the least useful website for English learning Crosstabulation

			Barnaby Bear	Adult Learning Activities	Randall's ESLCyber Listening Lab	none	Total
Department	Business	Count	9	4	2	7	22
		% within Department	40.9%	18.2%	9.1%	31.8%	100.0%
		% of Total	9.1%	4.0%	2.0%	7.1%	22.2%
	Information	Count	7	2	2	15	26
		% within Department	26.9%	7.7%	7.7%	57.7%	100.0%
		% of Total	7.1%	2.0%	2.0%	15.2%	26.3%
	Industrial	Count	8	2	2	13	25
		% within Department	32.0%	8.0%	8.0%	52.0%	100.0%
		% of Total	8.1%	2.0%	2.0%	13.1%	25.3%
	Textile	Count	13	3	4	6	26
		% within Department	50.0%	11.5%	15.4%	23.1%	100.0%
		% of Total	13.1%	3.0%	4.0%	6.1%	26.3%
Total		Count	37	11	10	41	99
		% within Department	37.4%	11.1%	10.1%	41.4%	100.0%
		% of Total	37.4%	11.1%	10.1%	41.4%	100.0%

Over 40% of the students from the Business Administration group thought that the *Barnaby Bear* website was the least useful. The other three groups, shared their view that the *Barnaby Bear* was the least useful website. The following comments may explain why the *Barnaby Bear* website attracted these learners at first, but was later regarded as the least useful website for learning. Participants' comments about the content of the *Barnaby Bear* website were categorised as '*insufficient practice*', while comments on the design of the website were coded as '*visual distraction*'. Examples from the data are displayed as follows.

Insufficient Practice

Compared to the other two websites, the contents of the Barnaby Bear website were rather sparse. Moreover, although the cartoon feature was cute, it had nothing to do with learning English.

(Business Administration)

Visual Distraction

The pictures on the Barnaby Bear website were fairly pretty, but this distracted my attention from listening to the audio clips and reading the text. Therefore, I did not get the full meaning of the story.

(Business Administration)

The above comment indicates that the *Barnaby Bear* website indeed attracted a certain number of learners especially the Business Administration group (41% in Table 7.2). However, after the learners had reviewed the *Adult Learning Activities* and *Randall's ESL Cyber Listening Lab* websites, the usefulness of the *Barnaby*

Bear website was reduced, when compared to the two other websites, which contained valuable and exploitable content such as topics or exercise for long-term learning.

From the statistical results shown in Table 7.5, it was not surprising that 50% of the respondents from the Department of Textile Engineering chose the *Barnaby Bear* website as the *'least useful'* for learning English. Their reasons were similar to the categories of question 4: problematic design and insufficiency.

Problematic Design

The Barnaby Bear website appeared to be more for kids. I am not a child and   I did not like the cute Bear. It felt foolish to me.

(Industrial Management)

Insufficiency

The Barnaby Bear website did not provide further exercises or any stories for more self-study. I do not think I would access this website outside the class.

(Textile Engineering)

A comparison of students' opinions of the three websites is given as follows. Table 7.6 lists the ranking for each website.

Table 7.6 A Comparison of the Three Websites

The favourite website for learning English	1. Adult Learning Activities	(53%)
	2. Barnaby Bear	(34%)
	3. Randall's ESL Cyber Listening Lab	(13%)
The most useful website for listening activities	1. Adult Learning Activities	(56%)
	2. Randall's ESL Cyber Listening Lab	(31%)
	3. Barnaby Bear	(13%)
The least favourite website for learning English	1. None	(46%)
	2. Barnaby Bear	(27%)
	3. Randall's ESL Cyber Listening Lab	(19%)
	4. Adult Learning Activities	(8%)
The least useful website for learning English	1. None	(42%)
	2. Barnaby Bear	(37%)
	3. Adult Learning Activities	(11%)
	4. Randall's ESL Cyber Listening Lab	(10%)

7.2.4 A Discussion of the Three Websites Used in this Study

The uses and benefits of integrating website materials into English lessons were determined in the three action cycles and reconfirmed from the data of Table 7.1. This illustrated the learners' preferred learning materials to be used in English class. Of all respondents, 86% showed a preference for the use of website materials in future English lessons. The finding should be able to encourage teachers to use website resources as supplementary teaching materials in English lessons. Meanwhile, learners' opinion about the use of a coursebook is necessarily taken into account. Having established the benefits of websites in motivating and supporting learners, the discussion that follows is based on the strengths and limitations of the three websites, with suggestions for possible improvements, both in choice of website and in relevant teaching practices.

Website 1: Barnaby Bear

The *Barnaby Bear* website, whose topic is sightseeing, can be used, with its rich images, to initiate an English lesson. The contents are so vivid that they may engage learners within an English context. However, a number of challenges, related to the use of the *Barnaby Bear* website for adult students, remain.

First of all, this website is designed for learners aged 4 to 11, with its cartoon style and voices. In this study, the data indicates that a website with cute cartoon characters may attract some female learners but may lose male learners' interest (Table 7.2). Based on the findings in Table 7.6, 34% of the respondents stated that this was their favourite website for learning English, but 27% of the respondents disagreed. Further, 37% of the respondents thought that it was the least useful website for learning English (Table 7.6). Many learners regarded it as their least favourite website, because it seemed too childish. Some of them stated that they liked it at first, because it was a new learning experience, but after viewing the content of the other websites, which tended to be more academic, they are quickly tired of the *Barnaby Bear* website.

Second, the design of the website resembles a '*living book*' focusing on the text with rich sound effects and high quality pictures. No exercises are offered to reinforce specifically targeted language skills. Teachers would required to design a handout for communicative activities or specific language practice, if they adopted this website for an English lesson.

The application of a website like *Barnaby Bear* may be useful as a lead-in feature to discuss related topics. The colourful website with child-like stories may be used as a 'starter' to be integrated into part of an English lesson to entice reluctant learners with short attention spans. The stories on this website may inspire learners to develop their language practice using such things as role play or an imaginary itinerary. However, teachers need to be aware that this kind of children's website may not attract male learners, based on the findings of this study (Table 7.4).

Website 2: Adult Learning Activities

The *Adult Learning Activities* website, after considerable research, actually garnered comments stating that the World Wide Web can provide authentic learning materials, and a variety of real-life learning (Teeler & Gray, 2000). According to participants' feedback and my own reflection, several positive aspects are stated to use this website for teaching and learning.

First, this website provides authentic topics which are from real news that happened in the world. The issues involved are fairly varied, such as nature, housing, money, school, family, working, science and technology and these enabled the site to achieve the most obvious pedagogical advantage of websites as the source of authentic material. Second, it contains a more comprehensive list of hyperlinks. Teachers can focus on a target language skill for learners to practise by clicking on a certain icon. Third, this website utilises task-based learning activities for learners which facilitates more student-centred approaches.

Website 3: Randall's ESL Cyber Listening Lab

The pros and cons of using the *Randall's ESL Cyber Listening Lab* website are discussed in this section. This website provides rich and authentic topics, incorporating either audio or video clips as well as a number of listening exercises. Each of the categories is stated below.

First, it has a variety of listening materials. The topics include campus issues, daily life context, travel information and so on. Second, it comprises three distinct sections: general listening, academic purpose listening, and long conversations with RealVideo, with each section being divided into three levels of difficulty. Third, the greatest advantage of this website seems to be the number of quizzes provided, based on authentic topics. Students became accustomed to the context of English-speaking countries and also mastered listening skills.

From my own teaching practice and reflections on Cycle 3, it appears that this website may be used more effectively in a class environment, than for self-study. The reason for this is that the authentic context provides teachers with rich ideas for classroom activities. The classroom activity design can help bring learners together and keep their attention. As learners recognise the advantage of this website, they are more likely to be motivated to access it after class. This is a key of autonomous learning, under computer assisted language learning. As Yumuk (2002: 143) mentions, '*learners can understand that learning is not a process in which teachers have complete control, but one in which they themselves can actively make decisions*'.

7.2.5 Learner Perceptions of Using these Three Websites for Self Study

Website materials can be regarded as a rich source for learners to use as self study materials and to direct their own learning. Table 7.7 presents learners' perceptions of the three websites in regards to self-study.

Table 7.7 Learners' Perceptions of the Three Websites Regarding Self Study

Department * Q3 the website for self-study Crosstabulation

			Barnaby Bear	Adult Learning Activities	Randall's ESLCyber Listening Lab	none	Total
Department	Business	Count	2	8	11	1	22
		% within Department	9.1%	36.4%	50.0%	4.5%	100%
		% within Q3 the website for self-study	16.7%	17.0%	33.3%	14.3%	22.2%
	Information	Count	4	10	10	2	26
		% within Department	15.4%	38.5%	38.5%	7.7%	100%
		% within Q3 the website for self-study	33.3%	21.3%	30.3%	28.6%	26.3%
	Industrial	Count	3	16	6		25
		% within Department	12.0%	64.0%	24.0%		100%
		% within Q3 the website for self-study	25.0%	34.0%	18.2%		25.3%
	Textile	Count	3	13	6	4	26
		% within Department	11.5%	50.0%	23.1%	15.4%	100%
		% within Q3 the website for self-study	25.0%	27.7%	18.2%	57.1%	26.3%
Total		Count	12	47	33	7	99
		% within Department	12.1%	47.5%	33.3%	7.1%	100%
		% within Q3 the website for self-study	100.0%	100.0%	100.0%	100%	100%

Of the learners surveyed, 47% favoured accessing the *Adult Learning Activities* website for self-study in most cases. In fact, 50% of the Business Administration group preferred the *Randall's ESL Cyber Listening Lab* website for self study. Learners' reasons for choosing the different websites for self-study were judged to fall into four broad categories. Comments about the rich content were categorised as '*authentic topics*'; the comments about the audio setting were regarded as '*clear speech*'; comments about the level of the content were identified as '*medium complexity*'; learners opinions about the design of practice mode were coded as '*variety of exercises*'.

Authentic Topics

There are many topics in various fields, so I can choose the one I am interested in. I thought the issues mentioned in this website bring language learning to life.

(Information Management - Randall's ESL Cyber Listening Lab)
The topics are in a real-life context. The topics were very useful to me and made learning fun.

(Industrial Management – Adult Learning Activities)

Clear Speech

The speech was delivered clearly, which helped me to practise my listening skills.

(Industrial Management - Adult Learning Activities)

Medium Complexity

The level was appropriate for me, so the content was not too difficult.
(Information Management - Adult Learning Activities)
The content was neither difficult nor too easy, which provided a certain level of challenge. I did not spend too much time simply listening to a story.
(Textile Engineering - Adult Learning Activities)
The content was not too complicated. I was able to feel a sense of achievement by finishing a short article each time.
(Industrial Management - Randall's ESL Cyber Listening Lab)

Variety of Exercises

Many types of exercises were offered, including a multiple-choice mode, matching exercises and spelling. I enjoyed practising the vocabulary as I was able to immediately find out whether my spelling was right or wrong.
(Business Administration - Randall's ESL Cyber Listening Lab)
The reason I chose this website was because it provided a vocabulary list with pronunciation for each word. There was also vocabulary dictation, which helped me to memorise each word.
(Industrial Management - Adult Learning Activities)

The above comments showed that many of the same issues about website material seem to occur, such as variety, match to ability, exercises and immediate feedback. The potential website advantages mentioned above have been indicated in several CALL research projects (Gitsaki & Taylor, 1999; Hémard, 2004; Warschauer & Healey, 1998). The participants' points of view revealed that these features of website had different levels of meaning for them. If learners thought that exercises were important to them, the *Randall's ESL Cyber Listening Lab* website with a lot of quizzes might be their favourite. Alternatively, if learners liked to know more about the information of daily life, they may have chosen the *Adult Learning Activities* website.

Of all respondents, seven learners answered '*none*' to this question. They stated that they were not interested in English at all. Consequently, they had no intention of making an effort after class. Interestingly, four of these students were all from the Textile Engineering group. When learners were asked if they would use the *Randall's ESL Cyber Listening Lab* website for self study, the Textile Engineering group had the highest proportion of negative responses, too. This observation reminds me that learners may be interested in class activities, but it does not mean that they would like to engage in self-study.

7.2.6 Reflection on Website Choices

Much research claims the Internet '*as a vast treasure trove of authentic material*' (Krajka, 1999:154) which can '*enhance learners' desire and curiosity to learn more*' (Yumuk, 2002). In reality, finding an appropriate website, which included different language skills, was not easy. In choosing websites, I was guided by notions of accessibility, readability, multimodal presentations and course requirement. First, I checked to see if the website was still accessible. Then, the quality of the audio or video clips was tested. After that, I went through each link to explore how the website could be used in class. However, some websites or web links were no longer operational and it took a long time to select an alternative and appropriate website for a class setting. Moreover, students had to have the opportunity to use the website to practise their listening skill after class. In my research journal, I have described my frustration at my attempts to access an appropriate website for classroom use.

I tried to search for another appropriate website for the next stage. However, some websites are well designed but have no audio clips for listening exercises. Sometimes, the website had sound effects, but did not work properly. More often, the website included too many advertisements. It was frustrating to discover just how few appropriate websites there were for English listening teaching. The other problem was that some of the authentic materials were too difficult for learners.

(Research Journal, 5 October, 2004)

Actually, there are a number of websites with links related to English learning skills, such as the links on the *Internet TESL Journal* website:

(URL: http://www.aitech.ac.jp/~iteslj/). Many resource links are provided by this website, including articles, research papers, lesson plans, classroom handouts, as well as teaching ideas for those teaching and learning English as a Foreign Language. However, some of these links were no longer available or useful in the required context. The creation of a local bulletin board for use by English teachers is expected to explore in future; this would give up-to-date details of websites that provide materials suitable for instruction of English at various levels.

7.2.7 Technology Issues

Technology is still a main issue when discussing the application of website resources. Although Internet facilities are upgraded annually, school facilities are often not capable of keeping pace with the progress. For example, some websites were accessible on my home desktop. However, the school computer was unable to access several hyperlinks on that website. Furthermore, a technical problem was met when accessing the website, *Randall's ESL Cyber Listening Lab* in the class. The audio clips did not work at the beginning of the lesson until the sound files had been updated.

In addition, there were many unpredictable situations which arose during the semester. We had a computer, a CD player, a DVD player and a video player in the lab. When I presented the *Barnaby Bear* website, the audio clips did not work properly on several web pages. Sometimes students only listen to one page and then had to read the next page without audio. Alternatively, the first web page did not link smoothly to the next web page. When I clicked on 'Back', it did not work, either. When encountering this kind of problem, I merely cancelled the use of the computer. Instead, I turned on the video player machine and played one unit of the coursebook. In brief, the lesson of the coursebook was only used to replace the website material for the duration of that class if the network system did not work properly.

My teaching experience with technology enforces the need for teachers to always have a back-up plan when using technological tools in the classroom. When the technology fails to work, teachers must have an alternative ready. This indicates that a coursebook is still required, although most students preferred website materials to a coursebook in this study. As mentioned in section 7.1, 11% of the students who had no access to a computer experienced difficulty practising language skills after class (Table 7.1). They thought that the coursebook was more useful for revision and more clearly structured. Inspired by the comments from these students, my personal view is that website materials may be better used in conjunction with a unit from the coursebook.

7.2.8 Summary Answers for Research Question 1

The major results, deriving from the analysis of the data, are stated below:

1.Classroom use

The data showed that the majority of students would prefer website based learning material for their English lessons in the future. The main reason was that the presentation of multimodality on the website could cater for students with different needs. Moreover, written text helped learners understand how the spoken language is used in real life situation. The audio and video design of the website also introduced variety into the teaching approach.

In my study, I presented website material with the aid of a data projector and a projection screen, to draw the attention of the whole class. This method can help teachers overcome '*both accessibility and availability limitation*' in the computer classroom which is considered a great problem by language teachers (Linder, 2004: 11). They are not confined to a situation in which learners practise language skills with the computer only. The various activities derived from website materials can provide more learning interaction.

Researchers have criticised coursebooks, stating that they are '*not good enough to be the only sources of materials and teaching aids*' (Krajka, 1999:158). The positive student reactions (Table 7.1) to the use of the website in my study, suggest that website can be used alongside a coursebook to overcome this limitation. Teachers can choose websites related to the topics mentioned in their coursebook. In other words, a coursebook can provide learners with clear language structures and exercises related to the theme in each unit, while multimedia websites can supplement the coursebook by providing further examples of language in use and further practice.

2.Self-study

The variety of resources on the Internet can also provide a number of after-class tasks. Teachers can design a series of homework activities which exploit the website content. Such tasks ensure that learners visit a given website and practise a particular section regularly in order to improve a target language skill. Take the *Randall's ESL Cyber Listening Lab* website as an example -- half of the Business Administration group preferred to practise listening with this website for self study (Table 7.7). In addition, the Internet is a useful tool to reflect learners' learning as it allows them to post their work and comments on a certain website such as a class homepage. Moreover, the findings of this research project indicate that teachers need to remember that learners can engage in learning with a website after class when they are told to do so. Beforehand, the websites have to be evaluated as interesting or authentic. The *Adult Learning Activities* website is the example. Learners were assigned the task of choosing their preferred topic and responding to the question provided on that topic. In this way, learners were able to use this website to become involved in language learning.

3.Technology issues

Teachers need to have a back-up lesson plan prepared in case a technology problem is encountered. A crucial point is that teachers must still be aware of the problems and challenges limiting the integration of website materials into English classes. For example, the audio clips may not work properly on some web pages or the network system does not process.

7.3 Research Question 2

Which sort of web page design appears more likely to engage learners? Audio? Visual? Text?

This question concerns the ways in which students experienced the website resources as listening materials. In fact, this research question was explored continuously during all three action cycles. In the exploration of Cycle 1, the pictures in the *Barnaby Bear* website were identified as the first feature to draw learners' attention and help them understand the story. Cycle 2 showed that learners got the most benefit from reading the text of the *Adult Learning Activities* website. This indicated that text was an element that helped learning. Then, in Cycle 3, it was determined that listening with video clips in the *Randall's ESL Cyber Listening Lab* website was learners' preferred learning mode. The discussions are based on

(1) learners' preferred learning approaches,

(2) the website elements that draw learners' attention, and

(3) learners' perceptions of important website features.

7.3.1 Learners' Preferred Learning Approaches

As mentioned previously, a website usually involves multimodal communication which provides learners with the opportunity to follow their learning preference. This section explores what kind of modality appealed to learners and if the websites motivate their willingness to learn English. Learners' preferred learning approaches are outlined in Table 7.8.

Table 7.8 Students' Preferred Learning Approaches

Department * Q9.b the preferred learning approach Crosstabulation

			Q9.b the preferred learning approach				
			do not like learning English	reading the text	listening to the audio clips	watching the video	Total
Department	Business	Count		4	9	9	22
		% within Department		18.2%	40.9%	40.9%	100.0%
		% within Q9.b the preferred learning approach		14.8%	33.3%	29.0%	22.2%
	Information	Count	7	6	9	4	26
		% within Department	26.9%	23.1%	34.6%	15.4%	100.0%
		% within Q9.b the preferred learning approach	50.0%	22.2%	33.3%	12.9%	26.3%
	Industrial	Count	4	6	5	10	25
		% within Department	16.0%	24.0%	20.0%	40.0%	100.0%
		% within Q9.b the preferred learning approach	28.6%	22.2%	18.5%	32.3%	25.3%
	Textile	Count	3	11	4	8	26
		% within Department	11.5%	42.3%	15.4%	30.8%	100.0%
		% within Q9.b the preferred learning approach	21.4%	40.7%	14.8%	25.8%	26.3%
Total		Count	14	27	27	31	99
		% within Department	14.1%	27.3%	27.3%	31.3%	100.0%
		% within Q9.b the preferred learning approach	100.0%	100.0%	100.0%	100.0%	100.0%

The proportions of each preferred learning approach were similar. 31% of the students defined 'watching the video' via the website was the best way to understand website information. Further, 27% of them felt 'listening to the audio clips' was helpful and 27% also chose 'reading the text' as a useful approach to understanding the context.

Interestingly, each group had different opinions about the preferred learning approach to the website materials. The Business Administration group liked to listen to the audio clips or watch the video. The Information Management group preferred listening to the audio clips. Watching the video was chosen by the Industrial Management group as the favourite approach. Finally, the Textile Engineering group preferred reading the text. To collect further evidence relevant to this question, follow-up interviews were carried out to explore why learners preferred a specific learning approach to others. Therefore, three different preferred learning approaches, from the respondents' perspectives, are given below: reading the text, listening to the audio clips and watching the video.

Reading the Text

I was able to understand the content better by reading the text. If I did not know a word, I could look it up in the dictionary.

(Information Management)

I am used to reading the text to understand the context of a story. I am not familiar with how the other methods can help me learn English.

(Industrial Management)

I preferred reading the stories and I wanted to improve my reading skills.

(Industrial Management)

My listening was not good enough, so I had to read the text to understand the contents.

(Industrial Management)

I think reading the text is helpful in practising my writing. Through reading the articles, I can learn how to use syntax.

(Textile Engineering)

The above comments indicate that students seemed to have different personal goals for their learning in the context of a semester on listening. Some of them tried to read the text in order to understand the story, while others attempted to improve their writing skill by reading more articles.

Listening to the Audio Clips

Listening ability is important so I wanted to practise developing a main idea or getting information for the comprehensive questions.

(Business Administration)

Among the four skills, my listening was the worst. Therefore, I wanted to improve my listening skills using the website sound files.

(Business Administration)

The characters spoke with different intonations, which helped me understand the context. I was unable to make any sense of the text until I heard it read aloud.

(Information Management)

I want to improve my ability to understand what people are saying.

(Information Management)

I could practise listening after class by clicking on any story from the website with sound files. In previous English courses, I could not practise my listening skills after class. This is because none of the coursebooks included tapes or CDs. I still found it troublesome to play the CD player even if the coursebook was equipped with a CD. Now, I only need to click on a single item, which is convenient.

(Textile Engineering)

According to the above comments, these students seem to be completely focused on listening practice even when they found the improvement is not that easy.

Watching the Video

Influenced by the Barnaby Bear website, I felt that authentic visual presentations helped comprehension.

(Business Administration)

Watching the video was more enjoyable. There were many intrinsically interesting features. For example, when we watched the slides in the Randall's ESL Cyber Listening Lab website, I found the characters in the story 'Our Family Roots' to be very funny. They looked like ancient people

(Industrial Management)

Watching the video helped my comprehension. I could figure out what was happening from the sequential plot.

(Industrial Management)

These students saw video as a way of using one kind of input (pictures) to help with the other (audio). Their view is echoed in Kang's study that *'visual enhancement in instruction can help students become more involved in the teaching-learning process'* (Kang, 2004:65).

Participants' opinion about different ways of receiving information in terms of sensory modes, such as auditory, text, or visual, suggests that multiple input approaches should be considered by the teacher. Learners' views also indicate that multimedia were valuable because *'support for second language learners involves learning styles and individual needs*' (Kamil, 2002:18). In addition, 14% of the students said that they did not like to learn English at all. Because of this, they were not concerned with the types of learning. Half students of this category were Information Management majors.

It is interesting that some students recognised the importance of listening and persisted with listening tasks even when they were difficult, but that students also showed a range of other goals for their work in these sessions. This may explain why different students valued different aspects of the websites though why these differences were related to the students' major course affiliation is not clear.

7.3.2 Website Elements that Draw Learners' Attention

As the data below shows, for students who had different favourite websites, different website features first drew their attention. According to Table 7.9, over 52% of the students stated that their favourite website for learning was the *Adult Learning Activities* website.

Table 7.9 The Most Popular Website Elements to Draw Learners' Attention

Q1.b the website element drew attention first * Q1.a the favourite website for learning English Crosstabulation

			Barnaby Bear	Adult Learning Activities	Randall's ESLCyber Listening Lab	Total
Q1.b the website element drew attention first	visual	Count	29	13	3	45
		% within Q1.b the website element drew attention first	64.4%	28.9%	6.7%	100.0%
		% within Q1.a the favourite website for learning English	85.3%	25.0%	23.1%	45.5%
	text	Count	2	17	3	22
		% within Q1.b the website element drew attention first	9.1%	77.3%	13.6%	100.0%
		% within Q1.a the favourite website for learning English	5.9%	32.7%	23.1%	22.2%
	audio	Count	3	22	5	30
		% within Q1.b the website element drew attention first	10.0%	73.3%	16.7%	100.0%
		% within Q1.a the favourite website for learning English	8.8%	42.3%	38.5%	30.3%
	others	Count			2	2
		% within Q1.b the website element drew attention first			100.0%	100.0%
		% within Q1.a the favourite website for learning English			15.4%	2.0%
Total		Count	34	52	13	99
		% within Q1.b the website element drew attention first	34.3%	52.5%	13.1%	100.0%
		% within Q1.a the favourite website for learning English	100.0%	100.0%	100.0%	100.0%

The above table indicates that the website chosen by the learners was related to the website features that first attracted their attention. To put it more simply, if visual things caught learners' attention first, their favourite website was the *Barnaby Bear* website. Similarly, if an audio feature caught learners' attention first, their favourite website was *Adult Learning Activities*.

The reasons for choosing the *Adult Learning Activities* website as the favourite were based on three factors: visual presentation, simple text, and smooth operation of the audio files.

Visual Presentation

The slide show in the story, 'My family roots' seemed slow. Although each slide was shown in black and white, I could still link the character with the description.

(Industrial Management)

Simple Text

The structure of each sentence was not too difficult for me to comprehend.
(Business Administration)

Smooth Operation

The rhythm was just right. I could understand what the speaker was saying without reading the text.

(Information Management)

In addition, 34% of the respondents who chose the *Barnaby Bear* website as their favourite said that the '*visual*' was the first element to draw their attention. This was also evident from the first cycle. Among these respondents, 29% indicated that the *Barnaby Bear* website was their favourite website because of the visual elements, such as animation and pictures. This finding is echoed in the data in Table 4.4, which showed that pictures drew 58% of the student attention first. Both the findings in Table 7.9 and Table 4.4 indicate that visual elements play an important role in determining whether a website will attract learners or not. Nevertheless, an interesting issued raised here is that the audio feature appears to determine if learners felt benefit in a long term. The most popular elements of the websites previewed, to help learning, are presented in Table 7.10.

Table 7.10 The Most Helpful Element for Learning

Q2.b the website element helped learning * Q2.a the website with the best listening activities
Crosstabulation

			Q2.a the website with the best listening activities			
			Barnaby Bear	Adult Learning Activities	Randall's ESL Cyber Listening Lab	Total
Q2.b the website element helped learning	visual	Count	11	10	3	24
		% within Q2.b the website element helped learning	45.8%	41.7%	12.5%	100.0%
		% within Q2.a the website with the best listening activities	84.6%	18.2%	9.7%	24.2%
	text	Count		20	8	28
		% within Q2.b the website element helped learning		71.4%	28.6%	100.0%
		% within Q2.a the website with the best listening activities		36.4%	25.8%	28.3%
	audio	Count	1	24	20	45
		% within Q2.b the website element helped learning	2.2%	53.3%	44.4%	100.0%
		% within Q2.a the website with the best listening activities	7.7%	43.6%	64.5%	45.5%
	others	Count	1	1		2
		% within Q2.b the website element helped learning	50.0%	50.0%		100.0%
		% within Q2.a the website with the best listening activities	7.7%	1.8%		2.0%
Total		Count	13	55	31	99
		% within Q2.b the website element helped learning	13.1%	55.6%	31.3%	100.0%
		% within Q2.a the website with the best listening activities	100.0%	100.0%	100.0%	100.0%

Over 55% of the respondents thought that the *Adult Learning Activities* website helped learning most. The data showed that text and audio functions on this website helped learning most. Among these respondents, 24% agreed that '*audio*' was the most helpful element in learning English overall. Moreover, 20% of the participants thought that text in the *Adult Learning Activities* website was helpful. In comparison with the other two websites, the *Barnaby Bear* one was viewed as being of the greatest help as a visual (45%). It indicates how the pictures in the *Barnaby Bear* website worked to create a meaningful scenario for learners.

As mentioned in Table 4.8, participants regarded reading the text as being the greatest benefit they received from the *Adult Learning Activities* website. In Table 7.10, the finding does not agree with the data in Table 4.8 but indicates that learners received the most benefit from audio features. The reasons for these different findings were clarified in the follow-up interviews.

When the Adult Learning Activities website was used for listening materials, I found it difficult to understand the content. Hence, I had to read the text provided by the website. After that, the Randall's ESL cyber listening lab website was often used for listening practice. The content of the Randall's ESL cyber listening lab website was more difficult than the Adult Learning Activities website. After a series of listening practice, I did not have to depend on the 'text' too much. I believe the quality of audio clips can affect learning.

(Business Administration)

The above comments indicate that learners tended to understand the content by reading the text at the beginning of learning. They did not need to depend heavily on '*text*' after they have received a series of listening training. Learners quickly became used to listening to a passage without the aid of the text. Moreover, 45% of the learners agreed that audio features helped them most for learning. It indicated that this proportion of learners may use audio functions of the websites to practise their listening. In addition, the above comments imply that the link between text and audio on the *Adult Learning Activities* was better than on the other two websites.

7.3.3 Learners' Perceptions of Important Website Features

This section considers learners' opinions of the website elements influencing their English learning. Table 7.11 gives an overview of students' perceptions of important website features for English learning.

Table 7.11 Students' Perceptions of Important Website Features for English Learning

Report

Department		Q6.a visual	Q6.b text	Q6.c audio
Business	Mean	3.64	4.50	4.27
	N	22	22	22
	Std. Deviation	.902	.673	.827
Information	Mean	3.65	3.04	4.19
	N	26	26	26
	Std. Deviation	.892	1.076	.849
Industrial	Mean	3.16	4.16	4.52
	N	25	25	25
	Std. Deviation	1.434	.746	.770
Textile	Mean	3.42	4.00	4.38
	N	26	26	26
	Std. Deviation	1.206	.980	.898
Total	Mean	3.46	3.90	4.34
	N	99	99	99
	Std. Deviation	1.137	1.035	.835

The mean value of '*audio*' ranged around 4.3.4 points, which indicated that the majority of the respondents thought '*audio*' was the most important feature for English learning. Apart from the Business Administration group, the others thought that the quality of the audio clips could most affect their learning to listening activities. A possible reason for '*audio*' being rated the highest is that the course was essentially a listening one. Although the other three skills, reading, speaking, and writing were sometimes involved in the lesson, the main teaching still focused on listening practice throughout the whole semester. Consequently, students regarded audio as an important feature of website design for their English learning. Table 7.11 also indicates that '*text*' and '*visual*' elements were important to learners, being measured at 3.46 points and 3.90 points, respectively.

7.3.4 Summary Answers for Research Question 2

Major points arising from the analysis of the data are as follows:

1.Learners' preferred learning approaches
Basically, the proportions of the three preferred learning approaches were similar in size: reading the text, listening to the audio clips and watching the video. However, the total numbers of learners who preferred to watch the video was higher than for the other two approaches. It implies that many learners are more visually oriented as is stated in LeLoup and Ponterio's (1996) study. Website materials presented in a variety of modalities maintain students' interest and in this way help to reinforce a target language skill (LeLoup & Ponterio, 1996). At the beginning of the listening stage, some learners needed to read the text to understand the meaning of a listening task. According to the multimodality theory (Kress, 2003), this supported the view that text makes a semiotic contribution towards facilitating listening. After a period of listening-training, learners were able to make some progress in comprehension, without reading the text, thus showing that multimodality in website design can function as a form of scaffolding.

2.Attractive website elements

Basically, the first attractive feature to draw learners' attention was visual. The colour combination of the three websites was that of a dark text on a lighter background which produced better readability. Apart from *Randall's ESL Cyber Listening Lab* website, the directory tools of the other two websites were navigated by picture icons. All the directories on *Randall's ESL Cyber Listening Lab* website were textually written. The impact of this kind of design affected two types of learners: holist and serialist (Pask, 1976). Some students stated that they had difficulty in selecting a specific exercise from the website which had at least 100 items. Such learners may build up their knowledge sequentially. In contrast, learners stated that the three categories of easy, medium and difficult were helpful for them to select their own entry level. Once started on the topic in this way, these learners explored the material based on their preferred subject. It implies that those learners preferred topic-based learning.

3.Learners' perceptions of important website features

Many learners were attracted by a website with strong visuals which indicates that visual aids are helpful. However, the main elements engaging learning did not depend on visual presentation only, but also on the needs of learners. In the listening lesson, learners tended to pay attention to the listening exercises provided by the websites. Accordingly, the design of audio functions could affect learners' choice about a helpful website for practising a target language skill. In addition, a certain number of learners stated that a combination of text and audio helps learning most (Table 7.10). This observation should be taken into account in the issues of web design.

7.4 Research Question 3

How can teachers implement the theory of multiple intelligences in a web-assisted language learning setting?

Research question number three explores a practical form of multiple intelligences, the entry point approach, used in web-assisted language teaching. Explicitly, in order to examine the entry point approach as an element of teaching instruction, the research was conducted via action research. In this way, the teacher as researcher could recognise the strengths and limitations of this method of implementing MI ideas in a practical teaching situation. Accordingly, the answers for this question are based on discussion of

(1) how the entry point approach was incorporated into teaching,

(2) the students' perspectives on entry point activities, and

(3) the strength of the entry point approach when used in English teaching.

The section below addresses these issues. Further reflections on the entry point approach used in this study are discussed in Section 7.5.5.

7.4.1 The Entry Point Approach in Language Teaching

According to Kallenbach and Viens:

Providing a greater variety of entry points of ways to engage in a topic or skill area is perhaps the most common MI-informed practice. (Kallenbach & Viens, 2002:66).

Their explanations of the entry point approach offer a reminder to teachers that they should keep learner differences in mind and therefore use a variety of activities to engage students in learning. Accordingly, this study has attempted to apply a series of entry point activities for learners with multiple strengths, in order to enhance English learning. To understand the impact of this multiple entry point approach, it is useful to know something about the MI profiles of the participants. Their profiles were therefore studied in a survey that was based on Armstrong's '*An MI Inventory for Adults*' shown in Appendix 1 (Armstrong, 2000). Table 7.12 displays the students' preferred intelligences of the students in each of the four groups.

Table 7.12 MI Profiles for the Four Groups

Departments Intelligences	Business Administration	Information Management	Industrial Management	Textile Engineering	Total Numbers
Linguistic	1	0	0	1	2
Logical	3	4	6	9	22
Spatial	1	0	0	6	9
Bodily	7	7	6	5	25
Musical	6	3	5	2	15
Interpersonal	3	5	3	2	13
Intrapersonal	4	3	5	2	13
Nature	0	5	0	2	5
Total	25	27	25	27	104

In this study, participants' strengths did not reside in linguistic areas. In the Textile Engineering group, the most common strength is logical intelligence; for the other three groups, it is the bodily-kinesthetic.

The inventory was not used to design teaching to match each learner's personal style. Instead, the inventory results were used to reinforce the idea that building an adaptable learning environment was more important, so as to present the material in a range of ways for students to learn as deeply as possible. In Chapter 2, it was mentioned that this range was achieved by using aesthetic, narrative, logical, and experiential multiple entry points. These were the entry points consistently discussed by Gardner. Moreover, the aesthetic and narrative entry points complied with the demand of the input theory. The survey makes it clear that the logical and experiential entry points appealed directly to individual strengths in the four groups. Accordingly, the following discussion focuses on these four entry points.

First, the entry point used at the beginning of each lesson was usually related to aesthetic and narrative activities. With the rich information available from the websites and the aid of the projection screen, a visual presentation was expected to engage the learners' attention and increase their understanding. In fact, each web page was equipped with a visual presentation and a narration which provided a multimodal presentation. Students were able to comprehend the materials either through the visual presentation or through the narration or through interaction between them. With the enriched input, learners were expected to make more sense of the learning materials. Data collected in this study suggested that visual materials and narration did indeed engage the learners' attention. Most learners felt that they were able to become involved with the learning materials, as visual or audio modes made them seem more real.

Apart from the visual and audio presentations, the next entry points were often related to logical and experiential approaches, where learners could employ logical reasoning as a way into understanding and '*build something, manipulate materials, or carry out experiments*' (Gardner, 1999:171). In other words, an experiential entry point activity aims to offer students a variety of meaningful experiences to engage thinking and learning. For example, participating in role play or clicking on an answer in front of the whole class often required learners to get outside of their own characters. In fact, they also need to get out of their own way of thinking and take on other people's characteristics. In addition, posting a writing task on the Internet required learners to logically construct a paragraph and post it on an assigned discussion board. This task involved a problem-based learning approach which is regarded as an experiential process of learning. As Gardner (1999:33) states, intelligence is '*the ability to solve problems or to create products that are valued within one or more cultural settings*'. In other words, the writing and posting of tasks provided learners with the chance to use their strengths to solve problems (writing difficulties or technological problems) and develop new products (pieces of completed work posted on the discussion board).

7.4.2 Students' Perspectives on Entry Point Activities

In this study, the jargon of entry point approaches based on Gardner's definition was not explained to the students in order not to confuse them. Students were expected to concentrate on the language practice through displayed visual presentations, providing answers in front of the class, completing a variety of tasks including listening, speaking, writing, and posting activities. Students were offered a broad range of opportunities to practise listening skills through activities during the period of the whole semester. At the end of the semester, participating students provided valuable feedback about classroom activities which underpinned the entry point approaches. The data came from the last question in the questionnaire, *The Learner Perspective of Website Evaluation* (Appendix 3) -- 'Do *you have any comments you would like to make about the listening and speaking class*?' Student comments about how these entry point approaches through classroom activities helped their English learning fell into three categories: aesthetic entry point approaches, narrative entry point approaches, and logical/experiential entry point approaches.

Aesthetic entry point approach

The aim of aesthetic entry point is to use '*sensory features*' that may capture learners' attention (Gardner, 1991:246). The aesthetic entry point in the context of this research meant the way that the websites displayed content. The website material consisted of pictures, slide, or video and was presented from a data projector which was expected to attract learners' attention. According to Table 4.4 (Chapter 4, section 4.5.3), pictures drew on learners' first impression. When asked in what form they preferred the listening exercise, over half of the participants chose listening with video clips based on Table 6.4 (Chapter 6, section 6.5.1).

I knew the Barnaby Bear story was about travelling in Paris, because I saw the famous museum and Eiffel Tower.
(Business Administration)

As Gardner notes, an entry point perspective has the advantage of *'arousing their interest'* (Gardner, 1999:172). A website like *Barnaby Bear* based on pictures can attract certain learners' attention. As for the other website, *Randall's ESL Cyber Listening Lab*, students' comments confirm that the aesthetic entry point served as a means of introducing the students to the issues.

I thought that listening using the Internet was a very positive method of instruction. Firstly, I could see the topic which I was going to listen to. When you played the story of 'My Family Roots', I did not understand the content. However, I saw the family photos and got some idea even though those pictures were black and white.
(Business Administration)

Narrative entry point approach

The narrative entry point approach *'addresses students who enjoy learning about topics through stories'* (Gardner, 1999:169). The websites used in the study all provide audio function for learners to listen to a story (*Barnaby Bear*, *Randall's ESL Cyber Listening*

Lab) or a news topic (*Adult Learning Activities*). This approach attempted to help learners to understand the topic from the vivid voice and clear speech and from the context created by the story itself. Consequently, learners' comments about audio presentation were under this category.

The learning materials were much more practical than those found in other of English courses. I can improve my listening through audio clips. Moreover, I knew how to use the Internet to practise listening.

(Business Administration)

This class provided some websites with listening exercises. I listened to the audio clips and did the quizzes at the same time after class. In this way, I could test how much I understood the listening topic.

(Industrial Management)

These comments indicate that the spoken words in a narrative context tend to benefit students' listening practice and enhance their understanding and, subsequently, their knowledge base. Moreover, the story itself was helpful for enhancing learners' interests in English learning. Take the *Barnaby Bear* story as an example. The last question in the *Barnaby Bear* story handout (Appendix 4) asked learners '*Would you like to go to Paris?*' Over 90% of the students replied 'Yes', because they would like to visit the places mentioned by Barnaby Bear. Learners' response indicates that the content of the story affects learners' attention to learning material to some extent. If the story is not attractive enough, learners will not have a positive reaction to the context of the story. It can thus be assumed that the story itself has a certain affect on English learning.

Logical and Experiential entry point approaches

The logical and experiential entry points engage students learning by expressing their ideas in response to the article (writing), making their own work using elements from this article (role play), presenting themselves (posting). Therefore, activities included role play, writing task, posting work on the Internet and guessing games.

The lessons were very exciting, because there were a variety of activities for us. Sometimes, we needed to run to the front and provided an answer.
(Business Administration)

Compared with other English courses, this listening course was more fun. Although it was a listening course, we often had to speak English in front of the class. At the beginning, I was very nervous. However, role play helped push me to listen how the sentences were said. Then, I can know how to speak a long sentence. I agree that the more I have the chance to practise, the better I can speak.
(Business Administration)

Practising speaking through role play was very interesting. I had never had this kind of experience before. I wanted to have more chances to speak in front of the whole class.
(Information Management)

The teaching styles within the listening course varied. We not only practised listening skills, but also had to speak English in front of the whole class. We either listened to the audio clips provided by the websites or participated in some activities. It was very different from other English lessons, where I usually just sat passively and listened to the lecture.
(Textile Engineering)

The listening materials content was quite authentic and close to daily life topics. I was more motivated when we practised listening exercises.
(Industrial Management)

The above statements indicated that many of the same issues emphasised in the MI-inspired instruction seem to come up. Some learners' reactions to role play can be consistent with the view that *'MI-inspired instruction increases the authenticity of learning experiences'* in Kallenbach and Viens' study (2002:71). Kallenbach and Viens identify student reports about enjoying MI-inspired learning activities as *'authentic or meaningful'* (2002:71). When asking about learners' feedback about writing task, posting task, and role play, many of them kept mentioning 'exciting', 'fun' or 'challenge' in the questionnaires. For some learners in this study, they regarded being able to speak English in front of the class as evidence of the learning outcome in the context of a listening class. When they were able to present a piece of work, learning becomes meaningful.

Apart from an increase in their interest, responsiveness, and motivation from the entry point activities, some learners from the Business Administration group mentioned that they would be willing to spend time on learning English. This indicates how website resources with multiple entry points can contribute to help learners move towards learning autonomy. It is my belief that students will take responsibility for their own learning when they see that learning is meaningful.

Gardner (1993) defines intelligence as a way to solve a problem and develop a product. In this study, the problem students encountered was writing difficulty. However, most of them were able to post their completed work on the Internet (develop a product). Learners' comments about writing and the posting task have been discussed in Chapter 5. Their comments reveal that the entry point activities paid off, with high levels of student engagement. Since these aspects of the lesson were inspired by the entry point idea, it suggests that this model is useful.

7.4.3 The Strength of the Entry Point Approach

The idea of multiple entry points is to initiate learning experiences from a variety of perspectives. For example, learning materials displayed through a big screen can be clear to the target audiences. At the same time, the explanation made by the audio clips or teachers themselves can enhance the understanding of the text. In other words, these multiple teaching instructions try to engage students with different strengths in mastering English skills.

Compared to traditional teaching instruction, in which lessons are introduced primarily through verbal instructions, the entry point activities required students to make decisions and take responsibility for their own learning. These different entry point activities e.g., writing tasks, posting tasks, giving answers in front of the whole class, and role play were designed to provide an initial choice, based on their potential strengths. Students who are used to learning passively may not be able to look to themselves for direction, when they are given the opportunity. Over time, as students experienced diverse learning activities, they began to take more control over the content or direction of the activities.

The other advantage is that learners began to express preferences through choice-based activities. One example is given here. At stage 3, students had the choices either presenting themselves during role play or writing an itinerary report. In role play, some students may like a certain topic, but they had to negotiate with other classmates. On the other hand, the writing questions in some topics may have seemed to have been more easily answered. However, learners found that writing logically was not that easy. Some of them changed the topic, while others tried to consult with other classmates or the teacher. By having a choice, students could share in the decision-making and, in this way, create a more learner-centred classroom. This is a crucial principle in Computer Assisted Language Learning mentioned in a wide range of research (Bickel & Truscello, 1996).

A way to add value to entry point activities, and make learning more meaningful, is to increase the authenticity of the learning experience. Accordingly, the authenticity of learning materials becomes a major input. Computer technology and website resources are able to provide rich information for language learners. Also, the audio and visual functions are potentially very attractive in language teaching. In order to utilise these technological tools, teachers must act as the bridge from these rich resources to both classroom activities and learning objectives. In this way, classroom instruction using website material can increase students' motivation to learn. As showed in Table 4.5, most learners agreed that website features helped understanding. However, few students thought the teacher's explanation was the most helpful for comprehension. This observation figures prominently in the findings of studies related to MI-inspired activities.

In addition, interaction is often questioned in computer assisted language learning research (Garrett, 1998). Garrett points out that control and interaction are still questioned and examined. In entry point activities, the computer becomes a means to provide a powerful platform for students to engage in the learning process. From the process of participation, organisation and completion, more interaction can occur between the teacher and the students or with the students themselves. The interaction can be in the form of an instruction from the teacher in reaction to questions on the task or students' peer evaluation of their own performance.

7.4.4 Summary Responses to Research Question 3

The theory of multiple intelligences is employed in this study by utilising one aspect, the approach of multiple entry points. The application of multiple entry points inspires educators to maximise the Internet's capabilities to engage many different kinds of learners. The entry point is used as an implementation of MI theory, because the approach accommodates a range of intelligences. Websites with a variety of information and different functions, i.e. audio or video modes, offer a number of entry point activities. The two initiatives (web-based learning and entry-point inspired instruction) neatly support one another. The audio or visual features of websites are available for teachers to make information explicit. Teachers can present the target language through a projection screen to learners who favour visual presentations. Alternatively, learners who are used to practise English through a listening approach can benefit from the audio clips.

The follow-up entry point activities provide many hands-on opportunities for learners to enhance their learning goals. Learners are afforded greater choices from website topics with which to demonstrate their understanding. Through their favourite topics, they work out the best way to learn for themselves. Students become active participants in learning. Hands-on activities are based on forms of interactive problem-solving and help students master language skills, such as listening or speaking. Teaching approaches informed by MI theory transfer a large portion of the responsibility for learning from the teacher to the learner. The idea behind entry point activities is not to prescribe the steps of an exercise to find a right approach, but to allow students the freedom to experiment and construct their own ideas.

7.5 Research Question 4

How do website materials and MI-inspired instructions shape language learning?

This question is explored based on

(1) student performance in the General English Proficiency Tests,

(2) students' perceptions of their performances in the GEPT,

(3) discussions of student performance in the GEPT,

(4) reflections on the GEPT test, used in the study, and

(5) reflections on the entry point approach, used in the study.

The display of the exploration is served by simple descriptive statistics at first. More complex inferential techniques are then used such as ANOVA (analysis of variance) and t-test. The use of statistics aims to reveal similarities and differences between groups of respondents, and relationships between variables, that may be difficult to identify in other ways. This will be displayed in section 7.5.1. After that, qualitative techniques are used such as in-depth interviews and observation to acquire information about participants' performance and comments. In other words, qualitative data is expected to serve and extend the findings from the quantitative strand (Postlethwaite & Maull, 2003). The qualitative data will be presented in section 7.5.2.

7.5.1 Student Performance in the General English Proficiency Tests

According to the statistical results of all the questionnaires reported, the majority of students preferred using website material for practising English listening skills instead of coursebooks. In addition to this, qualitative data collected in interviews were also positive about the three websites used for listening practise. However, many universities in Taiwan require that students take the General English Proficiency Test before graduation, as a means of assessing their general English proficiency. The GEPT pre-test and post-test were therefore used in this study to explore whether the framework of the entry point approach and the website resources could help learners prepare for nation-wide language tests.

There are four sections in the General English Proficiency Tests: listening, reading, writing and speaking. Only data related to the listening section was used for assessing students' listening competence in this study, because the course is called '*listening comprehension*'. The four groups of students took pre- and post-General English Proficiency Tests at both the beginning and the end of the semester, to measure whether any improvement had taken place. The total score of the General English Proficiency Test was set as 100 points. The pre-test and post-test descriptive statistics for the four groups in the General English Proficiency Test are displayed in Table 7.13.

Table 7.13 Descriptive Statistics for the Pre-test and Post-test GEPT

Descriptives

		N	Mean	Std. Deviation	Std. Error	Minimum	Maximum
PRE	business administration	25	60.48	13.507	2.701	34	82
	information management	27	56.67	9.182	1.767	40	76
	industrial management	26	54.23	18.412	3.611	20	96
	textile engineering	27	50.59	10.493	2.019	28	68
	Total	105	55.41	13.607	1.328	20	96
POST	business administration	25	59.68	12.632	2.526	36	80
	information management	27	60.15	10.582	2.036	40	82
	industrial management	26	64.46	12.176	2.388	46	98
	textile engineering	27	54.22	8.967	1.726	34	68
	Total	105	59.58	11.578	1.130	34	98

Table 7.14 displays the average scores of the pre- and post-tests for the four groups. It shows that the Business Administration group achieved a level of 60.48 points in the pre-test of the General English Proficiency Test (GEPT) with the other three groups being some distance behind. The Information Management and Industrial Management groups gained scores slightly below those of the Business Administration group (56.67 points and 54.23 points, respectively); whereas the scores of the Textile Engineering students were quite a lot lower than the Business Administration group (50.59 vs. 60.48).

The highest score achieved in the pre-test was 96 from the Industrial Management group, while the lowest score was 20, also from this group. In the score distribution at the pre-test, the standard deviation of the Industrial Management group was 18.412. This indicated that the range was much higher in this group than in the other three groups.

As for the post-tests, the Industrial Management group gained the highest average score (64.46 points) which surpassed the Business Administration group by about 4.78 points (64.46-60.96). The lowest average score was 54.22, from the Textile Engineering group. The Information Management group had similar scores to the Business Administration group (60.96 v.s.59.68). The highest score again came from the Industrial Management group (98 points), whereas the lowest score was from the Textile Engineering group (34 points). For the post-test, the standard deviation of the Business Administration group was 12.632 which indicated that the highest range of the score distribution fell within this group. The average score of the pre-test in the four groups was 55.41 points, while for the post-test, it was 59.58 points. In total, the additional points for the improved scores of the four groups amounted to 4.17. It was important to establish whether or not the groups were similar at the start of the study, because differences at this point could affect any changes brought about by my intervention. Therefore, a one-way ANOVA was used to check further, as shown in Table 7.14.

Table 7.14 ANOVA Results for the Pre-test Scores in the GEPT

ANOVA

PRE

	Sum of Squares	df	Mean Square	F	Sig.
Between Groups	1348.017	3	449.339	2.534	.061
Within Groups	17907.37	101	177.301		
Total	19255.39	104			

The results of the ANOVA test revealed that the pre-test scores were not significantly different among the groups. So, although some differences did exist among the groups, these differences could be attributed to chance.

A comparison was then made between the pre-test and the post-test scores using a paired samples t-test across the sample as a whole. Descriptive statistics and t-test results are displayed in Table 7.15 and Table 7.16.

Table 7.15 Descriptive Statistics

Paired Samples Statistics

		Mean	N	Std. Deviation	Std. Error Mean
Pair 1	PRE	55.41	105	13.607	1.328
	POST	59.58	105	11.578	1.130

Table 7.16 Results of T-test in Pre/Post-test Differences

Paired Samples Test

		Paired Differences							
					95% Confidence Interval of the Difference				Sig.
		Mean	Std. Deviation	Std. Error Mean	Lower	Upper	t	df	(2-tailed)
Pair 1	PRE - POST	-4.17	10.796	1.054	-6.26	-2.08	-3.959	104	.000

The analysis showed that there was a significant difference (t=-3.959, df=104, p<0.001), indicating that the post-test score was higher than the pre-test, the means differing by 4.17 points. A t-test run between the scores of the pre-test and post-test suggested that the learners had made some progress in the post-test. In order to understand if the groups had changed in different ways, as a result of my intervention, the increase in scores between the pre-test and the post-test was subjected to one way ANOVA ; the results are presented in Table 7.17.

Table 7.17 One Way ANOVA Results for the Increase in Scores

Descriptives

DIFF

	N	Mean	Std. Deviation	Std. Error	Minimum	Maximum
business administration	25	-.80	8.406	1.681	-22	14
information management	27	3.48	7.837	1.508	-10	24
industrial management	26	10.23	14.744	2.892	-14	50
textile engineering	27	3.63	8.321	1.601	-20	18
Total	105	4.17	10.796	1.054	-22	50

The output confirms the frequency of the different groups and shows the distribution of differences for each group. The last three groups had positive ranges of improvement, which was in contrast to the Business Administration group. This group's score decreased by an average of 0.8 points in the post-test results. In contrast, the Industrial Management class, which managed average scores of 54.23 in the pre-test, ended up improving the most of any group (by 10.23 points).

An additional analysis was carried out on the means of the improved scores for the four groups. An ANOVA was performed to look for differences between the four groups on the change in scores. The results are presented in Table 7.18.

Table 7.18 ANOVA Results for the Change in GEPT Scores

ANOVA

DIFF

	Sum of Squares	df	Mean Square	F	Sig.
Between Groups	1593.262	3	531.087	5.095	.003
Within Groups	10527.652	101	104.234		
Total	12120.914	104			

The overall ANOVA was significant at the .003 level (F=5.095, p<0.05). The results showed statistically significant differences among the increases in scores of the four groups in the General English Proficiency Test.

As noted in Chapter 3.7, the p<0.05 level of significance is used, not to indicate that generalisation to a population is acceptable, but simply as a consistent yardstick, for the particular group of students currently being investigated (Postlethwaite & Maull, 2003). It attempted to find how the same teaching practice worked with different groups of students and obtained different results. A post hoc test (Tukey's b) was used to further investigate these differences (Table 7.19).

Table 7.19 Homogeneous Subsets

DIFF

	MAJOR	N	Subset for alpha = .05	
			1	2
Tukey HSD [a,b]	bus admin	25	-.8000	
	info man	27	3.4815	3.4815
	textile eng	27	3.6296	3.6296
	indust man	26		10.2308
	Sig.		.400	.085

Means for groups in homogeneous subsets are displayed.

a. Uses Harmonic Mean Sample Size = 26.223.

b. The group sizes are unequal. The harmonic mean of the group sizes is used. Type I error levels are not guaranteed.

The results of the post hoc test showed that the main difference was between the Business Administration and the Industrial Management groups. The Business Administration group went down by 0.8 point, whereas the Industrial Management group improved by 10.23 points. The other two groups (Information Management and Textile Engineering) were not significantly different from one another and not significantly different from either of the other two. The relationships among the four groups are presented in Figure 7.1.

Figure 7.1 Grouping the Four Departments

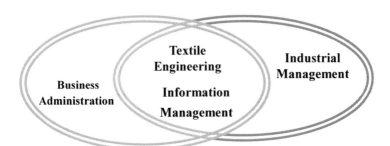

The step reviews differences between these four groups which is hard to see in other ways. The purpose of reporting this is prompt further exploration of why these differences may have come about.

As a further check, the different levels of improvement among the four groups are shown in Table 7.20. Table 7.20 displays the number of students in each of the ranges of improved and declining scores in the GEPT. It shows that the greatest number of students who improved were those in the 1 to 10 range (35). In reality, almost half (14) of these came from the Textile Engineering group. However, there were only two Business Administration students in this range. As for the remainder of the most improved scores (11 points to 20 points), student numbers were similar for the four groups. In addition, seven students improved by over 21 points, six of them being from the Industrial Management group.

Table 7.20 The Improvement Range of the GEPT Scores for the Four Groups

RANGE * MAJOR Crosstabulation

			MAJOR				
			business administration	information management	industrial management	textile engineering	Total
RANGE	-21~	Count	1			1	2
		% within MAJOR	4.0%			3.7%	1.9%
	-11--20	Count	1	2	2	1	6
		% within MAJOR	4.0%	7.4%	7.7%	3.7%	5.7%
	-1--10	Count	11	5	3	4	23
		% within MAJOR	44.0%	18.5%	11.5%	14.8%	21.9%
	0	Count	6	4	1	2	13
		% within MAJOR	24.0%	14.8%	3.8%	7.4%	12.4%
	1-10	Count	2	10	9	14	35
		% within MAJOR	8.0%	37.0%	34.6%	51.9%	33.3%
	11-20	Count	4	5	5	5	19
		% within MAJOR	16.0%	18.5%	19.2%	18.5%	18.1%
	21~	Count		1	6		7
		% within MAJOR		3.7%	23.1%		6.7%
Total		Count	25	27	26	27	105
		% within MAJOR	100.0%	100.0%	100.0%	100.0%	100%

On the other hand, of the 13 students who retained static scores, 6 were Business Administration students. In addition, 23 students in the four groups showed a slight decline of 1 and 10 points. Of these 23 students, 11 were from the Department of Business Administration, while 2 students (one of whom was from Business Administration) had far worse scores the second time around, decreasing by more than 20 points. In total, 29.5% of the four groups went down, 12.4 % remained the same, and 58.1% improved in the General English Proficiency Test.

Apart from the Business Administration group, the other three groups improved more or less. Meanwhile, Table 7.20 presents a significant contrast between the Business Administration group and the Industrial Management group. The total improved range of the Industrial Management group in the GEPT test was fairly high at 76.9% (34.6%+19.2%+23.1%), whereas 52% students from the Business Administration group went down (4%+4%+44%). The GEPT performance of the Business Administration group was perhaps the most surprising. Compared with the other three groups, the proportion of decline of the Business Administration group was significantly higher.

7.5.2 Students' Perceptions of their Performances in the GEPT

In respect of the findings from the GEPT results, follow-up interviews were carried out with the four groups, in order to deepen the understanding of participants' performances in the GEPT. The interviews were concerned about the perceptions of the participants towards the GEPT. Accordingly, during the interview, participants were asked about the level of difficulty and probable reasons for their improved or declining results. Each of these is displayed below.

(1) Level of Difficulty

Table 7.21 presents the perceptions of participants related to the listening section in the General English Proficiency Test.

Table 7.21 Learner Perceptions of Listening Tests

MAJOR * LEVEL Crosstabulation

			easy	medium	difficult	too difficult	Total
MAJOR	business administration	Count	1	9	7	8	25
		% of Total	1.0%	8.6%	6.7%	7.6%	23.8%
	information management	Count		15	9	3	27
		% of Total		14.3%	8.6%	2.9%	25.7%
	industrial management	Count		12	9	5	26
		% of Total		11.4%	8.6%	4.8%	24.8%
	textile engineering	Count		13	9	5	27
		% of Total		12.4%	8.6%	4.8%	25.7%
Total		Count	1	49	34	21	105
		% of Total	1.0%	46.7%	32.4%	20.0%	100%

As can be seen in Table 7.21, almost half of the learners rated the listening tests in the GEPT as being at a medium level (46.7%), 34% thought that the tests were difficult and 20% stated that the tests were too difficult. Among this 20%, the Business Administration group made up a greatest number (8 of the 21), indicating a higher proportion than in the other three groups. In addition, only one learner from the Business Administration group thought that listening tests were easy, which indicated that the range of students' listening competences in this group was quite wide.

(2) Reasons for Improved Results

The students' probable reasons for improved scores about the huge gap between their pre-test and post-test scores were categorised as '*better opportunity for improvement*'. Students mentioned class participation which was coded as '*class attendance*'. Moreover, description about the design of the test style was identified as '*familiarity with the test mode*'. Learners' thought about getting higher scores by chance was marked as '*good luck*'. Reflections about learner study process were regarded as '*self-study*'.

Better Opportunity for Improvement

At the pre-test, I received a very low score. Because of that, there was room for improvement. I did not think the GEPT was all that difficult.

(Information Management)

I did badly in the pre-test. Therefore, I had a great opportunity to improve in the post-test.

(Industrial Management)

Class Attendance

I only practised listening skills in the class, in which I maintained 100% attendance. I believe this to be the reason for my improved listening test scores.

(Information Management)

I did not find the GEPT to be too difficult. I thought that the class practice was very useful and indeed, this was the only time I practised listening skills.

(Industrial Management)

I found the listening tests to be very difficult. However, I think my class attendance was a key factor affecting my score. I only practised the listening exercises, more or less, in class. This was the only opportunity I had to listen to the audio clips.

(Textile Engineering)

Familiarity with the Test Mode

At the pre-test of the GEPT, I could not keep up with the speed of the audio clips. However, when it was time for the post-test, I had become used to the style of the exam. Therefore, I could manage my time better and knew what to expect.

(Industrial Management)

At the pre-test, I was not familiar with the form of the listening section in the GEPT would take. Consequently, I received a low score. During the post-test, I was aware that there would be three sections and had a better understanding of the exam style.

(Textile Engineering)

Good Luck

I thought that I was quite lucky on the test. I did not understand several of the questions; so, I simply guessed the answers, which all turned out to be correct.

(Information Management)

I was very lucky in the GEPT post-test. That is the reason I improved; I don't believe my listening competence had improved that much.

(Industrial Management)

When I could not answer a question, I chose an answer at random; luckily, those guesses turned out to be correct.

(Textile Engineering)

Self-study

I insisted on practising listening exercises every day, even if it was only for 10 minutes.

(Information Management)

I thought that the only approach to improving my listening skills was to listen to the audio clips as often as possible. So, I did my best to practise listening exercises every day.

(Textile Engineering)

(3) Probable Reasons for Declining Results

As for the possible reasons for declining results in the listening test, participants' feedback about their negative feeling to the test was categorised into '*anxiety*'. Description of a lower grade that can be 'by chance' was recognised as '*bad-luck*'. Furthermore, information about learners who were unable to concentrate on the testing was identified as '*distractions*'. In addition, learners' reflections on how they did not make any effort on review were coded as '*lack of review effort*'. The situation of students who were late for testing was coded as '*punctuality problems*'.

Anxiety

I did not understand some of the spoken words in the post-test. When I encountered such words, I kept thinking about them and fell behind with the next question.

(Industrial Management)

I worried that I had not answered the first question correctly. Then, I could not keep up with the following questions.

(Textile Engineering)

Bad Luck

I had bad luck that day. All my guesses turned out to be wrong.

(Information Management)

My listening competence was not good at all. I received a higher score in the pre-test because of beginner's luck. However, one cannot be lucky all the time; consequently, my score went down. Honestly, I hardly understood any of the questions I heard on the audio clips.

(Textile Engineering)

Distractions

I felt sleepy because I had stayed up recently to cram for other subjects. I could not concentrate on the test.

(Business Administration)

While listening to the questions, I was thinking of other things.

(Business Administration)

Lack of Review Effort

I did not review any listening exercises after class as I thought that listening practice during class was enough. Therefore, I did not try to access any website to practise my listening after class.

(Business Administration)

Honestly, I did not practise listening exercises outside of the class.

(Information Management)

Punctuality Problems

I was late and missed the first section of the listening test. Accordingly, it was difficult for me to concentrate on the remaining sections.

(Business Administration)

This feedback provided an understanding of how students felt about their performances in the GEPT. The reasons, both positive and negative, can be regarded as reflecting their learning attitudes. If they made an effort to practise the target skill, they tended to have different levels of improvement. When they did not take their learning seriously, they generally received lower scores.

In addition, an interesting factor was the '*luck*' category. Many students felt that the reasons their scores had improved or declined actually depended on luck. If the scores had improved, they believed they had experienced good luck. They had guessed correctly on the questions where they did not know the answers. If their scores went down, they also blamed that fact on not experiencing good luck in guessing the answers. This indicates that '*luck*' seems to be one important factor to some learners for improving or receiving lower scores in the General English Proficiency Test. Students' interpretation of their GEPT performance in this study is echoed with Weiner's definition of attribution theory. In Weiner' (1974) point of view, the most important factors affecting attributions for achievements are effort, task difficulty and luck. Interestingly, many of students attributed their success or failure to 'luck'.

7.5.3 Discussions of Student Performances in the GEPT

According to the student interview data as well as my own observations, this exploration focused on two sections: reasons for the lower scores of the Business Administration group and reasons for the improved scores of the Industrial Management group. The Business Administration students' feedback attempted to explain why they received lower scores for the GEPT post-test. Their problems were mainly attributed to study attitudes, such as promptness and effort. The probable reasons which resulted in the lower scores received by most students in the Business Administration group are discussed below.

The Promptness Issue

The listening course taken by the Business Administration students took place at 8:30 a.m. Some students did not manage to come to the class on time during the last month of the semester. Although they had been informed the previous week that they would be taking the GEPT post-test, some of them still did not take it seriously and did not get to class on time. Two students were even so late that they missed the first section of the listening test. Consequently, this affected their scores.

Self-study Efforts

The students' feedback showed that few students actually reviewed the lecture material or practised their listening skills. They spent little time reviewing listening exercises or accessing the website to practise their listening skills. This indicated that they viewed homework as being too easy. When students felt that the homework was not challenging enough, they could not be bothered reviewing the exercises. As for the Industrial Management group, the reasons for improvement may be that these learners had a greater opportunity to receive higher scores, and so made an effort to improve their listening skills.

Better Opportunity for Improvement

As several students from the Industrial Management group mentioned, they had very low scores in the pre-test. This was the main reason given that they were able to improve a lot in the post-test. According to Table 7.20, six learners improved by over 21 points. After a further check of their GEPT performances, it was found that three learners had dramatically improved, as shown in Table 7.22.

Table 7.22 The Range of Improvement for Industrial Management Students

Student	Pre-test	Post-test	Improved scores
1	20	60	40
2	28	78	50
3	32	62	30

These students might not have been familiar with the GEPT test mode or felt they had had '*bad-luck*' during the pre-test. These were the reasons they gave for receiving lower scores in the first test; thus, they were able to make a big improvement in the post-test.

Class Participation

As well, class participation was another important reason for improvements in the listening test. The listening lessons taken by the Industrial Management students began at 10:30 a.m. In general, few students skipped these lessons because they had another lesson prior to this. Some confessed that the listening exercises, during the class, were the only times they practised. They made no effort after class, but at least they did not skip the lesson and lose the opportunity for listening training. Meanwhile, several students also mentioned that they did practise some listening exercises on the chosen websites. In other words, learning attitudes more or less influenced the GEPT results.

7.5.4 Reflections on the GEPT Used in the Study

The setting for the English class in this study was a listening comprehension course. The main teaching materials were website resources and teaching instruction was based on the framework of multiple entry point activities. As explored in the three stages, a majority of students enjoyed the use of website resources as learning materials (86%-Table 7.1) and some of them appeared to learn with more positive attitudes through the variety of activities. However, the results of the General English Proficiency Test seemed to indicate that neither the website materials nor the teaching instruction helped some of the students prepare for the GEPT. Possible reasons for this may be due to the style of the General English Proficiency Test.

The listening section of the General English Proficiency Test was the only item applied in the study to measure student progress. The items in each part of the GEPT may be regarded as a standardized test. The test is based on multiple-choice questions and students are required to select an answer from four choices. As Diaz-Lefebvre (2004:51) asserts, '*paper-and-pencil testing is the only method used in assessing how they are smart*'. In other words, the standardized test '*provides results that can be fully understood only by a trained professional*' (Armstrong, 2000:91). If students want to gain higher scores on listening tests within a certain period, they need to participate in a listening training course, e.g., learning, so that they can achieve a good score. The results of the students' GEPT scores only illustrated that their listening competence did not improve much. However they may have been able to perform better in other ways, e.g. in speaking or writing.

The problem of standardized tests, e.g. the General English Proficiency Test is that the success of student linguistic can be predicted in school. However, Hoerr (2000:2) reminds educators that:

> *Real-world success, however, encompasses much more than skill in the linguistic and logical-mathematical arenas. Therefore, that same focus means standardized tests offer little useful predictive information about success in life.*

In this study, the positive attitudes of the Business Administration students to entry point activities and website materials tended to indicate that they enjoyed a problem-solving learning approach. However, they may not be able to master a standardised test over a short period.

7.5.5 Reflections on the Entry Point Approach Used in the Study

As mentioned before, the entry point approach '*draws on MI's conception of pluralistic intelligence by emphasizing multiple entry points (intelligences or domains) into the class material*'

(Kallenbach & Viens, 2002:58). Compared to conventional instruction, an entry point activity, using website materials, often requires time and commitment. As Gardner mentions, '*it is necessary to spend significant time on a topic*' (Gardner, 1999:176). However, it ended up with different types of achievement in this study.

The findings of the GEPT performance results showed that the Industrial Management group displayed a significant contrast to the Business Administration group. More surprisingly, their attitudes towards participation in classroom activities were less enthusiastic than those of the Business Administration group, based on the exploration of the three cycles. Their responses is summarised as below.

91% of the Business Administration students gave positive responses about the writing task. 77% of them felt that they had learned something from it. In contrast, 76% of the Industrial Management students were in favour of the writing task and yet, only 52% of them were satisfied with their written work. As for the role play activity, 88% of the Business Administration students liked it, but only 42% of the Industrial Management were favourable towards participation in it. The findings related to students' perceptions of entry point activities and the results of the General English Proficiency Test, seemed to indicate that entry point activities did not help in the preparation for the GEPT for some of the students in this study. In other words, the entry point approach tended to be less helpful in preparing for a standardised exam.

As emphasised by Gardner (1999), MI is not an educational prescription for the classroom. Teachers are the ones choosing the most appropriate teaching approaches for learners. He points out (Gardner, 1999:89):

Educators are in the best position to determine whether and to what extent MI theory should guide their practice

The critical issue illuminated by this study is that teachers must be aware of the different teaching approaches as an on-going process, since teaching involves dynamic and flexible procedures. For example, after the investigation of student perceptions of role play, the Industrial Management group was not often requested to do role play during the class. The Industrial Management group expressed that they did not like role play activities. Accordingly, the following classes included some paper-and-pencil quizzes for this group. The comments of the Industrial Management groups indicated that conventional instruction, e.g., teacher-centred lectures and standardised exams, should be integrated into a course. In this way, learners can recognise their weakness in listening skills and learn from their mistakes.

7.5.6 Summary Answers for Research Question 4

The survey and interviews illustrated that students enjoyed a variety of different activities and hoped for similar instruction in future English lessons. It indicates that the use of the entry point approach may be a promising tool for student-centred learning.

Students can make use of various website resources to develop their learning objectives. Moreover, they did make the effort to solve difficulties and produce a piece of work, which correlates with the principle of the multiple intelligences.

However, the results of the GEPT showed that the entry point approach may not help certain learners on the preparation of a standardised test. In contrast, conventional instructions were more appropriate in the class to help learners in the systematic learning of English. Based on the exploration of this study, teachers may feel dilemma when applying the entry point approach in class. However, the crucial point raised here is that teachers should be aware of teaching approach as an on-going process. Since teaching is dynamic and flexible, teachers do not need to follow all the MI theory. The use of the entry point approach in this study is hoped that teachers can maximise the advantages of website materials and computer technology.

CHAPTER

PROFESSIONAL LEARNING:

IMPLICATIONS AND CONCLUSIONS

8.1 Introduction

The results of this study have been discussed in detail in the previous chapters. In this chapter, an overview of the research, a summary of major findings, a reflection on the research approach, the implications of utilising website resources in English teaching and recommendations for further research and practice are given as follows.

8.2 Description of the Study

The purpose of this study was to investigate the effect of incorporating the theory of multiple intelligences (MI) into computer-assisted language learning in English listening classes. The teaching material was based on three websites plus a coursebook,

Atlas Video Lab Guide A. The resources were used in lesson plans that followed the entry point approaches which are one of the practical applications of multiple intelligences. The setting for this study was in a listening comprehension course in a university of science and technology in Taiwan. The participants involved in this study included first-year undergraduate students from four different departments.

The research project, which involved three websites, was undertaken in three stages. At each stage, one of the websites was used with several multiple entry point activities in order to offer the maximum possibility for motivation and enjoyment in learning. At the end of each stage, students' performance of language skills and comments on the website material were collected and used to inform reflection in order to improve teaching for the next stage. Reflection is a necessary part of action research and agrees with the action research principles. In particular, I have tried to develop an in-depth understanding of my practice including the consideration of how website resources can integrate with multiple entry point principles to support the learning of English. Furthermore, the aim of my action research was to improve the learning experience of students in English classes. It is also an account of my own learning because the results are actually '*relevant to the immediate needs and problems of teachers*' (Crookes, 1993:137).

8.3 Summary of the Findings of the Research Questions

The findings of this study reveal diverse results from integrating website material with the MI-inspired multiple entry point approaches in English lessons. The findings are summarised in relation to the study's four research questions, and to the literature reviewed.

8.3.1 The Use of Web Materials in English Teaching

The responses to the first research question, '*How can teachers use website resources more effectively as teaching materials for learners of English in a language classroom?*' showed that both advantages and drawbacks were identified in the use of the three websites during the three distinct stages.

During the first stage, a picture-based website with animation, '*Barnaby Bear*' was used in the class in order to attract the learners' attention. The detail of the action research process was examined in Chapter 4. Students' perceptions indicated that some of the students were, indeed, attracted by a predominantly visual website with cartoon features. This was especially true for the female students. However, the findings also indicated that a certain number of students were not interested in this type of website with its cute features and cartoon voices. More specifically, a particular problem with this website was that it did not provide sufficient content for learners to practise language skills. After considering several ways of circumventing this problem, the solution adopted at this stage was to design supplemental handouts or exercises before class, to accomplish the necessary target language practice. This proved to be one way in which teachers could use web materials effectively in class.

At the second stage, a website called *Adult Learning Activities*, with a number of different topics (see Chapter 5) was used during the class and for homework assignments. This website largely fulfilled the practical need for efficient language learning material. During the class, each story posted on this website was suitable as authentic listening or reading material, complete with comprehension questions attached. Afterwards, the website provided learners with opportunities to choose their favourite topics and complete small-scale projects concerned with writing a short essay and posting it on the Internet. After viewing the websites demonstrated in the class, learners had a clearer idea of how to access this website and what kinds of exercises were provided. They learned how to use audio or video functions as their preferred learning styles to facilitate language learning. After class, learners accessed this website, chose a topic, listened to the story, and answered the question provided on their chosen story. The whole process was actually demonstrated in the class which gave students a clear understanding of exactly what they had to do for homework. After that, students were asked to post their written work on the class homepage which was regarded as a small scale project. This approach was basically in accordance with Warschauer and Healey's definition of '*Integrative CALL*'. Learners are involved in authentic environments through '*task-based, project-based and content based approaches*' (Warschauer & Healey, 1998:58). It follows, therefore, that the process of task-based learning is another way in which teachers can use web resources effectively.

At the third stage, the website, '*Randall's ESL Cyber Listening Lab*', was used in class for listening practice. This website raised some disagreement among the students because of its information-rich listening exercises, which were categorised into three levels. Most of the students regarded the listening exercises on this website as a very useful source of information. However, they only accessed it on their own when they were required to do so as part of their homework. In class, the website was used as the focus for a competitive approach to learning. The results showed that learners were keener to participate in learning when they felt that they could earn a personal reward. Motivation was therefore boosted by a tangible reward system, e.g. by scoring points. The competitive approach indicates how a website can be exploited effectively in an English class by a teacher.

Students' comments about giving answers in front of the whole class (see Chapter 6, Section 6.5.3) suggested that the method of rewarding more points did indeed enhance learners' participation in the class. Those students who were not well motivated to learn English also liked this activity. They regarded it as an exciting way of learning and enthusiastically participated in the activity. Crookes and Schmidt (1991) define one of the motivational conditions as satisfaction, being the outcome of an activity, referring to the combination of extrinsic rewards, such as praise or good marks, and intrinsic rewards, such as enjoyment and pride.

The Internet seems to have a positive impact on students' learning experience. This view is based on data about their perception of that experience. Among the interview data about the advantages of the three websites provided, the 'authentic' nature of the website resources was often mentioned. The reason why learners emphasised the importance of authenticity to them was that from the Internet they have a chance to know how English is used in the real world. More specifically, the Internet offers them the opportunity of an active interface for English learning purpose which is an important factor to maintain their learning. Although the three websites used were primarily intended to provide listening practice, students utilised other advantages of the websites such as reading and writing practice. Levy argued that '*native speakers of the target language are able to become active participants in the learning process*' (Levy, 1997:171) by using website resources. This research showed that non-native speakers are also able to benefit in this way as well.

In reflecting upon the teaching practice used in these three stages, it can be said that my approach was based on task-based teaching. Nunan (2004) presents seven principles for task-based language teaching: scaffolding, task dependency, recycling, active learning, integration, 'reproduction to creation', and reflection. There is a similarity between my practice and his framework.

According to Nunan, learners are not expected to produce language. He (2004:35) suggests that *'materials should provide supporting frameworks within which the learning takes places'*. In my teaching, a website was displayed from a data projector in order to give learners an idea of what they were going to learn at the beginning of each stage. The multimodal presentation of visual and verbal material helped students develop and use their cognitive capabilities to comprehend the content of the website (scaffolding). In the first action research stage, learners were provided with a handout which contained ten questions based on a specific story on the website. The handout offered learners clues that they were going to explore some specific information step by step (task dependency). Likewise, the requirements for an assignment were posted on the class homepage to help learners complete the task in the second action research stage. From choosing a preferred topic to posting a piece of work on the Internet, learners experienced a more complicated task in the second stage. The design of an itinerary and presentation in the third action research stage helped learners use English to construct a coherent document. These activities tried to match Nunan's categories: recycling, active learning, integration, and 'reproduction to creation'. Through hands-on activities, learners realised how to manage their own learning. Finally, *'learners should be given opportunities to reflect on what they have learned'* (Nunan, 2004:37). This idea was put into practice in the second stage when learners were asked to write a brief feedback about the writing and posting tasks.   The principle of task-based learning is echoed in a native American proverb, *Tell me and I'll forget. Show me, and I may not remember. Involve me, and I'll understand.*

8.3.2 Visual and Audio Aids for Learning

Research question two asked, '*which sort of web page design appears more likely to engage learners*?' The findings, as shown in Chapter 7, Section 7.3, suggest that visual features drew a certain level of attention from the learners, while audio was the key to facilitating their in-depth understanding of the context. In reality, much research has proved that a learning environment equipped with both visual and audio facilities can help learners in a language learning environment (Brett, 1997; Coniam, 2001). For example, Brett investigated whether learners benefited from a multimedia-based environment in listening comprehension. His study proved that '*higher levels of comprehension and language recall were achieved while listening in the multimedia environment*' (Brett, 1997:49).

The reason for addressing both audio and visual issues in this study was to convince language teachers that the use of audio cassettes is not the only teaching tool in the language laboratory tool-kit. As Hanson-Smith (1999:190) notes, multimedia allows learners to listen to voices in a visual context which can '*create stronger memory links than voices alone can*'. In other words, multimodal presentations on the Internet provide a different communication system which is expected to meet learners' needs (Snyder, 2001). Many classrooms and laboratories in the university used in this study were equipped with a network system, video player, a data projector, and projection screen. However, my observations indicate that a cassette player with a cassette still seems to be the main teaching tool used in a listening comprehension course. The findings from this study indicate that students are likely to respond well to a more imaginative web-based approach: a majority of students liked the three websites because of the availability of information and the well-designed audio-visual effects (see Chapter 7, Table 7.6). Moreover, they enjoyed the combination of audio and visual aids in language learning (see Chapter 7, Table 7.9). Their comments were consistent with the statement proposed by Chun and Plass' research summary that '*dynamic visual advance organizers are more effective in aiding global comprehension of a text than other forms*' (Chun & Plass, 1996:505).

Therefore, it is incumbent upon me to remind those teachers used to using traditional cassette players that there may be better ways of achieving their goals. At the same time, the display of visual and verbal materials tends to better satisfy students' preferences.

8.3.3 The Comprehensive Approach

Research question three asked: '*How can teachers implement the theory of multiple intelligences in web-assisted language learning setting?*' This question explored how, to enhance students' English learning by utilising website material with multiple entry points, which are a practical framework provided by MI theory. The reasons for applying multiple entry points in class instruction were to aid comprehension of learning topics and make learning meaningful. As Krechevsky and Seidel (2001:49) stated regarding the *'implications of MI theory for instruction'*, if a teacher can explain the target concept in more than one way, students will understand it better. Consequently, multiple entry points are likely to promote understanding from a variety of perspectives.

According to students' responses, multiple entry point activities were felt to be useful to them by increasing the opportunities for them to approach their learning through their own unique strengths. For example, aesthetic and narrative entry point approaches captured students' attention and focussed them on the learning material by giving them a solid idea of the material that they were about to learn. Then, logical and experiential entry point activities helped enhance learners' understanding of the topic, by requiring them to speak, write and post their work on the Internet. The multiple entry point approaches integrated with Internet features, e.g., a discussion board, class homepage and website material which provide learners with a concrete learning experience by allowing them to share their work with others making their learning more meaningful. Students' perspectives on the four entry point approaches have been discussed in detail in Chapter 7, Section 7.4.2.

8.3.4 The Impact of Website Materials and MI-inspired instructions on Language Learning

Research question four was: *How do website materials and MI-inspired instructions shape language learning?* The results of listening skills component of the General English Proficiency Test showed that students of different majors showed different levels of improvement when they were taught using a website. The Textile Engineering group improved by about three points as did the Information Management group, while the Industrial Management group improved by over ten points. However, many learners from the Business Administration group went down. The reasons why this group received lower scores for the second listening test have been analysed in Chapter 7, Section 7.5.3. For example, they did not take listening test seriously and few of them actually made efforts to practise listening task after class. On the other hand, the post-test result of this group indicated that teaching based on MI theory did not help every student prepare for a standardised test. The analysis in previous chapters showed that these students were indeed fond of multiple entry point activities (Table 5.8 and Table 5.10). However, there was little evidence that the MI theory itself was helpful to the Business Administration group to prepare a standardise test. This notion was also a concern of Diaz and Heining-Boynton:

> How can educators teach to multiple intelligences, evaluate consistently with their goals and objectives, and still have their students do well on standardized tests? *(Diaz & Heining-Boynton, 1995:616)*

In addition to these varied findings relating to changes in GEPT listening scores, I found that website material with MI-based instruction provided a variety of learning opportunities for students who responded positively to the MI-inspired tasks. Therefore, Research Question Four can be considered from two perspectives. First, multiple entry point approaches can make use of learners' strengths and encourage an initial effort in English learning. For example, students found role play a welcome challenge and provided useful oral practice. Moreover, posting their writing work on the Internet for real audiences was another achievement that encouraged learners to take responsibility for their own learning. In this respect the website activities could be seen as providing a context for authentic assessment which '*refers to the procedures for evaluating learner performance using activities and tasks*' (Kohonen, 2001:50). These tasks should be able to represent learning goals and instruction in realistic conditions of language use. Learners' response to class activities proved that the entry point activities such as oral presentation, writing and posting can be regarded as a means of authentic assessment. The General English Proficiency Test basically was basically a pencil and paper test. Moreover, only the listening section of the GEPT was used in my research. While it is useful to know if learners' listening scores change the overall learning progression of learners is not specifically tested by the General English Proficiency Test. In other words, the test had limitations in its ability to map the results of web-based teaching '*in products that have value to students*' (Armstrong, 2000:91).

As for the second perspective, the results of the General English Proficiency Test suggest that higher achievement can be attained by use of the web-based teaching. However, this was not universally the case. Performance on standardised tests is a complex domain which cannot always be altered by the use of entry point teaching only. Students agreed that MI-based activities with website resources were interesting. However, few of them actually used these websites as self study. They only reviewed the listening exercises when they were informed that there would be a test in the next class. This issue of why one group did so much less well than the rest has been discussed in Chapter 7, Section 7.5.3. In this study, the style of listening quizzes on the third website, *Randall's ESL Cyber Listening Lab*, was similar to the General English Proficiency Test mode. In other words, if teachers want students to improve their General English Proficiency Test results by utilising the exercises on *Randall's ESL Cyber Listening Lab*, they may need to implement paper-and-pencil tests linked to the website content during language classes. In practice, paper-and-pencil instruments can be used in ways that offer students concrete ideas to practise in preparation for standardised tests. Without this practice, the potential of the website to improve standardised test score may not always be realised. Such tests may offer learners a general idea about their listening competence. If they see that their score on a standardised test is higher than the previous one, learners will feel a sense of achievement.

8.4 Implications

This study meant to explore how first-year undergraduates from four different academic programmes learn English and also examine the feedback on their use of website materials in class. The research presented in this study tried to aid teachers' choices for instruction in Computer Assisted Language Learning courses and at the same time, it consulted the theory of multiple intelligences to enhance classroom instruction. Based on the research results, some pedagogical implications are made for English teaching practice including the inclusion of website materials in language teaching and the incorporation of multiple intelligences into web assisted language teaching.

8.4.1 The Inclusion of Website Materials in Language Teaching

The results of this study agree with the generally accepted view that a variety of website resources with a multimodal presentation offers learners the opportunity to experience how the target language is used in the real world by means of a virtual environment. Moreover, the up-to-date details of websites provide materials suitable for instruction of English at various levels.

The implications of web assisted language teaching are that teachers no longer have to be confined to a computer classroom. This study presented a practical mode of web assisted language teaching. A computer with a network connection was adopted in the language class. With rich website information, teachers select a target language skill, e.g. listening and a specific topic at one time to proceed to many different language activities.

This study suggests that teachers should look at computer assisted language learning (CALL) from a wider definition. Computer technology can be used as a powerful teaching tool to deliver authentic materials to learners. English language teachers are encourage to acknowledge the effect of a data projector. Website materials are presented via a projection screen, a method that is very useful to get students' attention. Moreover, it can present teaching materials in an impressive manner. As mentioned in the reflection of Chapter 4, the first website, *Barnaby Bear*, indeed caught the learners' attention at first. When this website was displayed in the class, some students who sat at the back actually moved their chairs to the front desk. Those were students that would normally either copy other classmates' answers or fall asleep in a traditional teacher-centred lesson. With the aid of a data projector, rich website information becomes a live coursebook. Students no longer listen passively to the lecture. They participate in learning through a series of activities. The research emphasises that a CALL lesson does not necessarily mean that every student has to work with a computer in order to practise language skills. This kind of approach can reduce teachers' fear in which they regard technology as '*potentially frustrating*' (Debski & Gruba, 1999:228).

The other advantage of displaying a particular website in front of the whole class is that learners can receive better instructions and get a clearer idea of what they are going to learn. According to previous experiences, students usually feel ambiguous about the concept they have to learn and the task they have to complete. By displaying learning materials in front of the whole class, learners acquire the initial idea and pay attention to a specific concept. With the aid of a projection screen, the teachers are able to explain the learning materials concretely. Afterwards, students have a better understanding of a certain website and are able to manage their homework.

In addition, when teachers choose website materials, learners' ages and/or genders is often taken into account. The cute cartoon pictures may attract certain learners at first sight while on the other hand other learners may regard a website like '*Barnaby Bear*' as childish. Furthermore, visual-based websites can be taken into account, because they may '*mean more cognitive capacity can be released to deal with linguistic decoding*' (Kellerman, 1992:250). Nevertheless, teachers who tend to choose visual-based materials should check if the pictures or animation can aid comprehension or are in fact only decoration. A lot of research about second language learning has shown that comprehension can be improved by visual cues while listening to spoken text (Kellerman, 1992). In contrast, pictures do not always help in certain contexts (Zhang & Elliott, 1998). For example, Zhang and Elliott's (1998) research shows that pictures do not really help the understanding of prepositions.

Although website resources have shown the ability of offering many advantages to the foreign language classroom, a coursebook may also be necessary. As shown from learners' comments in Chapter 7, Section 7.2.1, certain students preferred the coursebook as learning material because of its well-organised structure. It give them clear instructions for review after class. The use of website materials alongside a coursebook not only meets learners' expectations on authenticity, but also satisfies those learners who would like a structural syllabus based on defined linguistic items.

8.4.2 Incorporating Multiple Entry Points into Web Assisted Language Teaching

The greatest difference between traditional instruction based on lecturing and multiple intelligences inspired instruction is the transformation from a teacher-centred to a student centred learning environment. Many elements of practical instruction mentioned in the theory of multiple intelligences, e.g. task-based learning and authentic learning material actually have already been addressed as crucial issues in the context of teaching English. As Kallenbach and Viens (2002:58) mention, one of MI-inspired educational theories is the idea of multiple entry points which *'refer to activities that engage students in a particular subject area or content'*. A framework for the various elements of learning which can be informed by MI theory is the entry point. The idea of the entry point approach was incorporated in the present study in order to help students to develop a greater capacity for learning through resource-rich environments. Moreover, the entry point approach can be regarded as the criteria of teaching practice to help learners practise and acquire English from a variety of perspectives.

First, the World Wide Web which consists of visual features is presented via a projection screen thereby providing an aesthetic approach. It allows learners to acquire concrete ideas about what they are going to learn.

Second, the audio function and web text, plus teachers' explanation offer a narrative entry point. This study has shown that some learners can make a connection between the visual images and the contents, while others feel learning is facilitated through the listening. In addition, a few learners regard the explanation by the teacher as essential for understanding.

Third, exercises on the website can provide a logical entry point. Learners are asked to describe a perspective of a topic through speaking (role play) or writing. According to Gardner's (1999) definition, this approach helps learners present a concept by deductive reasoning. The questions provided by the second website for writing tasks often require learners to describe what they will do when they meet a similar problem in the story. In other words, learners have to construct a logical argument to convince their audiences. If they do not understand what the question means and therefore write an inappropriate essay, they have a chance to rewrite it. Learning from mistakes is often an effective way of learning. This approach actually involves an authentic assessment for learners to use the knowledge and understanding gained from the lesson. Learners are given a chance to reflect on their learning and to show to what degree they understand of the topic.

Fourth, the Internet related activities proposed by teachers such as a discussion board and publishing on the Internet offer an experiential approach. Teachers can use Internet functions, e.g. a class homepage and a discussion board allow learners to express what they have learned English through hands-on activities like performances and experiments. This approach tries to encourage students to take responsibility for their learning, because they have to post their outcome on the Internet and share it with their peers. These four entry points can be regarded as an instructional framework to help learning become meaningful.

8.5 Suggestions on Applying Multiple Intelligences in English Teaching

After Gardner mentioned the theory of multiple intelligences (MI), much research has proven that MI-based instruction is able to provide more opportunities for learners to explore learning with their potential strengths (Diaz-Lefebvre, 2004; Kallenbach & Viens, 2002; Lazear, 1991). That motivated this study to try and implement a practical form of the theory of multiple intelligences (MI) in computer assisted language teaching. After the experiment in this study, some suggestions are mentioned as a reference for teachers who may want to adopt the application of multiple intelligences in their classes.

First, language teachers should focus on language practice but not on intelligences. The primary purpose of using learners' potential strengths is to get them interested in the English language and master language learning. As Gardner advises, the entry point approach can '*help the teacher introduce new materials in ways in which they can be easily grasped by a range of students*' (1991:245). On this basis, the design of entry point activities in this study continuously aims to enhance learners' language skills. The use of the aesthetic approach tries to acquire learners' attention but not to develop their spatial or visual intelligences. Neither does this research intend to explore how to assess and develop learners' other multiple intelligences. Language teachers should focus on how to improve students' language skills and not how to develop their multiple intelligences.

Second, the MI inventory can help teachers acknowledge learner differences and then provide them with multiple activities to encourage learning. Awareness of students' strengths can help the teacher introduce new materials in ways in which the topic can be easily grasped by a wide range of students. However, students' MI profiles should be regarded as a reference and not as definite information. Because of cultural differences and personal backgrounds, the outcomes of MI profiles may not be exactly the same with different inventories. In reality, the main benefit of the MI approach is to remind teachers as well as learners that it is the learners themselves that must take responsibility for their own learning. Teachers only play a role as a mediator. This idea has been mentioned before in Campbell's (1995) research about the impact on teachers using the framework of multiple intelligences. As he stated, '*the teacher also finds that he/she is working with students, rather than for them*' (Campbell, 1995:205). In particular, '*in planning for such diverse modes of learning, the teacher becomes more creative and multimodal in his/her own thinking and learning.*

A teacher might well ask: 'Who is changing the most, students or teachers?' (Campbell, 1995:205)

Third, a language teacher does not own all intelligences, so it is not possible to help students to develop all the intelligences. Many MI related books focus on how teachers identify students' individual differences. MI educators tend to design a series of activities which are concerned with how to help learners build on each intelligence, e.g. Armstrong's *Multiple Intelligences in the Classroom* (Armstrong, 2000). Similarly, in Lazear's book, *Seven Ways of Knowing: Teaching for Multiple Intelligences* (1991), he presents numerous teaching ideas for teachers who want to apply the theory of Multiple Intelligences in their classroom. The author designs a series of activities based on how to *'awaken'*, *'amplify'*, *'teach'* and *'transfer'* the intelligence (Lazear, 1991: 9-17). However, it is my personal opinion that a sourcebook on expanding learners' multiple intelligences is not appropriate in an English language class. Many activities designed in this book are about enhancing spatial or musical intelligences which likely are not English teachers' subjects. When teaching English, the teacher only needs to design activities for learners to use their potential strengths in order to master their own language learning pace. It is not the job of an English language teacher to improve learners' multiple intelligences.

8.6 Reflections on the Research Process

The primary model of this study was based on individual teacher action research, in which the teacher first identifies the problems then implements website resources and multiple entry point instructions, carefully evaluating each experimental cycle. This action research process included plan, action, observation and reflection, which helped me take charge of the class and improve instructional methodologies at different stages. During the research process, insights into what learners thought and felt about learning English with website materials, gathered through questionnaires and interviews, contributed to a more thorough comprehension of the process. Discussion included how and why the students had benefited from website resources as they learned the target language. This is consistent with Lousberg and Soler's (1998:4) study, which found that '*students also play an invaluable role as active researchers, as frank informants and as critics*'. In the present study, student perceptions were helpful in reaching an objective understanding and evaluation of the teaching process.

The process of documentation and collection of data provided a record of reflection, which led to change over time. Reflections of teaching practices at each stage provided a focus for moving towards a greater understanding of particular '*problems and concerns in the classroom*' (Thorne & Qiang, 1996:256). The benefit of this reflective process is the assimilation of a greater insight into the researcher's teaching experience and leads to a change in teaching practice (Block, 1997). While reviewing teaching practice, colleagues' comments, along with self-reflection, helped me generate, organise and expand upon ideas. I came to be more confident of how instruction, using a multiple intelligences approach, can be integrated with website materials. In regard to the process, action research provided a point of common interest to begin discussions about the work, and the opportunity to try particular innovative and new practices. The value of the reflective approach can be a reference for teachers in Taiwan who would like to reflect on their teaching practice in Taiwan. They may benefit from what I have learned from my own action research and use it as a guideline for their own teaching practice.

8.7 Limitation

This study has several limitations. The first limitation is that issues of multiple entry points and computer assisted language learning were fairly new to many language teachers. Moreover, teachers who were familiar with computer assisted language learning had little knowledge about the theory of multiple intelligences. Therefore, it was not possible to find a colleague who understood both issues to observe the teaching practice and also provided feedback. Consequently, one colleague who had applied computer assisted language teaching was invited as a critical friend in the class to provide feedback about website resources used in the English class. As for the other colleague, the main focus of feedback was on MI-inspired instruction as well as the development of students' strengths. In other words, none of them could provide a holistic opinion.

The second limitation is the gap in the existing literature review between computer assisted language learning and the theory of multiple intelligences. Although some English teachers have applied MI-inspired approaches in class, most of them do not integrate computer technology with their teaching. In contrast, CALL research does not mention issues of multiple intelligences even though both these principles are sometimes compatible.

8.8 The Significance of this Research

This study has explored how website resources integrated with MI-inspired instruction can be used in English teaching in a university in Taiwan. Being a preliminary attempt to explore the possibilities of using website resources under MI-inspired instruction to teach a listening lesson, it is hoped that the study can contribute to the scant studies available in the literature on the MI theory in a computer assisted language learning context.

This research could be regarded as a resource book for teachers who would like to apply multiple entry point activities in their language classes. On-line sources are particularly valuable in learning situations where we usually expect authentic materials. The lesson plan mentioned in this research incorporates MI theory including multiple entry point activities which could help teachers to outline their classroom management. The positive comments mentioned by learners should encourage teachers to try and use different approaches in their teaching instruction. At the same time, teachers should be aware of potential pitfalls such as occurred in this research project as they may be similar to those they have also experienced in a computer assisted language learning class.

In addition, this research builds a bridge from theory to practical approach aiming to assist teachers who believe intrinsically in the use of technology, but have not been trained in its use. My reflection on teaching practice suggests that Internet resources can improve our ability to capture the attention of second language learners' attention, which is at the heart of my thoughts on authentic learning. Moreover, I believe that each learner has the ability to learn according to their own individual strengths. This is also the main reason why this study has drawn so often on Gardner's MI theory.

8.9 Recommendations

In this section, recommendations for future practice and research are made.

8.9.1 Recommendations for Further Practice

The teaching practice in this study can be a reference for teachers who would like to adopt the theory of multiple intelligences in their computer assisted language learning courses. However, different technology functions and MI-inspired activities will serve learners' diverse needs in English learning. The World Wide Web is a valuable resource for both teachers and students as a means of instruction and learning. Thus, I like to make some recommendations for teachers who would like to use MI theory in computer assisted language learning courses.

First, the framework of multiple intelligences emphasises the understanding of a target subject and it demonstrates learners' outcome through multiple activities. In addition, Internet activities do indeed can provide numerous opportunities for learners to explore language learning. However, teaching with different technology functions such as audio and visual equipment needs to be aware of a different approach to present learning materials. The point should be made that teachers should present a website with specific concepts, one at a time.

Second, the theory of multiple intelligences can be regarded as a rubric for teachers to design their syllabus of Internet activities. However, teachers should not regard class activities as a compulsory pedagogical mode. The traditional lecture mode based on a coursebook is sometimes necessary in an adapted teaching curriculum. Alternatively, teachers can use website resources for supplementary activities.

Third, teachers need to take multidimensional assessments into account to evaluate students' performances and improvement apart from standardised tests. A sample authentic assessment can be a project, a learning journal, or a portfolio. Implementing an assessment can focus on students' self-reflection.

8.9.2 Recommendations for Further Research

This study has explored the experience of website material integrated with MI-inspired approaches and set the stage for further research in the area of MI theory with Internet activities. When conducting further research involving teachers' use of MI theory, this study has some recommendations.

First, further research should explore the influence of multiple intelligence theory in the CALL context. In order to investigate those influences, other studies could be conducted that are descriptive and experimental in nature. Their findings would provide criteria to examine the support for the intrinsically attractive MI theory in effective computer assisted language learning.

Second, teachers can explore the relationship between their own strengths and teaching approaches. This raises the questions: Do teachers' potential strengths affect their chosen Internet activities? What kinds of teaching approaches do teachers like to apply in a computer assisted language learning lesson based on their preferred intelligences?

Last, it is recommended that teachers, who are interested in implementing CALL or MI contexts in their instructional setting, use the action research methodology to promote their professional development. By observing, the learning of their students, teachers can reflect continuously on their teaching instruction continuously in order to benefit both learners and themselves in the diverse classroom.

8.10 Personal Benefit

Through the action research process, I have introduced CALL, and a particular framework of multiple intelligences - the entry point approach into my practice of teaching. From the evaluation and comments of students, it seems that the MI-inspired instruction offers them additional opportunities for practising English. Their response suggests that they feel that I had improved the way in which I am teaching. Also, the use of website resources and the principles of multiple intelligences were of positive benefit to students who earlier were not very interested in learning English. Using the entry approach increased not only the students' motivation for classroom participation, it also boosted my enthusiasm for varying my teaching methods. Teaching in this kind of mode has made learning plausible and enhanced the interaction between my students and myself. I learned a new way of thinking about teaching with technology for second language learners. The Internet has particular strengths for second language learners because its websites can offer authentic materials. Moreover, the integration of MI principles can help maximise the potential of Internet resources. However, a coursebook has its own advantages – a fact we should not forget. Therefore, teaching methods need to be adopted in a variety of ways so as to engage learners a love of learning and to exploit, to their advantage, their different methods of learning.

Action research helped me bridge the gap between theories such as multiple intelligences, second language learning, computer assisted language learning and practice, e.g., classroom management and instruction. While engaging in critical self-reflection about my own role in the action research process, I realised how it is important to be sensitive to learners' feedback and to use it as a criteria for one's own teaching approach. The more data I review, the more understanding I gain. The process of reflection, including reviewing learners' interview data, discussing matters with colleagues, and writing a research journal helps me establish a context in which individuals are able to reach their goals. The entire research process made me appreciate the value of a teacher's personal practical knowledge. More important, it has brought a refinement to the theory mentioned in the study, and how to adjust it to a learners' particular learning context.

As I have stressed throughout this book, the ideas of CALL and MI are certainly not the be-all and end-all of second language teaching. One must remain alert and keep an eye on how Internet resources will influence second language learning, and how the MI theory will affect classroom instruction in the future.

APPENDICES

APPENDIX 1

Inventory of Multiple Intelligences

This is an inventory of multiple intelligences to help you understand your eight intelligences. Using the scale below, give each statement a number that best represents your view.

0	1	2
not at all	little	a lot

Linguistic Intelligence

_____ 1. Books are very important to me.

_____ 2. I can hear words in my head before I read, speak, or write them down.

_____ 3. I get more out of listening to the radio or a spoken-word cassette than I do from television or films.

_____ 4. I enjoy word games like Scrabble, Anagrams, or Password.

_____ 5. I enjoy entertaining myself or others with tongue twisters, nonsense rhymes, or puns.

_____ 6. Other people sometimes have to stop and ask me to explain the meaning of the words I use in my writing and speaking.

_____ 7. Chinese, social Studies, and history were easier for me in school than math and science.

_____ 8. Learning to speak or read another language (e.g., English) has been relatively easy for me.

_____ 9. My conversation includes frequent references to things that I've read or heard.

_____ 10. I've written something recently that I was particularly proud of or that earned me recognition from others.

_____ **Total**

Logical-Mathematical Intelligence

_____ 11. I can easily compute numbers in my head.

_____ 12. Math and/or science were among my favorite subjects in school.

_____ 13. I enjoy playing games or solving brainteasers that require logical thinking.

_____ 14. I like to set up little "what if" experiments (for example, "What if I double the amount of water I give to my rosebush each week?")

_____ 15. My mind searches for patterns, regularities, or logical sequences in things.

_____ 16. I'm interested in new developments in science.

_____ 17. I believe that almost everything has a rational explanation.

_____ 18. I sometimes think in clear, abstract, wordless, imageless concepts.

19. I like finding logical flaws in things that people say and do at home and work.

20. I feel more comfortable when something has been measured, categorized, analyzed, or quantified in some way.

_____ **Total**

Spatial Intelligence

21. I often see clear visual images when I close my eyes.
22. I'm sensitive to color.
23. I frequently use a camera or camcorder to record what I see around me.
24. I enjoy doing jigsaw puzzles, mazes, and other visual puzzles.
25. I have vivid dreams at night.
26. I can generally find my way around unfamiliar territory.
27. I like to draw or doodle.
28. Geometry was easier for me than algebra in school.
29. I can comfortably imagine how something might appear if it were looked down on from directly above in a bird's-eye view.
30. I prefer looking at reading material that is heavily illustrated.

_____ **Total**

Bodily-Kinesthetic Intelligence

_____ 31. I engage in at least one sport or physical activity on a regular basis.

_____ 32. I find it difficult to sit still for long periods of time.

_____ 33. I like working with my hands at concrete activities such as sewing, weaving, carving, carpentry, or model building.

_____ 34. My best ideas often come to me when I'm out for a long walk or a jog, or when I'm engaging in some other kind of physical activity.

_____ 35. I often like to spend my free time outdoors.

_____ 36. I frequently use hand gestures or other forms of body language when conversing with someone.

_____ 37. I need to touch things in order to learn more about them.

_____ 38. I enjoy daredevil amusement rides or similar thrilling physical experiences.

_____ 39. I would describe myself as well coordinated.

_____ 40. I need to practice a new skill rather than simply reading about it or seeing a video that describe it.

_____ **Total**

Musical Intelligence

_____ 41. I have a pleasant singing voice.

_____ 42. I can tell when a musical note is off-key.

_____ 43. I frequently listen to music on radio, records, cassettes, or compact discs.

_____ 44. I play a musical instrument.

_____ 45. My life would be poorer if there were no music in it.

_____ 46. I sometimes catch myself walking down the street with a television jingle or other tune running through my mind.

_____ 47. I can easily keep time to a piece of music with a simple percussion instrument.

_____ 48. I know the tunes to many different songs or musical pieces.

_____ 49. If I hear a musical selection once or twice, I am usually able to sing it back fairly accurately.

_____ 50. I often make tapping sounds or sing little melodies while working, studying, or learning something new.

_____ **Total**

Interpersonal Intelligence

_____ 51. I'm the sort of person that people come to for advice and counsel at work or in my neighborhood.

_____ 52. I prefer group sports like badminton, volleyball, or softball to solo sports such as swimming and jogging.

_____ 53. When I have a problem, I'm more likely to seek out another person for help than attempt to work it out on my own.

_____ 54. I have at least three close friends.

_____ 55. I favor social pastimes such as Monopoly or bridge over individual recreations such as video games and solitaire.

_____ 56. I enjoy the challenge of teaching another person, or groups of people, what I know how to do.

_____ 57. I consider myself a leader (or others have called me that).

_____ 58. I feel comfortable in the midst of a crowd.

     59. I like to get involved in social activities connected with my
_____   work, church, or community.
     60. I would rather spend my evenings at a lively party than stay
_____   at home alone.

_____ **Total**

Intrapersonal Intelligence

     61. I regularly spend time alone meditating, reflecting, or
_____   thinking about important life questions.
     62. I have attended counseling sessions or personal growth
_____   seminars to learn more about myself.
_____ 63. I am able to respond to setbacks with resilience.
     64. I have a special hobby or interest that I keep pretty much to
_____   myself.
     65. I have some important goals for my life that I think about
_____   on a regular basis.
     66. I have a realistic view of my strengths and weaknesses
_____   (borne out by feedback from other sources).
     67. I would prefer to spend a weekend alone in a cabin in the
        woods rather than at a fancy resort with lots of people
_____   around.
     68. I consider myself to be strong willed or independent
_____   minded.
     69. I keep a personal diary or journal to record the events of
_____   my inner life.
     70. I am self-employed or have at least thought seriously about
_____   starting my own business.

_____ **Total**

Naturalist Intelligence

_____ 71. I like to spend time backpacking, hiking, or just walking in nature.

_____ 72. I belong to some kind of volunteer organization related to nature (e.g., Sierra Club), and I'm concerned about helping to save nature from further destruction.

_____ 73. I thrive on having animals around the house.

_____ 74. I'm involved in a hobby that involves nature in some way (e.g., bird watching).

_____ 75. I've enrolled in courses relating to nature at community centers or colleges (e.g., botany, zoology).

_____ 76. I'm quite good at telling the difference between different kinds of trees, dogs, birds, or other types of flora or fauna.

_____ 77. I like to read books and magazines, or watch television shows or movies that feature nature in some way.

_____ 78. When on vacation, I prefer to go off to a natural setting 9park, campground, hiking trail) rather than to a hotel/resort or city/cultural location.

_____ 79. I love to visit zoos, aquariums, or other places where the natural world is studied.

_____ 80. I have a garden and enjoy working regularly in it.

_____ **Total**

APPENDIX 2

The open-ended questions of the three websites

Part I   Barnaby's Story

http://www.bbc.co.uk/schools/barnabybear/stories/

1. What do you think you have learned or now understand better from this website?
2. Is there anything on this website that you do not understand? Please explain.
3. What did you like or dislike about this website?
4. Did you think that the listening on this website is easy or difficult? Please explain your reasons.
5. Which element in this website drew your attention first? Please explain your reasons.
6. Which one element on this website helped you to understand the content most? Please explain your reasons.

Part II   Adult Learning Activities

http://www.cdiponline.org/

7. Which topic and article did you choose? Why?
8. Did you (a) read the text (b) listen to the audio (c) watch the video? In which order did you do these activities?
9. Did you get most benefit from reading, listening or watching the video?

10. Did you use a dictionary to look up words?

11. What did you like or dislike about the writing tasks? Whether it was too easy, okay, or too difficult?

12. How do you evaluate performance on your writing task?

13. How did you feel about posting your writing task? What did you learn from posting your writing and looking at others' writing?

Part III   Randall's ESL Cyber Listening Lab

http://www.esl-lab.com/

14. What did you think of the quiz from this website we did in the class?

	easy	medium	difficult
Listening exercises			
Text completion quiz			

15. Which kind of listening exercises you like to practice?

Listening with audio clips	Listening with video clips

16. Did you try the exercises as self-study?

yes	no

If yes, which level did you do?

easy	medium	difficult

17. Did you answer the questions after the listening or did you find the answer from the quiz scrip?

18. Were any problems encountered while using this website? How did you solve them?

19. How did you feel about giving answers in front of the whole class?

20. Did you like role play in front of the whole class?

yes	no

Please explain the reasons.

APPENDIX 3

The Learner Perspective of Website Evaluation

Thank you for taking the time to complete this questionnaire.

Compare the following 3 websites. Please answer Question 1-9 below by placing a tick (√) in the appropriate box.

Barnaby's Story http://www.bbc.co.uk/schools/barnabybear/stories/

Adult Learning Activities   http://www.cdiponline.org/

Randall's ESL Cyber Listening Lab   http://www.esl-lab.com/

1a. Please tick (√) the website you liked best for learning English.

Barnaby's Story	Adult Learning Activities	Randall's ESL Cyber Listening Lab

1b. Which element in the website you chose drew your attention first?

visual	text	audio	others

2a. Which website had the best listening activities?

Barnaby's Story	Adult Learning Activities	Randall's ESL Cyber Listening Lab

2b. Which element in the website you chose helped your learning?

visual	text	audio	others

3. Which website would you use for self-study?

Barnaby's Story	Adult Learning Activities	Randall's ESL Cyber Listening Lab

Why?

4. Which website did you dislike most?

Barnaby's Story	Adult Learning Activities	Randall's ESL Cyber Listening Lab

Why?

5. Which website did you think was least useful for your English learning?

Barnaby's Story	Adult Learning Activities	Randall's ESL Cyber Listening Lab

6. Which of following elements in the website design is important for your English learning?

Please rate the importance of each element on a 1-5 scale

	visual	text	audio

Not at all important	1	1	1
Quite important	2	2	2
important	3	3	3
Very important	4	4	4
Extremely important	5	5	5

7. Which aspect of the website visual features was most beneficial to your studies?

Please rate the importance of each element on a 1-5 scale

	colour	picture	animation	video
Not at all important	1	1	1	1
Quite important	2	2	2	2
important	3	3	3	3
Very important	4	4	4	4
Extremely important	5	5	5	5

8. Which materials would you like to use in the future English listening and speaking class?

website	coursebook

Why?

9a. Do you like learning English with website materials?

Yes	No

9b. If yes, do you like learning via…

reading the text	listening to the audio clips	watching the video

Why?

10. Do you have any comments you would like to make about listening and speaking class?

If you would like to share your opinion about teaching material or classroom instruction, please write in the space below or email to cla_ss4@yahoo.co.uk
Many thanks!

APPENDIX 4

Part I

The handout of Barnaby's day trip to Paris

It looks like a long way to go for a day!	That's because the River Seine goes right through the middle of the city.
Not really, Barnaby. We're going by train.	They're called baguettes, Barnaby.
Gosh, that's fantastic. I hope it doesn't leak.	
I'm going to France for the day.	Then you'll need some Euros. This is the money used in France and Europe.
Can I see your passport and your train ticket please?	Yes, it is – the engine must be very powerful.
Please don't laugh at my passport photo!	It's a very long train, isn't it Barnaby?
There are lots of bridges around Paris.	It's very, very tall, isn't it?
We're going so fast it looks like those cars are not moving.	The Metro is the underground railway. It goes all over Paris.
It's much quicker than walking.	Gosh, these sandwiches are very big.
Look over there at the size of those boats.	The Ile de la Cite is an island in the middle of Paris. The river flows past on both sides.
It doesn't look very big does it?	Oh Barnaby, that's just the entrance, the gallery is huge!
Oh Barnaby, she smiles at everyone!	I'm sure she's smiling at me.
Yes, I don't know if I could eat	They eat things in France that we're

frog's legs.	not used to.
Oh! Barnaby, you've learnt a French word!	That was fantastique!
I hope this picture is better than my passport photograph!	You can walk up it if you like. It's only 1652 steps!

Part II

Your Name: _____

Title: Barnaby's Day Trip to Paris

Website: http://www.bbc.co.uk/schools/barnabybear/stories/

1. What currency is used in France?

2. How did Barnaby get around in Paris?

3. Which river did they go for a boat cruise on?

4. What did they eat for lunch?

5. What is the Louvre?

6. Who painted the Mona Lisa?

7. How many steps are there in the Eiffel Tower?

8. How did Barnaby and his friends get to the top of the Eiffel Tower?

9. What did Barnaby have for dinner?

10. Would you like to go to Paris? Why? Why not?

REFERENCES

Aiken, L. (1988). *Psychological Testing and Assessment*. Boston: Allyn and Bacon, Inc.

Arhar, J., M. Holly, & W. Kasten. (2001). Action Research for Teachers. New Jersey: Merrill Prentice Hall.

Armstrong, T. (2000). *Multiple Intelligences in the Classroom, 2nd Edition*. Alexandria VA: Association for Supervision and Curriculum Development (ASCD). http://www.ascd.org/

Armstrong, T. (2003). *The Multiple Intelligences of Reading and Writing: Making the Words Come Alive*. Alexandria VA: Association for Supervision and Curriculum Development (ASCD).

Backhouse, J.K. (1984). Inferential and Non-inferential Tests, *Educational Research*, Vol.26(1):52-55.

Baker, A. & E. Greene. (1987). *Storytelling: art and technique*. New York: Bowker.

Baum, S., J. Viens. & B. Slatin. (2005). *Multiple Intelligences in the Elementary Classroom*. New York: Teachers College Press.

Bassey, M. (1995). *Creating education through research: a global perspective of educational research for the 21st century*. England: Kirklington Moor Press.

Bax, S. (2000). Putting technology in its place: ICT in Modern Foreign Language Teaching. In K. Field, (Ed.), *Issues in Modern Foreign Languages Teaching* (pp. 208-219). London: RoutledgeFalmer.

Bax, S. (2003). CALL-past, present and future. *System*, Vol.31(1):13-28.

Beatty, K. (2003). *Computer-assisted Language Learning*. London: Pearson Education Limited.

Berman, M. (1998). *A Multiple Intelligences Road to an ELT Classroom*. Wales: Crown House Publishing Limited.

Bickel, B. & D. Truscello. (1996). New opportunities for learning: style and strategies for computers. *TESOL Journal*, Vol.6(1):15-19.

Black, P. & D. Wiliam. (1998). Inside the Black Box: Raising Standards Through Classroom Assessment. *Phi Delta Kappan*, Vol.80(2): 139-148.

Block, D. (1997). Learning by listening to language learners. *System*, Vol.25(3):347-360.

Brett, P. (1997). A Comparative Study of the Effects of the Use of Multimedia on Listening Comprehension. *System*, Vol. 25(1):39-53.

Brett, P. (1995). Multimedia for listening comprehension: the design of a multimedia-based resource for developing listening skills. *System*, Vol. 23(1):77-85.

Brown, H.D. (1994). *Principles of Language Learning and Teaching*. New Jersey: Prentice Hall Regents Prentice Hall, Inc.

Brown, H.D. (1991). TESOL at twenty-five: What are the issues? *TESOL Quarterly*, 25(2): 245-260.

Brualdi, A. C. (1996). Multiple intelligences: Gardner's theory. *Practical Assessment, Research & Evaluation*, Vol.5(10). (ED410226). Retrieved October 20, 2004 from http://www.ericfacility.net/ericdigests/ed410226.html

Buck, G. (2001). *Assessing Listening*. Cambridge: Cambridge University Press.

Burmark, L. (2002). *Visual Literacy: Learn to See, See to Learn*. Alexandria VA, Association for Supervision and Curriculum Development (ASCD).

Burns, A. (1999). *Collaborative Action Research for English Language Teachers*. Cambridge: Cambridge University Press.

Burns, R. (2000). *Introduction to Research Methods*. London: Sage Publications.

Butler-Pascoe, M. E. & K.M. Wiburg. (2003). *Technology and teaching English language learners*. Boston: Pearson Education.

Calhoun, E. (1994). *How to Use Action Research in the Self-Renewing School*. Alexandria VA, Association for Supervision and Curriculum Development (ASCD).

Calhoun, E. (1999). *Teaching Beginning Reading and Writing with the Picture Word Inductive Model*. Alexandria VA, Association for Supervision and Curriculum Development (ASCD).

Campbell, B. (1995). Multiple Intelligences in Action. In R. Fogarty & J. Bellanca (Eds.). *Multiple Intelligences: A Collection* (pp.195-206). Illinois: IRI/SKYlight Piblishing, Inc.

Campbell, L. (1997). Variations on a Theme – How Teachers Interpret MI Theory. *Educational Leadership*, Vol.55(1):14-19.

Campbell, L & B. Campbell. (1999). Multiple Intelligences and Student Achievement: Success Stories from Six schools. Alexandria VA, Association for Supervision and Curriculum Development (ASCD).

Carr, W. & S. Kemmis. (1986). *Becoming Critical*. London: Falmer Press.

Chapelle, C.A. (1996). CALL-English as a second language. Annual Review of Applied Linguistics. Vol.16: *Technology and Language* (pp139-157).

Checkley, K. (1997). The first seven...and the eighth: A conversation with Howard Gardner. *Educational Leadership,* Vol.55(1). Retrieved July 18, 2006, from   http://www.ascd.org/

Chisholm, I. & F. Beckett. (2003). Teacher Preparation for Equitable Access through the Integration of TESOL Standards, Multiple Intelligences and Technology. *Technology, Pedagogy and Education*, Vol.12(2):249-275.

Christison, M.A., (1996). Teaching and Learning Languages Through Multiple Intelligences. *TESOL Journal*, Vol.6(1):10-14.

Chun, D. & J. Plass. (1996). Facilitating Reading Comprehension with Multimedia. *System*, Vol. 24(4): 503-519.

Cohen, L., L. Manion, & K. Morrison. (2000). *Research Methods in Education 5th Edition*. London: RoutledgeFalmer.

Collins, J., M. Hammond, & J. Wellington. (1997). *Teaching and Learning with Multimedia*. London: Routledge.

Comstock, D. (1982). A method for critical research. In Bredo, E. & Feinberg, W. (Eds.), *Knowledge and values in social and educational research*. Philadelphia: Temple University Press.

Coniam, D. (2001). The use of audio or video comprehension as an assessment instrument in the certification of English language teachers: a case study. *System*, Vol. 29(1):1-14.

Crookes, G. (1993). Action Research for Second Language Teachers: Going Beyond Teacher Research. *Applied Linguistics*, Vol.14(2): 130-144.

Crookes, G., & R. Schmidt. (1991). Motivation: reopening the research agenda. *Language Learning,* Vol. 41(4):469-512.

Crotty, M. (1998). *The foundations of social research*. London: Sage.

Cunningsworth, A. (1995). *Choosing your Coursebook*. Oxford: Heinemann.

Dara-Abrams, B. (2005). Reaching Adult Learners through the Entry Point Framework and Problem-based Learning in a Croquet-based Virtual Environment. *Proceedings of the Third International Conference on Creating, Connecting and Collaborating through Computing.*

Davis, P., B. Garside & M. Rinvolucri. (1998). Ways of Doing. Cambridge: Cambridge University Press.

Debski, R. & P. Gruba. (1999). A Qualitative Survey of Tertiary Instructor Attitudes towards Project-Based CALL. *Computer Assisted Language Learning*, Vol.12(3): 219-239.

Diaz, L. & A. Heining-Boynton. (1995). Multiple Intelligences, multiculturalism, the teaching of culture. *International Journal of Educational Research*, Vol. 23(7):607-617.

Diaz-Lefebvre, R. (2004). Multiple Intelligences, Learning for Understanding, and Creative Assessment: Some Pieces to the Puzzle of Learning. *Teachers College Record*, Vol.106(1):49-57.

Dickinson, L. (1987). *Self-instruction in language learning.* Cambridge: Cambridge University Press.

Doughty, C. & T. Pica. (1986). Information gap tasks: Do they facilitate second language acquisition? *TESOL Quarterly*, Vol. 20(2):305-325.

Elliott, J. (1991). *Action Research for Educational Change.* Buckingham: Open University Press.

Ellis, R. (2003). *Task-based Language Learning and Teaching.* Oxford: Oxford University Press.

Ellis, R. (1994). *The study of second language acquisition.* Oxford: Oxford University Press.

Ellis. R. & X. He. (1999). The roles of modified input and output in the incidental acquisition of word meaning. *Studies in Second Language Acquisition*, Vol.21(2):285-301.

Erickson, F. (1999). Qualitative Methods in Research on Teaching. In M.C. Wittrock (Ed.), *Handbook of Research on Teaching* (pp.119-161). New York: Macmillan.

Felix, U. (1999). Web-Based Language Learning: A Window to the Authentic World. In R. Debski & M. Levy (Eds.), *WORLDCALL: Global Perspectives on Computer-Assisted Language Learning* (pp.85-98). Lisse: Swets & Zeitlinger.

Ferrance, E. (2000). *Action Research.* Brown University. Retrieved July 12, 2006, from http://www.alliance.brown.edu/pubs/themes_ed/act_research.pdf

Field, J. (1998). Skills and strategies: towards a new methodology for listening. ELT Journal, Vol.52(2):110-118.

Fox, L. & R. Johnson. (2001). The Next Generation Internet and the Schools. *Insight*, Vol.(1):63-90.

Fried-Booth, D. L. (1986). *Project work*. Oxford: Oxford University Press.

Gardner, H. (2006). The Development and Education of the Mind. London: Routledge.

Gardner, H. (2004). Audiences for the Theory of Multiple Intelligences. *Teachers College Record*, Vol.106(1):212-220.

Gardner, H. (1999). *Intelligence Reframed: Multiple Intelligences for the 21st Century*. New York: Basic Books.

Gardner, H. (1995). Reflections on multiple intelligences: Myths and messages. *Phi Delta Kappan*, Vol.77(3):200-209.

Gardner, H. (1993). *Multiple intelligences: the theory in practice*. New York: Basic Books.

Gardner, H. (1991). *The Unschooled Mind: How Children Think and How Schools Should Teach*. New York: Basic Books.

Gardner, H. (1983). *Frames of Mind: the theory of multiple intelligences*. Heinemann: London.

Garrett, N. (1998). Where do research and practice meet? Developing a discipline. *ReCALL*, Vol.10(1): 7-12.

Gass, S. M. & L. Selinker. (1994). *Second Language Acquisition: An introductory course*. New Jersey: Lawrence Erlbaum Associates, Inc.

Gass, S.M. (2003). Input and Interaction. In Doughty, C & M. Long (Eds.), *The Handbook of Second Language Acquisition* (pp. 224-255). Malden, MA: Blackwell Publishing Ltd.

Gitsaki, C. & R. Taylor. (1999). Bringing the WWW into the ESL Classroom. In K. Cameron (Ed.), *CALL & the Learning Community* (pp.143-159). Exeter: ELM Bank Publications.

Good, T. & J. Brophy. (1978). *Looking in Classrooms*. New York: Addison Wesley Educational Publishers.

Gunn, C. & G. Brussino. (1997). An evolutionary approach to CAL. *Active Learning*, Vol. 6:20-22.

Haley, M. H. (2004). Learner-Centered Instruction and the Theory of Multiple Intelligences with Second Language Learners. *Teachers College Record*, Vol. 106(1):163-180.

Hanson-Smith, E. (1999). Classroom Practice: Using Multimedia for Input and interaction in CALL Environment. In J. Egbert & E. Hanson-Smith (Eds.), *CALL Environments* (pp.189-215). Alexandria, Va.: Teachers of English to Speakers of Other Languages.

Hémard, D. (2004). User Interface Design Applied to Online CALL: Design Considered as a Process of Negotiations between Designers and Users (pp.153-159). In J. Colpaert et al (Eds.), *CALL Research Methodologies* (Proceedings of the 11th International CALL Conference, University of Antwerp, 5-7 September, 2004).

Hémard, D. (2003). Language learning online: designing towards user acceptability. In U. Felix (Ed.). *Language Learning Online: Towards Best Practice*. Lisse: Swets & Zeitlinger.

Herrnstein, R & C. Murray. (1994). *The Bell Curve: Intelligence and Class Structure in American Life*. New York: The Free Press.

Herring, J. (2004) *The Internet and Information Skills*. London: Facet Publishing.

Herron, C., J. Hanley & S. Cole. (1995). A comparison study of two advance organiser for introducing beginning foreign language students to video. *The Modern Language Journal*, Vol.79(3):387-395.

Hill, A. and L. Scharff. (1999). Readability of computer displays as a function of color, saturation, and background texture. In D. Harris (Ed.), *Engineering Psychology and Cognitive Ergonomics*, Vol. 4:123-130.

Hoerr, T.R. (2000). *Becoming a Multiple Intelligences School.* Alexandria VA, Association for Supervision and Curriculum Development (ASCD).

Hopkins, D. (1987). Teacher research as a basis for staff development. In M.F. Widden, & Andrews, I. (Eds.), *Staff development for school improvement: A focus on the teacher* (pp.111-128). Philadelphia: Falmer Press.

Hopper, B. & P. Hurry. (2000). Learning the MI Way: The Effects on Students' Learning of Using the Theory of Multiple Intelligences. *Pastoral Care in Education*, Vol.18(4):26-32.

Hoven, D. (1999). A Model for Listening and Viewing Comprehension in Multimedia Environments. *Language Learning & Technology*, Vol.3(1):88-103.

Husén, T. (1997). Research Paradigms in Education. In J. P. Keeves (Ed.), *Educational Research, Methodology and Measurement: An International Handbook* (pp.17-20). Oxford, England: Pergamon.

Ikeda, N. (1999). Effects of different types of images on the understanding of stories: basic research to develop Japanese teaching materials for use on the internet. *System*, Vol.27:105-188.

Isbell, K. & J. Reinhardt. (2000). Web Integration: A Model for Task-Based Learning. In E. Hanson-Smith (Ed.), *Technology-Enhanced Learning Environments* (pp.45-56). Alexandria, Va.: Teachers of English to Speakers of Other Languages.

Kallenbach, S. & J. Viens. (2002). Open to Interpretation: Multiple Intelligences Theory in Adult Literacy Education. *National Center for the Study of Adult Learning and Literacy Reports #21*. Retrieved July 31, 2006, from http://www.gse.harvard.edu/~ncsall/research/reports/ami.html

Kamil, M.L. (2002). The Future of Reading and Learning to Read. *Insight*, Vol.2:7-27.

Kang, S. (2004). Using visual organizers to enhance EFL instruction. *ELT Journal*, Vol.58(1):58:67.

Kellerman, S. (1992). 'I See What You Mean': The Role of Kinesic Behaviour in Listening and Implications for Foreign and Second Language Learning. *Applied Linguistics*, Vol.13(3):239-258.

Kemmis, S. (2001). Exploring the relevance of critical theory for action research: Emancipatory action research in the footsteps of Jurgen Habermas. In P. Reason & H. Bardbury (Eds.), *Handbook of Action Research* (pp.91-102). Thousand Oaks: Sage.

Kemmis, S. (1997). Action Research. In J. P. Keeves (Ed.), *Educational Research, Methodology and Measurement: An International Handbook* (pp.173-179). Oxford, England: Pergamon.

Kemmis, S. & R. McTaggart. (1988). *The Action Research Planner*. Australia: Deakin University.

Kern, R. & M. Warschauer. (2000). Theory and practice of network-based language teaching. In M. Warschauer & R. Kern (Eds.), *Network-based Language Teaching: Concepts and Practice*. New York: Cambridge University Press, (pp.1-19).

Kezar, A. (2001). Theory of Multiple Intelligences: Implications for Higher Education. *Innovative Higher Education*, Vol.26(2):141-154.

Kincheloe, J.L. & P. McLaren. (1998). Rethinking critical theory and qualitative research. In N.K. Denzin & Y.S. Lincoln (Eds.), *The Landscape of Qualitative Research* (pp.260-299). Thousand Oaks: Sage Publications.

Kitao & Kitao, (2001). Teaching Students to Find Internet Resources Related to Culture. In K. Cameron (Ed.), *C.A.L.L. - The Challenge of Change* (pp.143-150). Exeter: Elm Bank Publications.

Klein, P. (2003). Rethinking the multiplicity of cognitive resources and curricular representations: alternatives to 'learning styles' and 'multiple intelligences'. *Journal of Curriculum Studies*, Vol.35(1):45-81.

Ko, C. (2002). *A Case Study on Applying MI Theory to Improve Low English Proficiency Student's Learning Competences in Senior High*. Unpublished master's thesis, National Chengchi University, Taiwan.

Kohonen, V., R. Jaatinen, P. Kaikkonen, & J. Lehtovaara. (2001). *Experiential Learning in Foreign Language Education*. Harlow: Pearson Education.

Kolb, D. (1984). *Experiential learning: experience as the source of learning and development*. Englewood Cliffs : Prentice-Hall.

Krajka, J. (2001). Online Lesson-Using the Internet to Help the Coursebook. In K. Cameron (Ed.), *C.A.L.L. - The Challenge of Change* (pp.151-160). Exeter: Elm Bank Publications.

Krashen, S. (1985). *The Input Hypothesis: Issues and Implications*. London: Longman.

Krechevsky, M. & H. Gardner. (1990). The Emergence and Nurturance of Multiple Intelligences: The Project Spectrum Approach. In M. Howe (Ed.), *Encouraging the Development of Exceptional Skills and Talents* (pp.222-245). Leicester: The British Psychological Society.

Krechevsky, M. & S. Seidel. (2001). Minds at Work: Appling Multiple Intelligences in the Classroom. In J. Collins & D. Cook. (Eds.), *Understanding Learning: Influences and Outcomes*. London: Paul Chapman Publishing Ltd.

Kress, G. (2003). Literacy in the New Media Age. London: Routledge.

Kress, G. (1997). Before Writing: Rethinking the paths to literacy. London: Routledge.

Kress, G & van Leeuwen. (1996). The Grammar of Visual Design. London: Routledge.

Ladousse, G.. (1995). *Role Play*. Oxford: Oxford University Press.

Lazear, D. (1991). *Seven Ways of Knowing: Teaching for Multiple Intelligences*. Illinois: IRI/SkyLight Training and Publishing, Inc.

LeLoup, J. & R. Ponterio. (2005). On the Net. First, you have to hear it! ESL Oral Language Practice. *Language Learning & Technology*, Vol.9(3):4-8.

LeLoup, J. & R. Ponterio. (1996). Choosing and using materials for a 'net' gain in FL learning and instruction. In V. B. Levine, (Ed.), Reaching Out to the Communities We Serve. *NYSAFLT Annual Meeting Series*, 13; 23-32. Retrieved July 31, 2006, from http://www.cortland.edu/flteach/articles/nysaflt96.html

Levy, M. (1997). Computer-Assisted Language Learning: Context and Conceptualization. Oxford: Clarendon Press.

Lightbown, P. & M. Spada. (1999). *How Languages are Learned*. Oxford: Oxford University Press.

Linder, D. (2004). The Internet in every classroom? Using outside computers. *ELT Journal*, Vol.58(1):10-17.

Ling J. & P. Schaik. (2002). The effect of text and background colour on visual search of Web pages. *Displays*, Vol.23:223-230.

Littlewood, W. (1994). *Foreign and Second Language Learning*. Cambridge: Cambridge University Press.

Long, M.H. & G.. Crookes. (1992). Three Approaches to Task-Based Syllabus Design. *TESOL Quarterly*, Vol.26(1):27-56.

Lousberg, M. and J. Soler. (1998) Action research and the evaluation of IT projects. *Active Learning*, Vol.8(1):36-40.

Lyman, H. (1998). The Promise and Problems of English On-Line: A Primer for High School Teachers, *English Journal*, Vol.87(1):56-62.

Macintyre, C. (2000). *The Art of Action Research in the Classroom*. London: David Fulton Publishers.

Maun, I. & Myhill, D. (2005). Texts as Design, writers as designers. *English in Education*, Vol.39(2): 5-21.

Mayer, R.E. & R. Moreno. (2002). Animation as an Aid to Multimedia Learning. *Educational Psychology Review*, Vol.14(1):87-99.

Mayer, R.E. (1999). Multimedia aid to problem-solving transfer. *International Journal of Educational* Research, Vol.31(7):611-623.

McFarlane, L. (1998). Reviews the Letterland materials. *Journal of Speech-language Pathology and Audiology.* Vol.22(4). Retrieved July 31, 2006, from http://www.letterland.com/Teachers/LuanneMcFarlaneArticle.pdf

McGrail, E. (2005). Teachers, Technology, and Change: English Teachers' Perspectives. *Journal of Technology and Teacher Education.* Vol.13(1): 5-24.

McKernan, J. (1996). *Curriculum Action Research.* London: Kogan Page.

McNiff, J. & J. Whitehead. (2002). *Action Research: Principles and Practice.* London: Routledge.

McNiff, J. (1988). *Action Research: Principles and Practice.* London: Routledge.

McNiff, J., P. Lomax, & J. Whitehead. (1996). *You and Your Action Research Project.* London: Routledge.

Meskill, C. (1999). Computers as Tools for Sociocollaborative Language Learning. In K. Camerson (Ed). *Computer assisted language learning (CALL) : media, design and applications* (pp.141-162). Lisse: Swets & Zeitlinger.

Miles, M. & A. Huberman. (1994). Qualitative data analysis. Thousand Oaks: Sage Publications.

Mitchell, R. & F. Myles. (1998). *Second Language Learning Theories.* London : Arnold.

Moreno, R. & Mayer, R.E. (2000). A coherence effect in multimedia learning: the case for minimizing irrelevant sounds in the design of multimedia instructional messages. *Journal of Educational Psychology,* Vol.92(1):117-125.

Moore, D.M. (2003). Visual Literacy: A Vision from the Past, Insight for the Future. _Insight_, Vol.3:91-112.

Morton, J. (2001). The Multi-Dimensional Effects of Color on the World Wide Web. The 9th Congress of the international Colour Association Symposia. Retrieved February 12, 2006, from http://www.iscc.org/aic2001/abstracts/poster/

Mueller, G. (1980). Visual Contextual Cues and Listening Comprehension: An Experiment. _The Modern Language Journal_, Vol.64(3):335-340.

Murray, D.E. (1987). Computer-Mediated Communication as a Tool for Language Learning. _TESOL Newsletter_, Vol.21(3):13-14.

Murray, L. (1998). CALL and Web training with teacher self-empowerment: a departmental and long-term approach. _Computers & Education_, Vol.31(1):17-23.

Nagata, N. (1996). Computer vs. Workbook Instruction in Second Language Acquisition. _CALICO Journal,_Vol.14(1):53-75.

Nettelbeck, T. & R. Young. (2002). Intelligence and savant syndrome: Is the whole greater than the sum of the fragments? _Intelligence_, Vol.22(1):49-68.

Nielsen, J. (1997). How user read on the web. Retrieved July 31, 2006, from http://www.useit.com/alertbox/9710a.html

Norman, D. (2002). _The Design of Everyday Things_. New York: Basic Books.

Nunan, D. (2004). _Task-Based Language Teaching_. Cambridge: Cambridge University Press.

Owston, R.D. (1997). The world wide web: a technology to enhance teaching and learning? _Educational Researcher_, Vol.26(2)27-33.

Pask, G. (1976). _Conversation theory: applications in education and epistemology_. Oxford: Elsevier.

Peterson, M. (1997). Language teaching and networking. _System_, Vol.25(1):29-37.

Pirie, B. (1995). Meaning through Motion: Kinesthetic English. *English Journal*, Vol.84(8):46-51.

Plass, J. L., D. Chun, R. Mayer & D. Leutner. (1998). Supporting visual and verbal learning preferences in a second language multimedia learning environment. *Journal of Educational Psychology*, Vol.90(1):25-36.

Postlethwaite, K. & W. Maull. (2003). Similarities and Differences amongst Learning Sites in Four Further Education Colleges in England, and Some Implications for the Transformation of Learning Cultures. *Journal of Vocational Education and Training,* Vol.55(4):447-469.

Postlethwaite, K. (2004). *PhD Programme Lecture: Action Research.* University of Exeter.

Preece, J., Y. Rogers, & H. Sharp. (2002) *Interaction design: Beyond human-computer interaction.* New York: John Wiley & Sons, Inc.

Rainey, I. (2000). Action Research and the English as a Foreign Language Practioner: time to take stock. *Educational Action Research*, Vol.8(1):65-91.

Richards, J. (2001). *Curriculum Development in Language Teaching.* Cambridge: Cambridge University Press.

Richard, W. (1996). Some Principles and Procedures for the Conduct of Action Research. In O. Zuber-Skerritt (Ed.), *New Directions in Action Research* (pp.13-27). London: Falmer Press.

Ritchie, J. & J. Lewis. (2003). *Qualitative research practice.* London: Sage Publications.

Rodrigo, V., S. Krashen & B. Gribbons. (2004). The effectiveness of two comprehensible-input approaches to foreign language instruction at the intermediate level. *System*, Vol.32(1):53-60.

Rollinson, P. (2005). Using peer feedback in the ESL writing class. *ELT Journal*, Vol.59(1): 23-30.

Rossman, G. & S. Rallis. (1998). *Learning in the Field: An Introduction to Qualitative Research*. Thousand Oaks: Sage Publications.

Rost, M. (2002). *Teaching and Researching Listening*. Harlow: Person Education Limited.

Salaberry, M. R. (2001). The use of technology for second language learning and teaching: A retrospective. *The Modern Language Journal,* Vol. 85(1):39-56.

Sanderson, P. (1999). *Using Newspapers in the Classroom*. Cambridge: Cambridge University Press.

Scott, D. & R. User. (1999). *Researching* education *data, methods and theory in educational enquiry*. London: Cassell.

Scrivener, J, (1994) *Learning Teaching*. Oxford: Heineman.

Secules, T., C. Herron & M. Tomassello. (1992). The effect of video context on foreign language learning. *Modern Language Journal* Vol. 76(4):480-490.

Shacklock, G. & J. Smyth. (1998). Behind the 'cleansing' of socially critical research accounts. In G. Shacklock & J. Smyth (Eds.), *Being reflexive in critical educational and social research* (pp. 1-12). London: Falmer Press.

Sheen, R. (1994). A critical analysis of the advocacy of the –task-based syllabus. *TESOL Quarterly*, Vol.28(10):127-151.

Shieh, K. & C. Lin. (2000). Effects of screen type, ambient illumination, and color combination on VDT visual performance and subjective preference. *International Journal of industrial Ergonomics*. Vol. 26(5):527-536.

Simeone, W. (1995). Accommodating Multiple Intelligences in the English Classroom. *The English Journal*, Vol.84(8): 60-62.

Simpson, J.M. (2000). Practicing multiple intelligences in an EFL class. *TESOL Journal*, Vol.9(1):30-32.

Singhal, M. (1997). The Internet and Foreign Language Education: Benefits and Challenges. *The Internet TESL Journal*, Vol. 3(6). Retrieved July 31, 2006, from http://iteslj.org/Articles/Singhal-Internet.html

Skehan, P. (1996). A Framework for the Implementation of Task-based Instruction. *Applied Linguistics*, Vol.17(1):38-62.

Smagorinsky, P. (1995). Multiple intelligences in the English class: An overview. *English Journal*, Vol.84(8):19-26.

Smith, B. (2003). Computer-Mediated Negotiated Interaction: An Expanded Model. *The Modern Language Journal*, Vol.87(1): 38-57.

Snape, D. & L. Spencer. (2003). The Foundations of Qualitative Research. In J. Ritchie, J & J. Lewis (Eds.), *Qualitative research practice* (pp. 2-23). London: Sage Publications.

Snyder, I. (2001). A new communication order: researching literacy practices in the network society. *Language and Education*, Vol.15(2&3):117-131.

Sternberg, R. J. (1985). Human Intelligence: The Model is the Message. *Science*, Vol. 230(4730):1111-1118.

Sternberg, R. J. (1996). *Cognitive psychology*. London: Harcourt Brace College Publishers.

Tanner, R. (2001). MI and you. *English Teaching Professional*, Vol.21:57-58.

Teeler , D. & P. Gray. (2000). *How to Use the Internet in ELT*. Harlow: Longman.

Thorne, C. & W. Qiang. (1996). Action research in language teacher education. *ELT Journal*, Vol.50(3):254-261.

Tindall-Ford, S., P. Chandler & J. Sweller. (1997). When two sensory modes are better than one. *Journal of Experimental Psychology: Applied,* 3(4): 257-287.

Ting, K. & K. Cameron. (2004). Exploring the Website Visual Forms as an Aid to Learning for Adult Learners of English (pp.287-297). In J. Colpaert et al (Eds.), *CALL Research Methodologies* (Proceedings of the 11th International CALL Conference, University of Antwerp, 5-7 September, 2004).

Toyoda, E. (2001). Exercise of learner autonomy in project-oriented CALL. *CALL-EJ Online*, Vol. 2(2). Retrieved July 31, 2006: http://www.clec.ritsumei.ac.jp/english/callejonline/5-2/toyoda.html

Tsou, W., W. Wang & H. Li. (2002). How computers facilitate English foreign language learners acquire English abstract words. *Computers & Education*, Vol.39(4):415-428.

Unsworth, L. (2001). *Teaching multiliteracies across the curriculum*. Buckingham: Open Universitiy Press.

Ur, P. (1984). *Teaching listening comprehension*. New York: Cambridge University Press.

Vandergrift, L. (2004). Listening to learn or learning to listen? *Annual Review of applied Linguistics*, Vol.24(1):3-25.

Veenema, S. & H. Gardner. (1996). Multimedia and Multiple Intelligences. *The American Prospect*. Vol.7(29). Retrieved July 31, 2006, from http://www.prospect.org/print-friendly/print/V7/29/veenema-s.html

Viens, J. (1999). Understanding Multiple Intelligences: The Theory Behind the Practice. *Focus on Basics*, Vol.(3): Issue A. Retrieved July 31, 2006, from http://www.gse.Harvard.edu/~ncsall/fob/1999/viens.htm

Wallace, M. (1991). *Training Foreign Language Teachers: A reflective approach*. Cambridge: Cambridge University Press.

Wallace, M. (1998). *Action Research for Language Teachers*. Cambridge: Cambridge University Press.

Warschauer, M. & D. Healey. (1998). Computer and language learning: An overview. *Language Teaching*, Vol.31(1):57-71.

Warschauer, M. (2000). The death of cyberspace and the rebirth of CALL. *English Teachers Journal*, Vol. 53:61-67.

Weiner, B. (1974). *Theories of Motivation: from mechanism to cognition*. Chicago: Rand McNally College Publishing Company.

Wendon, L. (1993). Literacy for early childhood: learning from the learners. *Early Child Development and Care*, Vol. 86:11-22. Retrieved July 31, 2006, from http://www.letterland.com/Teachers/LiteracyArticle.html

Willis, J. (1996). *A Framework for Task-Based Learning*. England: Longman.

Winter, R. (1998). Finding a Voice – Thinking with Others: a conception of action research. *Educational Action Research*, Vol.6(1):53-68.

White, J. (1998). *Do Howard Gardner's multiple intelligences add up*? London : Institute of Education, University of London.

Woods, G. (2004). *Student Perceptions of Web-based Technologies Principles of Good Practice, and Multiple Intelligences*. Unpublished doctorate's thesis, Allian International University, USA.

Wright, A. (2003). The Place of Stories in ELT. In A. Paran & E. Watts. (Eds.), *Storytelling in ELT*. Whistable: IATEFL.

Wright, A. (1995). Storytelling with Children. Oxford: Oxford University Press.

Wright, A. (1989). *Pictures for Language Learning*. London: Cambridge University Press.

Yang, S.C. (2001). Integrating computer-mediated tools into the language curriculum. *Journal of Computer Assisted Learning*, Vo.17(1):85-93.

Yu, F. & H. Yu. (2002). Incorporating e-mail into the learning process: its impact on student academic achievement and attitudes. *Computers & Education*, Vol.38(3):117-126.

Yumuk, A. (2002). Letting go of control to the learners: the role of the Internet in promoting a more autonomous view of learning in an academic translation course. *Educational Research* Vol.44(2):141-156.

Zhang, Q. & R. Elliott. (1998). Interference of sentence and picture contexts on learning prepositions. *Journal of Behavioural Education*, Vol.8(4):439-456.

實踐大學數位出版合作系列
社會科學類　AF0061

Teaching English using the Internet and the Multiple Intelligences Approach
運用多元智慧於網路輔助英語教學

作　　者	丁廣韻 (Kuang-yun Ting)
統籌策劃	葉立誠
文字編輯	王雯珊
視覺設計	賴怡勳
執行編輯	詹靚秋
圖文排版	郭雅雯
數位轉譯	徐真玉　沈裕閔
圖書銷售	林怡君
網路服務	徐國晉
法律顧問	毛國樑律師
發 行 人	宋政坤
出版印製	秀威資訊科技股份有限公司
	台北市內湖區瑞光路583巷25號1樓
	電話：(02) 2657-9211
	傳真：(02) 2657-9106
	E-mail：service@showwe.com.tw
經 銷 商	紅螞蟻圖書有限公司
	台北市內湖區舊宗路二段121巷28、32號4樓
	電話：(02) 2795-3656
	傳真：(02) 2795-4100
	http://www.e-redant.com

2007 年 5 月
BOD 一版
定價：470元

請尊重著作權
Copyright©2007 by Showwe Information Co.,Ltd.

讀 者 回 函 卡

感謝您購買本書，為提升服務品質，煩請填寫以下問卷，收到您的寶貴意見後，我們會仔細收藏記錄並回贈紀念品，謝謝！

1. 您購買的書名：_____

2. 您從何得知本書的消息？

　　□網路書店　□部落格　□資料庫搜尋　□書訊　□電子報　□書店
　　□平面媒體　□ 朋友推薦　□網站推薦 □其他_____

3. 您對本書的評價：(請填代號　1.非常滿意 2.滿意 3.尚可 4.再改進)

　　封面設計____　版面編排____　內容____　文/譯筆____　價格____

4. 讀完書後您覺得：

　　□很有收獲　□有收獲　□收獲不多　□沒收獲

5. 您會推薦本書給朋友嗎？

　　□會　□不會，為什麼？_____

6. 其他寶貴的意見：_____

_____

_____

_____

讀者基本資料

姓名：_____　年齡：_____　性別：□女 □男

聯絡電話：_____　E-mail：_____

地址：_____

學歷：□高中(含)以下　　□高中　　□專科學校　　□大學
　　　□研究所(含)以上 □其他_____

職業：□製造業 □金融業 □資訊業 □軍警 □傳播業 □自由業
　　　□服務業 □公務員 □教職　□學生 □其他_____

請貼郵票

To：114

　台北市內湖區瑞光路 583 巷 25 號 1 樓

　秀威資訊科技股份有限公司　　　　收

寄件人姓名：

寄件人地址：□□□

(請沿線對摺寄回,謝謝!)

秀威與 BOD

BOD（Books On Demand）是數位出版的大趨勢，秀威資訊率先運用 POD 數位印刷設備來生產書籍，並提供作者全程數位出版服務，致使書籍產銷零庫存，知識傳承不絕版，目前已開闢以下書系：

一、BOD 學術著作—專業論述的閱讀延伸
二、BOD 個人著作—分享生命的心路歷程
三、BOD 旅遊著作—個人深度旅遊文學創作
四、BOD 大陸學者—大陸專業學者學術出版
五、POD 獨家經銷—數位產製的代發行書籍

BOD 秀威網路書店：www.showwe.com.tw
政府出版品網路書店：www.govbooks.com.tw

　　　永不絕版的故事・自己寫・永不休止的音符・自己唱